Library and Archives Canada Cataloguing in Publication

Flavell, David, 1947-, author

Community & the human spirit :
oral histories from Montreal's Point St. Charles, Griffintown & Goose Village / David Flavell.

Includes bibliographical references.
ISBN 978-1-927032-13-8 (pbk.)

1. Pointe-Saint-Charles (Montréal, Québec)--History--20th century.
2. Griffintown (Montréal, Québec)--History--20th century.
3. Goose Village (Montréal, Québec)--History--20th century.
4. Lachine Canal (Montréal, Québec)--History--20th century.
5. Irish Canadians--Québec (Province)--Montréal--History--20th century.
6. Italian Canadians--Québec (Province)--History--20th century.
7. Canadians, French-speaking--Québec (Province)--Montréal--History--20th century.
8. Montréal (Québec)--Social conditions--20th century.

I. Title.

FC2947.51.F53 2014   971.4'28   C2014-904885-8

Design, editing and layout by Petra Books
Ottawa Ontario Canada K1N 5W1
petrabooks.ca

Every attempt has been made to contact copyright holders;
the author and the publisher welcome any communications concerning
errors and omissions, which can be corrected in future editions.

Cover: Fortune Street, north of Wellington Street, Point St. Charles.
Acrylic on canvas by David Flavell, 2010.

Community and the Human Spirit

~

Oral histories from Montreal's

Point St. Charles, Griffintown and Goose Village

petrabooks.ca

I dedicate this book to the many generations of families
that called Griffintown, Point St. Charles or Goose Village their home.

Acknowledgements

First, I would like to thank all of the contributors to this book for taking the time to meet and develop these oral histories. Your support and patience was greatly appreciated, as was your help in arranging for introductions when requested. Thank you to Allen and Elmo Trepanier of the City of Montreal's Police Museum for providing a key introduction early in the process. I would like to extend my gratitude, as well, to Dr. Steven High, Director of the Concordia University Oral History program. Dr. High kindly gave me the opportunity to listen to several experts in the field just as the project was beginning. Thanks, also to Professor Emeritus, Michael Tritt (Marianopolis College, Montreal), for reviewing the introduction to this book. Thanks, as well to Donald Pidgeon, Historian for the United Irish Societies in Montreal. Donald lived in Griffintown and provided me with background material and advice on several occasions. To David O'Neill and Bill O'Donnell of Griffintown – thank you.

I extend my thanks to representatives of other organizations, as well, such as the Griffintown Horse Palace Foundation, the Ancient Order of Hibernians, the Point St. Charles Historical Society, the Erin Sports Association, the Point St. Charles Hall of Recognition, the City of Montreal's Fire Service Museum, the City of Montreal archives, as well as McGill University's McCord Museum, and McGill's Rare Books section at the McLennan library.

Various contemporary writers and researchers such as Richard Burman, Sharon Doyle Driedger, Patricia Burns, Yvon Desloges & Alain Gelly, D'Arcy O'Connor, as well as others have already shed light, in important ways on the history of Griffintown, Point St. Charles, Victoriatown (*Goose Village*), the Lachine Canal and surrounding areas. From their efforts I learned a great deal and encourage those interested in this topic to read their works.

I would like to extend a special thanks to Professor John Matthew Barlow, now of Salem State University (Department of History) in Massachusetts. Professor Barlow spent many years researching Griffintown while at Concordia University in Montreal. Matthew helped me during various stages of this work, even before the idea of a book took shape and my focus was on photography and painting. I look forward to Matthew's forthcoming book on Griffintown entitled "House of the Irish".

Lastly, I would like to thank George McRae for his help. George, a lifelong resident of the Point, volunteers tirelessly to photograph, film and document ongoing Point St. Charles activity on his website, www.thepoint.ca. George's site also supports a message board enabling people from the area, as well as from across Canada and elsewhere to stay in touch.

D. Flavell
JDF47@rogers.com

Note: Depending on the books, daily newspapers or web sites one reads, or the age of maps reviewed, the spelling of Point St. Charles / Pointe-Saint-Charles reflects the English or French background of the Montreal area. Both forms are used interchangeably in this book.

Table of Contents

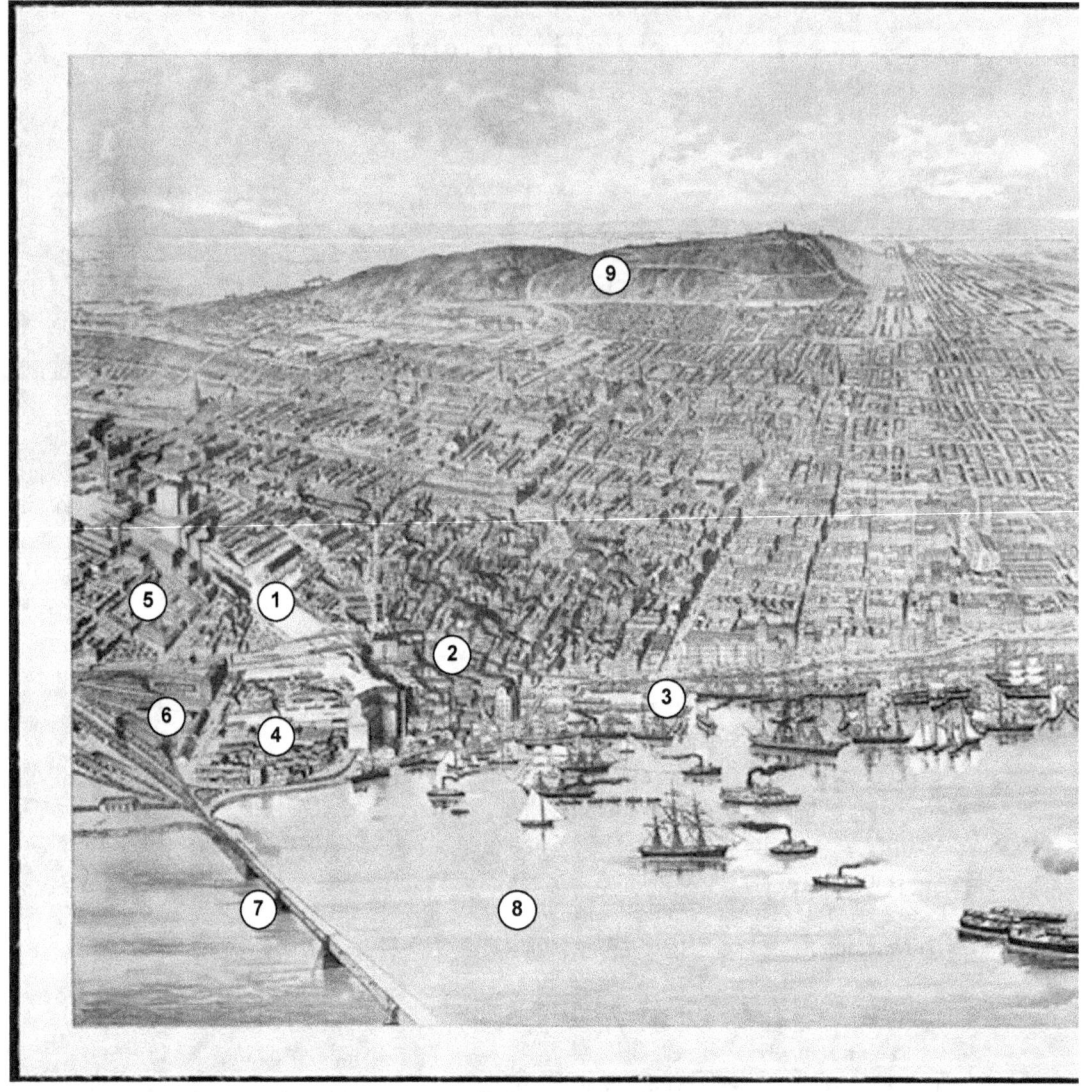

The legend points to several of the primary locations discussed in this book.

1) Lachine Canal   4) Goose Village   7) Victoria Bridge

2) Griffintown   5) Part of Point St. Charles   8) St. Lawrence River

3) Montreal harbour   6) Railyards   9) Mount Royal

An interpretation of Montreal looking north across the city from the St. Lawrence River and on to the slopes of Mount Royal. 1898.

Please note: all picture credits are listed in the Appendix starting on p. 346.

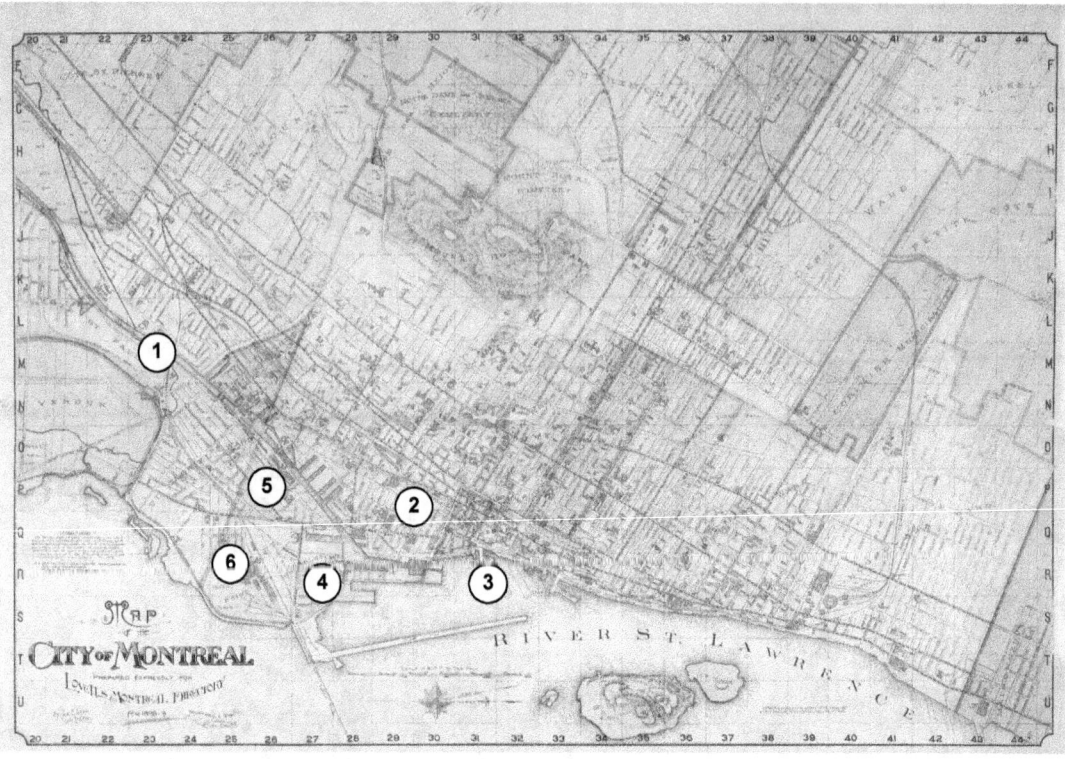

Charles E. Goad Map of Montreal from Lovell's Montreal Directory, 1898.

1) Lachine Canal
2) Griffintown
3) Montreal harbour / Old Port
4) Goose Village
5) Point St. Charles
6) Railyards

Montreal 1898

Introduction

D. Flavell, 2014

This book presents a collection of oral histories from people who were born between the 1920s and 1950s and who, for the most part, grew up in Montreal's Point St. Charles, Griffintown or Victoria-town (usually referred to as Goose Village). Those born during this period in these three storied neighborhoods at the east end of the Lachine Canal near the Montreal harbour were really the last demographic to experience the area as a closely intertwined trio of residential/industrial communities standing squarely at what was the heart of industrialization in Montreal.

For generations, the area's factories, foundries, breweries, meat packers, paint manufacturers, flourmills, railway yards, coal yards, the Port of Montreal and a host of other enterprises provided a livelihood for thousands of predominantly working class men and women of *the Point*, Griffintown and Goose Village.

It is a leisurely 20-minute stroll, much of it downhill, from today's fashionable downtown Montreal to the corner of Rue de la Montagne (Mountain Street) and Notre Dame. Cross this intersection and you have arrived in the rapidly gentrifying area of Griffintown. Walk five more blocks south and you arrive at the eastern reaches of the Lachine Canal, not far from Montreal's Old Port. A short walk west from here along the north side of the canal brings you to the historic St. Gabriel Locks. Here stands a tall fence surrounding the remnants of a sizeable old stone foundation that once supported the Ogilvie Four Mill. A sign on the fence reads:

> *Archeological intervention and environmental rehabilitation underway on one of the first*
> *industrial sites on the Lachine Canal, cradle of industrialization in Canada.*
>
> (author's translation)

A further 20-minute southeasterly walk from here across the canal and through Point St. Charles places you in the middle of a parking lot near the northern entrance to the Victoria Bridge that crosses the St. Lawrence River. Devoid of any housing, this is where the small community of Goose Village once stood.

The Lachine Canal

The canal was officially opened in 1825 and was closed completely to navigation by 1970. Extending over 14 km it stretches from Lachine in the west to the Port of Montreal in the east. The waterway enabled marine traffic on the St. Lawrence River to bypass the Lachine rapids located to the west of the City. Completion of the project was an important step in a canal-building era enabling marine traffic flow to and from the Atlantic Ocean and inland North America. In addition to providing safe passage, the Lachine Canal provided water and hydraulic power to the factories accumulating on its banks, thereby

Looking south from atop Mount Royal over downtown Montreal toward the St. Lawrence River. It is a relatively short walk down the hill from the centre of this cluster of buildings to the middle of Griffintown and the east end of the Lachine Canal. 2013.

helping to provide jobs for the people of the area. The Lachine Canal and Point St. Charles' once massive Railway yards complex served as critically important industrial lifelines to this area for decades – one by water, the other by land.

In their excellent book entitled, <u>The Lachine Canal – Riding the Waves of Industrial and Urban Development</u>, Yvon Desloges and Alain Gelly, experts on the subject, offer the following *(p. 14)*:

> *...not only was the canal used as a shipping lane and energy source, it was also a supplier of water to industries. Owing to this threefold use, between 1846 and 1945 the canal attracted more than 600 different firms covering the entire gamut of industrial manufacturing, whether light or heavy...In the process, the canal corridor became the epicenter of Canada's manufacturing sector, and Montreal the nation's leading metropolis.*

Montreal's downtown high-rises loom over Griffintown. This photo looks north across the Lachine Canal from the grounds of Point St. Charles' old Belding Corticelli factory (now Lofts Corticelli) adjacent to the St. Gabriel Lock. Early canal stonework is clearly visible. 2010.

In 1897, very near the mid-point in this 100-year period, Herbert Brown Ames published a study on Griffintown, some nearby streets, as well as parts of today's Point St. Charles. His work, entitled The City Below the Hill: A Sociological Study of a portion of the City of Montreal, Canada provides a detailed portrait of one of Canada's earliest industrial, working class areas. In discussing the differences between what he refers to as the more affluent "city above the hill" where some of the opulent mansions of Montreal's earlier business elites still grace the slopes of Mount Royal, versus the "city below the hill", just a short walk away, Ames writes:

> Looking down from the mountaintop upon these two areas, the former is seen to have many spires, but no tall chimneys, the latter is thickly sprinkled with such evidences of industry and the air hangs heavy with their smoke. (p.3)

This 1896 panorama provides an outstanding view of a significant part of Griffintown. The east end of the canal is visible in the middle right (facing page). Point St. Charles sits on the other side of the canal and the former location of Goose Village lies just before the entrance to the Victoria Bridge, also visible on the facing page.

Identities

A number of contributors to this book explained to me that the residents of Griffintown, the Point and Goose Village considered their respective neighborhoods as proudly distinct from each other, but that depending on the location of one's house, age, faith, skills, and other variables, the people of the three communities often interacted with each other on a routine basis. For example, many Goose Village children first attended St. Alphonsus School in the Village, then moved on to continue their studies in Griffintown. Depending on whether sports teams were parish, school, tavern or community-based, they played and took part in sports, either with or against each other. They worked side by side in the factories, railyards, dockyards, stockyards, and for the City of Montreal. They intermarried. They tell of a time when all three neighborhoods still bustled with industry and the links between the Village, the Point and Griffintown ran deep. Families were frequently large. Churches were numerous, active and influential.

The narrow streets, say contributors, were crowded with activity and teeming with children. Corner stores abounded and taverns thrived.

Terry McCarthy grew up in Griffintown and is one of the contributors to this book. Terry was born in 1937. He and others describe a time when young people from the area often went right to work in various local industries surrounding the eastern region of the Lachine Canal, including a number of large, well-known employers. Says Terry:

Back in those days, you could pretty much step outside your door all around the east end of the canal and get a job. In the eastern end of Griffintown where I lived it was very busy with industry. Mayer Shoes was across the street from our house. Kraft Foods was in the Griff before they and some others moved farther north toward the border of Montreal and St. Laurent. Darling Brothers' Foundry and Elevators, Liberty Smelting, Hydro Québec, and lots of others provided opportunities for people. We all worked.

—Terry McCarthy, Griffintown

This 1896 panorama, taken from the Griffintown (north) side of the canal, provides a view across the canal to Point St. Charles and then west en route to Lachine. Several "basins" at right angle to the canal are shown prominently in the foreground. Canada Sugar Refining Company Ltd. (the future Redpath) dominates the centre of the panorama on the Point St. Charles bank of the canal.

With available jobs in the factories and related businesses, low rents, and in some cases, a support network already in place, Goose Village, the Point and Griffintown were areas of Montreal that could offer a base for new immigrants to Canada. The Irish were well represented in all three communities. In tiny Goose Village, there was also a strong and vibrant Italian presence. Together with these and other ethnic groups, there was always a traditional Quebec Francophone population across the area. Street names tell their own story. Walking the streets of the Point, for example, there's no mistaking the French influence with street names like Charlevoix, D'Argenson and Bourgeoys. The same holds true in regard to the Irish with street names like Dublin, Hibernia, St. Patrick, Coleraine and others.

The end of an era

Adding to the challenges of an area already in decline, the late fifties and early sixties brought irrevocable shifts to the way of life at the east end of the Lachine Canal. The St. Lawrence Seaway mega project was completed and opened in 1959. This new waterway had a much larger capacity and it rendered the Lachine Canal obsolete. By 1970 the canal was closed to traffic completely. At the nearby Port of Montreal in the 1960s, technological advances on the waterfront led to major labour force downsizing. Readers will learn of how thousands of jobs vanished at the Port alone.

Goose Village's demise was quick and final. In 1964, the Village's six residential streets, all hemmed in tightly by industry, railyards and the St. Lawrence River, were demolished by the City of Montreal. The land was quickly repurposed and remains non-residential. With the exception of a small commemorative stone honouring Victoriatown (Goose Village), servicemen who lost their lives in World War II, one would never know the Village existed. Past residents explain that leading up to the demolition, the Village was home to just over 300 families.

Researchers, speakers and others that I spoke to about Griffintown's depopulation paint a different picture—one of how Griffintown, as a community of people, essentially withered away between the 1950s and the 1970s. A fascinating 1972 National Film Board of Canada production entitled simply Griffintown tells viewers that, at the time of production, under 300 families remained in the historic district. Thankfully, some substantial old Griffintown buildings remain in place to this day and are clearly identifiable by their architecture.

Things were changing in Point St. Charles as well. And by 1976, a National Film Board documentary entitled The Point tells of a proud community of people experiencing some extremely challenging times. Several people I spoke to who grew up there describe its own dramatic drop in population, yet the Point endured. And whereas most residential properties in Griffintown, as well as all of the homes in Goose Village fell to the wrecking ball and bulldozer, the Point retains plenty of its original architectural heritage. Remove the cars parked bumper-to-bumper down some of the long narrow streets, add some children skipping or playing road hockey, and it is easy to envision the scenes from 60-70 years ago that contributors to this book describe.

Looking ahead

In 2014, renovation and major new residential developments are on the rise both in Griffintown and the Point. Expansive billboards describe in-fill initiatives with names evocative of the areas' heritage. From month to month, particularly in Griffintown, it is any casual observer's guess as to where the next billboard or fence will appear announcing a new condo. During the weekend it is easy to spot potential buyers cruising the streets, stopping to take notes, or visiting sales offices.

The current Griffintown and emerging Point St. Charles renewal is attributed in large part to their proximity to Montreal's stylish downtown. Depending on location, residents can either walk up the hill or take a short ride uptown on public transit. Over the years some older industrial properties like Belding Corticelli, Redpath Sugar, the Sherwin Williams Paint Co. building in the Point, as well as the Lowney's Chocolate site in Griffintown had already been converted into elegant condos, but the current pace of redevelopment especially in Griffintown, is moving ahead with considerable speed. In some respects though, this is unsurprising. There is more land available for development in Griffintown than in the Point.

Other factors contribute to the overall renewal as well. The Federal Government has invested significantly in the revitalization of the Lachine Canal as a historic site. Smaller pleasure craft now cruise the canal. The adjacent parklands and bicycle paths are also popular destinations.

Some key public and private "anchor" locations have also been built in the area. For example, the Government of Quebec established a large post-secondary institution (École de Technologie Supérieure) at the northern border of Griffintown and the school is supported with a recently built student residence located near the centre of Griffintown. Boutique business enterprises, cafés, stores and other amenities are spreading across Griffintown from different points such as the eastern border adjacent to Old Montreal—one of the City's busiest tourist destinations.

As redevelopment moves ahead in such a storied and strategically located area, it should surprise no one that there are differing visions of the future. An internet search of Griffintown, for example, reveals much discussion in the Montreal media and elsewhere regarding the future of the area, and questions persist. What should be built? What should go where? What is the right balance between building for the future and preserving the rich, unique and colorful history of the area? What is the right blend of architecture and scale? What demographic should this area serve? Will gentrification hurt lower-income residents and eventually price them out of the Point. My own hope is that 30 years from now students of urban history and planning will look back on the fuller period of development in the Point, Griffintown and, eventually, the Goose Village site, and see a sound model for other cities to consider—and one that proved careful to pay homage to the people that lived and worked there for generations. The ongoing heritage work on the Lachine Canal as a historic site will go some distance in supporting this wish. As future generations walk the nearby streets around the east end of this historic waterway, may they see the same care and attention.

Developing these oral histories

The oral histories in this book were developed between late 2011 and early 2014. Initially, there was no plan for a book. At the outset of this project my intent was to document, through photography and painting, some of the history and ongoing changes in Griffintown. But it was during this earlier period, as I started speaking to past and current residents, that I began to understand the deep and enduring linkages between Point St. Charles, Griffintown and Goose Village. Eventually, I decided to begin approaching people from all three communities with a view to sharing their memories by way of a collection of oral histories.

I spent a lot of time on the road meeting with contributors and in many cases their spouses. We often met in their homes and I was always greeted with openness, generosity and patience. I attended a broad range of events in the Point and Griffintown such as bazaars, commemorations, fund-raisers, award presentations, sporting events, as well as festive and arts community events. I enjoyed many long chats at the Capri Tavern, Magnan's, and the Fine Pointe Restaurant in Point St. Charles.

For a number of the people featured in this book, religion was an important part of their upbringing. It remains so for some. In Ames' The City Below the Hill (1897) he indicates that, overall, the area was majority Roman Catholic. Several contributors to this book spoke to me of the enduring and substantial Roman Catholic presence in the area as they were growing up in the mid 1900s. Although not raised in the Roman Catholic faith, I received and accepted several invitations to attend special services and community events at St. Gabriel's Church in the Point.

All of the foregoing afforded me the opportunity to meet and talk to many past residents of the area in addition to those featured in this book. For the most part, given the era targeted, they ranged in age from their late 60s to 80s. For all of this, I am most grateful. Additional notes on methodology are in the Appendix.

A few words about what this book is not

This is not a history book in any classic sense. With only a few exceptions, the oral histories that follow reflect the memories of people who grew up, played, attended school, and in many cases worked in the area. Most of these stories trace the lives of the contributors into the present. My journey in developing this book led me, for the most part, to people of Irish, French or Italian heritage. Although this direction shouldn't surprise anyone familiar with the three neighborhoods at the east end of the canal, it is in no way meant to dismiss the history, impact or contribution of other ethnic groups that lived in the area. Nor is it meant to diminish the importance of nearby communities like Saint-Henri. Indeed, a number of contributors allude to these other groups and communities.

Nor is this book an exercise in investigative journalism. Roger Agnessi, a contributor to this book is a retired Montreal police detective and lifelong resident of the Point. Roger explained to me that he and others from the area are all well aware of what he refers to as the "caricature" or the "stereotype" of the Point, Griffintown and the Village that bubbles up from time to time—one involving crime, welfare etc. He says:

> In any community you'll always have the small minority that go the wrong way and get into trouble, and we had our share. And yes, the area had a welfare challenge. In one case I know of, a family has been on welfare for four generations—but that's not the Point as a whole— that's the caricature of the Point. The truth is that 95% of the people in the Point just wanted to do the right thing and build a better life for their families. I have known people from Griffintown and the Village for my whole life and they'll tell you the same thing.

—Roger Agnessi, Point St. Charles

For the most part, the focus of this work is the 95%.

Community and the human spirit

The people who share their stories in this book typically had little by way of material possessions as children. *"We were poor, but we didn't know it"* was a comment I often heard as contributors described their childhood. Some overcame early and very long odds on the road to a secure and rewarding future. Today, they speak with great affection and loyalty toward their old neighborhoods. For many, the bonds developed with childhood friends and institutions remain very strong. And when you sit down and listen to past residents as they speak of the sense of community that they knew in Griffintown, the Village and the Point, the feeling in their words is truly palpable.

> "The people in Goose Village cared about each other, and they helped each other. If I ever needed help in the Village there was always someone there. The closeness was really indescribable. I have never seen anything that compares with this in other communities."

—Linda Frainetti, Goose Village

In the end my sense is that, as much as anything else, this book tells stories of the importance and meaning of community, as well as the strength of the human spirit. It is my fervent hope that, over the coming years, others will continue to help documenting this fascinating story of the area and its people. This former industrial/residential area at the east end of the Lachine Canal, and the contributions made by those that lived there represent a profoundly important chapter in Montreal and Canadian history.

This 1930 aerial photograph provides a good view of :

1) The Peel Basin at the east end of the Lachine Canal
2) Griffintown
3) Western end of the port of Montreal.
4) Goose Village
5) The railway yards in Point St. Charles

1930

This 1920 photo shows the west end of the canal at Lachine and its route east to the Montreal harbour. Some sizeable industrial venues in Lachine are visible on the left side of the canal past the lock.

Lachine and the western end of the canal

The Library and Archives Canada title for this photo is "Shipping Lachine Canal". No further detail is given, although the horses, vehicle models and steam engine provide significant hints as to the era. In the foreground a ship is passing one of the canal's swing bridges. On each side of the canal, people await the bridge to swing back. The Montreal harbour is in the background.

Eastern end of the Lachine Canal in Montreal

The Library and Archives Canada title for this photo is "Montreal harbor—Shipping—Lachine Canal". No further detail is given, but it clearly provides a sense of the scope of industry in the area. Date unknown.

Montreal Harbor

An aerial view (1920) shows much of Griffintown, as well as the easternmost point of the Lachine Canal and the Port of Montreal's western end. The St. Lawrence River is in the background.

Griffintown

Aerial view of the primary areas under discussion. c. 1970s.

1) Lachine Canal
2) Griffintown
3) West end of the Montreal harbour / Old Port
4) Past site of Victoriatown (Goose Village)
5) Point St. Charles
6) Railyards
7) Victoria Bridge
8) St. Lawrence River
9) Stock yards
10) St. Gabriel Lock

Examples of earlier "Golden Square Mile" architecture such as this still grace the slopes of Mount Royal up the hill from Griffintown and the Point. 2012.

These four Goose Village street scenes were taken shortly before the 1964 demolition. See also p. 150-151.

Goose Village 1964

Griffintown 2010-2014

Point St. Charles 2010–2014

Towards the east end of the Lachine Canal. 2011–2013.

Canal Scenes

A sign at the corner of Coleraine and Liverpool in Point St. Charles. "Ireland Park. In tribute to the citizens of Irish origin who established themselves in this neighborhood during the construction of the Grand Trunk Railway and the Victoria Bridge" (author's translation). 2013.

The Maison St. Gabriel. The wording on this plaque provides visitors with some background on early Quebec and Point St. Charles. 2011.

A pleasure boat cruises the canal past the old LaSalle Coal Tower several kilometers west of Griffintown and the Point. 2011.
Below: Plaque. 2013.

The King's Wards

In the colony, circa 1666, there were 65 single women for 719 single men. To re-establish the balance, Louis XIV gave dowries to young orphaned girls who wanted to move to New France to find a husband. The first of the "King's Wards" arrived in 1663. Between that time and 1673, more than 800 made the crossing. Some stayed in Quebec while others settled in Montreal where they were welcomed by Marguerite Bourgeoys. About 50 of them stayed at Maison Saint-Gabriel.

A depiction of the Lachine Rapids.

Canadian Illustrated News (1879)

Part of the Port of Montreal looking west toward the east end of the Lachine Canal. The Montreal side of the Victoria Bridge is visible on horizon at the top left.

Canadian Illustrated News (1875)

Looking east during canal enlargement work at the St. Gabriel Lock, then on toward the Port of Montreal. Industrial enterprises frame both sides of the Canal.

Canadian Illustrated News (1877).

LACHINE CANAL ENLARGEMENT WORK AT THE ST GABRIEL LOCKS UNDER Messrs LOSS & McRAE.

Clearing away ice at the harbour and looking west toward the smokestacks of Montreal industry, a short walk away.

Canadian Illustrated News (1879)

MONTREAL — CLEARING AWAY OF THE ICE

"The Presentation Brothers from Ireland

were quite something.

I can truthfully say that

they were the first

to bring real first-rate education

to the English Catholic kids in the Point.

They started at the school in 1910…

They were great teachers.

They taught us our academics

and they taught us values."

Brendan Deegan

Brendan Deegan

Brendan Deegan grew up in the Point with his four brothers and four sisters. Brendan pursued a rewarding 50-year teaching career, although he will readily point out, with a wide smile, that he was 'no angel' in his younger days.

Brendan has been active in support of the Irish community of Montreal since his youth. He has served as President of the Catholic Youth Organization, President of the Ancient Order of Hibernians, and as a member of the executive of the United Irish Societies (UIC). In 2011 Brendan was chosen as Chief Reviewing Officer of Montreal's St. Patrick's Day Parade. Brendan continues to organize special events of importance to the Irish community.

Brendan and his wife Katie, have been involved

"Future generations reading about the Point, Griffintown and Goose Village should understand that the Irish that lived there were very, very proud of their heritage…St. Ann's Church in Griffintown and St. Gabriel's in the Point were very important to us."

in volunteer work in support of the needy for decades. Now in retirement, they volunteer their services with H.O.P.E. (Helping Other People Effectively), which works from St. Mary's Parish in Brossard. "When we receive a phone call from the dispatcher", says Brendan, "we're ready to go". Brendan loves to laugh and happily points to a calendar busy with upcoming commitments. He remains a man on the move.

Photo: Katie and Brendan Deegan at a United Irish Societies event in Montreal, March 2013.

My great grandparents came to Canada from County Clare, Ireland. They lived in Point St. Charles and so did my parents.

I was born on Grand Trunk Street in 1933, but grew up at 1294 Laprairie. That's right across the street from my old school, Canon O'Meara and the Presentation Brothers residence. The Brothers' address was 1295. I was the last of nine children to leave home.

I have always been very active in the church and in the Irish community. I have been working at it since I was in my teens. For a while when I was younger I was President of the Catholic Youth Organization. We held dances, organized sports and had other activities. The basement of the church was like a second home for us. I also began to get very seriously involved in various forms of charity work when I was young. Helping out at St. Gabriel's Church, or with organizations like the United Irish Societies and the Ancient Order of Hibernians has been an important part of my life. A number of us still work hard to keep all the Irish traditions alive here in Montreal,

Knights of Columbus, 2012 "Walk to the Stone" (The Black Rock). The inscription reads:

"To preserve from desecration the remains of 6000 immigrants who died of ship fever A.D. 1847-8,
this stone is erected by the workmen of Messrs. Peto. Brassey & Betts.
employed in the construction of the Victoria Bridge A.D. 1859"

but the younger ones today don't seem to be as interested as we were. I have been a member of the Ancient Order of Hibernians for over 30 years and served as President for one term. The Ancient Order of Hibernians is the oldest Catholic organization in the world. It was started in Ireland and it was dedicated to protecting the Catholic faith and Irish tradition. At the time it was started in Ireland, Irish catholic families in the north couldn't send their kids to school and they weren't allowed to attend Mass. Catholics in the north used to have to hold Mass out in the countryside in the bushes and things like that.

One of my annual responsibilities with the Order is organizing the annual "Walk to the Stone". This is held at the end of every May. This is very important to me. On the grass median in the middle of the road just a little north of the Victoria Bridge, there is a large monument commonly called the "black rock" or the "stone". It is dedicated to the 6000 Irish that died coming to Canada in the mid 1800s during the potato famine in Ireland. The monument stands in memory of those Irish immigrants. That rock represents an important piece of Irish history and the Ancient Order of Hibernians is committed to helping keep the memories alive.

The annual "Walk to the Stone" starts off with a Mass at St. Gabriel's Parish. Then we all walk to the stone together. We have a ceremony and then walk back to the church for a while. We have some refreshments and get some more time to talk to each other. In some cases we may not have seen some people for a year.

Father McEntee at St. Gabriel's really helped to keep the Ancient Order of Hibernians organization together over the years. He had a big influence on me. When I was a young guy, I thought long and hard about becoming a priest like him. I was always active in the church and I think Father McEntee was grooming me to move into the Priesthood. But when I met Katie in my late twenties, that was it. I got married. I think Father McEntee must have been very disappointed, because it took years after that before he would speak to my wife.

There are lots of stories about Father McEntee. I remember one year I went down to march in the New York City St. Patrick's Day Parade with Montreal's Erin Sports Club contingent. Father McEntee was with us. We won the "Most Outstanding Group" award. Every one of us was in the traditional dress that we use in the Montreal parade—top hat, long black coat, shamrocks etc. After the parade, a lot of the guys went out on the town and into the bars with the New York guys. I don't drink so I didn't go. Father McEntee and I decided to just do some sightseeing, so off we went. We came across the statue of Father Duffy. It is at the north end of Times Square. He was a Canadian, but he went to the U.S. and became a military chaplain. He served in the Spanish American War and the First World War. He was a teacher too. Anyway Father McEntee sees this and goes up to the statue and starts singing Irish songs. He really enjoyed singing. He was wearing his collar. He loved to wear it, and that was at a time when priests weren't wearing them all the time. Before you know it a big crowd started to gather around and they all began clapping for him. "Well", I told him, "after all the singing you've done, you finally made it to Broadway!" He was a very good man. I had great respect for him.

As well as the Ancient Order of Hibernians, I have been a member of the United Irish Societies here in Montreal for years. I served on the Executive Committee for one year. The United Irish Societies helps coordinate some activities in the Irish community in Montreal.

Where Brendan grew up on Laprairie Street. 2012.

Brendan, second step from bottom, centre right, with siblings. 1941.

Specifically, the UIS is responsible for organizing the annual St. Patrick's Day Parade. There are several other Irish organizations in Montreal like the Irish Protestant Benevolent Society, the St. Patrick's Society, the Erin Sports Association, Innisfail, and as I've mentioned, the Ancient Order of Hibernians.

The St. Patrick's Day Parade in Montreal is the biggest in Canada, and St. Patrick's Day is the biggest Day of the year for the Irish. For the Irish, St. Patrick's Day is like Christmas. I have marched in that parade for over 60 years. I felt very honoured last year when chosen as Chief Reviewing Officer for the parade.

Back in the 'seventies and 'eighties I was active in the Harp and Thistle Society as well. I even served as President for a while. The Society was established during the early days of Quebec's language laws like Bill 101. The focus of this organization was English rights. We crossed the lines of Protestant and Catholic interests to look at English rights as a whole. This is why we chose the Harp and Thistle as our emblem. We did some really good things. I also served as the Grand Knight of the Knights of Columbus for several years.

When I was growing up in the Point, we were a poor family, and we certainly weren't alone in that respect. But we had a lot of fun. We lived in a small three bedroom flat. There were five boys in one bedroom and four girls in another. My father and mother were in the third. There would have been ten kids in total but my mother lost one child at birth. I think we were all born under a year apart. Maybe that is why my mother died as young as she did. Big families like this were very commonplace in the Point at that time.

These big Point St. Charles families led to a lot of poverty. I didn't really realize just how much until I started to move around the Point a little more as I was growing up. The people below Grand Trunk Street thought we had more money on our side of the Point and vice versa.

Brendan (left) at home with twin brother Kevin. 1985.

Fellow pitcher Dave Lampton (left) with Brendan's father, Frank "Lefty" Deegan. Early 1950s.

The truth is that the poverty was all over and it often stemmed from the big families. I remember that on a bad day for us we'd be eating what we used to call a Point St. Charles bread pudding. For around 27 cents, when I was very young, you could go the store and get a loaf of bread, a quart of milk and a half a pound of sugar. My mother would break up the bread, pour in the milk and sugar and stir it up into a pudding. If we didn't have enough for milk we'd just use water. But, you know, that was ok with me. It was what we had, and I liked it cold.

The other thing is that back then a good number of the families in the Point had alcoholic fathers as well. That is why lot of young people stole. They didn't have much. We didn't have much either. I can remember when I used to walk in the St. Patrick's Day Parade with the Canon O'Meara School contingent when I was small. Sometimes I used to have to put cardboard in my shoes because of the holes. My feet would get soaked and cold. No, we didn't have much.

We grew up in the French section of the Point. As far as I can remember, our family and the Youngs, just down the street, were the only English families around that part of the Point at that time. The Youngs had six kids. Jackie Young was my age and other than my brothers he was my closest friend. He still is. Living on the French side was fine with me. I learned to speak French living there and it really helped me.

I remember one big French family that lived close to us. They had a lot of kids. They were from the Gaspésie region of Quebec. The children's mother had nicknames for all of the kids— "Ding-dong. Moo-moo, Da-da" and things like that. She'd yell for them down the street for dinner or to come home at night: "Hey, Ding-dong, Moo-moo…" When I first started hearing this I was very young and didn't know they were nicknames. I thought it was their real names. One day I'm in the store and Moo-moo walks in, so I said "Hey, Moo-moo!" He looks at me and tells me in French…"My name isn't Moo-moo. It's André!

When I was young I had two paper routes. I'd deliver the Montreal Star to English houses and LaPresse to French families. When I eventually started teaching it was in the French school system. If I hadn't grown up on the French side I would have missed that opportunity. I didn't speak the greatest French. It was what you call *Joual* in Quebec. It was street French, but I got by fine.

There were always the usual fights between the French and English, but I knew them all on both sides. And anyway, there were five Deegan brothers and we all stood up for ourselves. My older brothers, Freddie and Frankie were both Dominion Champion boxers as well. We always fought back. I really admired my brothers. We were like a clan.

My father was a semi pro baseball player. He was good and he made some money at it. He was a left-handed pitcher—Frank "Lefty" Deegan. He was always away a lot in the summer playing ball. When my twin brother Kevin and I were born he learned about it by reading one of the newspapers on the train coming home from a road trip. My father also worked in the shops at the Canadian National Railway (CNR) yards in the Point. Unfortunately he suffered from what I call the Irish curse. He liked to drink and he liked to gamble. In the off season when he wasn't travelling and playing baseball I can remember my mother sending my brother and me down to the railway yards on pay-day. She'd have us tell him that she wanted some money to do some food shopping. She'd want to make sure that we had money for food before he could go to the tavern.

A recent book came out called <u>Montreal's Irish Mafia</u>. It talks about a number of guys from around the Point and the west end in the '50s, '60s, and '70s as part of what is referred to as the "West End Gang". I didn't hang around with them, but I knew them through my father and my brother Frankie. The author of the book came to interview me when he was researching the book. He wanted to talk mostly about my brother Frankie. All the Deegan brothers except Frankie stayed out of any real trouble. Frankie was six years older than me. He was really a nice guy and a great boxer. Eventually everything worked out for Frankie, but he had quite a story. Frankie could rob your eyes and come back for the eyelashes! He was a pool shark, a con artist and a pickpocket. He was also very smart. They called him the "machine" for his ability with numbers. He was an amazing card player. He made money playing cards right up until he passed away.

There are so many stories about Frankie. I remember when he was young he joined the Navy but he eventually went AWOL. They never caught him. When he would come around the Point at that time, Jackie Young would sleep at our house and Frankie would sleep at Jackie's house. When Frankie was hustling he moved around a lot. When he was travelling, if he didn't want to pay for a hotel room he'd go to the nearest hospital and run around the building a few times as fast as he could. Then he'd stumble into the emergency room holding his heart, panting and complaining he couldn't breathe. That was his hotel room for the night. He did this all over the place.

Eventually, the lifestyle caught up with Frankie and he ended up spending some time in jail. But he did turn things around in life. Frankie loved hockey and he was a great talent spotter. He was so good, that when Scotty Bowman was with the Buffalo Sabres he gave Frankie a job as a

L-R: Brother Kevin, Jack Young and Brendan in front of the Laprairie Street home on St. Patrick's Day. 1951.

Brother Kevin with Brendan (right). c. 1954.

scout. My son Shannon went to the University of Vermont on a hockey scholarship. He even signed a pro contract. Scotty Bowman knew Shannon. One day he bumped into my son at a game and asked him if he was related to Frankie Deegan. Shannon told him yes, that Frankie was his uncle. Scotty Bowman told Shannon that Frankie was one of the best scouts he had ever hired.

Frankie died in 2006. He was over at our house here in Brossard on Boxing Day just a few days before he passed away. I hold a party at our house every Boxing Day. There were over 80 people at the last one. Sometimes I wonder how we fit them all in. In 2006 Frankie was at a palliative care hospital in Longeuil, and like I said, he was very near the end. He had cancer. He told me he wanted to come to the party, so we arranged for an ambulance to bring him over. At first, we set him up in a chair in the living room and gave him a beer. Then, as the night wore on we eventually put him in one of the beds. Everybody at the party knew Frankie's situation so people would go over and talk to him. When the party died down and people had left it was early in the morning. At around 4:00 a.m. I wondered where the ambulance was to take Frankie back to the Hospital so I phoned the hospital. "Oh, yes", they told me, "Frankie is fine. He's asleep in his room". Well, we straightened that out and they sent the ambulance right over. When they were carrying him out I remember joking with him and saying, "Well Frankie, how many people can say they participated in their own wake? You've just had your last drink! Now get the hell out!" Frankie passed away five days later.

I was no an angel myself growing up, but I never got into any real trouble. When we were young a day would often start for my brothers and me with an early morning run over to the railroad tracks beside the Lachine Canal to see what we could lift from boxcars. They weren't far from our flat. At that time there were railroad tracks serving the factories all around the Lachine

Canal. The Boxcars were everywhere. Sometimes other guys would have been there before us and have already broken some of them open. You never knew what you'd find. Some of the boxcars brought in fruit. They'd use big blocks of ice to keep the produce fresh. We'd grab those ice-blocks and bring them back and sell them in the Point. In those days they delivered ice door to door in the Point. So we would just look around and see who left a delivery marker outside for the iceman and we'd knock on the door. We knew what the iceman charged for his ice, so we'd sell ours for less but also give the person more ice than they'd get from the iceman. After we'd come home from doing stuff like this we used to often leave some money in different places in the house for our mother to find, then act surprised when she'd find it…"Oh, you found some money!"

We worked the railroad tracks from Bridge Street in the east to Charlevoix in the west. After that the Saint-Henri crowd took over. The French controlled the area between Charlevoix and points west on through Saint-Henri. I knew all the Saint-Henri guys to say hello to, and because I could speak French I could talk to them. There was never any trouble. Everybody respected each other's areas. And, you know, all these years after we were doing this as kids, some of those same guys from Saint-Henri showed up to pay their respects at Frankie's funeral. In fact, some of them came over and sat beside us.

My twin brother Kevin and I were born nine minutes apart and you couldn't tell the difference between us. I remember that McGill University sent a team down to the Point once to do a study on twins. There were four sets of twins they looked at in the Point: the Whites, Greens, Browns and Deegans. Hands down, Kevin and I were the closest. We could tell each other anything in complete confidence, and we did. We used to laugh and say "we know more about each other than God does!"

One night I met a girl from Goose Village at a dance and I was walking her home to the Village. We were almost there and she turns around for no reason and slaps me hard in the face, and then she says to me "you know what that's for!" It took me a minute but then I knew. I got home that night and asked my brother "did you recently meet a girl called "so-and-so"?" "Yeah", he said, "and I never even got to first base!"

Kevin was a very good athlete. He was a good tennis player and a very good hockey goalie, but he just never took sports all that seriously. He went on to become a teacher. In fact, he's the one who influenced me the most to become a teacher myself a little later on. He loved teaching and he used to tell me all about his classes and how much fun he had with the kids. He eventually became a Principal, and a very good one. He won an award as the top Principal in Canada. That's something! He really loved teaching. In the summer, he used to teach school at the same place I did. And even when he was a Principal he would volunteer to teach some courses. He didn't have to do that, but he did. He worked very hard. Right up to the point he was on his deathbed he talked about how rewarding it was when he was in the classroom. He taught right up until the end.

I remember sometimes we'd have family events and Kevin wouldn't show up. He'd say, "Sorry, can't make it, I'm really tied up", or something like that. Later on we'd find out that it was usually something to do with the school. For example, we learned that Kevin was going in on Saturdays to open up the gym for the kids during the day so they'd have someplace to go. He always put in that little extra for the kids at times like Halloween and that. Even at Christmas sometimes he wouldn't be at our family events. Eventually we learned that what he'd been doing was bringing some very poor families from the school over to his place for Christmas dinner. He wanted to make sure they had a proper Christmas dinner.

Kevin and I were very close. We shared a car for three years when we were young. We also had a deal that if either of us bought a lottery ticket and won, we'd share the winnings. The very last ticket I bought just before he passed away was a winner—$160. I shared the winnings with his widow, Roberta. That was the deal. During the last month of his life I spent every day with him. It was in the summer and we'd just sit in the sun and talk.

Freddie was the second boy born. Freddie was another great Point St. Charles boxer. He won the Dominion Golden Gloves Championship in his weight class, and just like Frankie he joined the Navy. They both boxed for Navy teams. At one time, they used to have something like a national championship in Navy boxing. Freddie was stationed in the east coast and Frankie was on the west coast. They both won it all in their own areas and they were in the same weight class. So, they were scheduled to fight each other for the national championship. My father stepped in and said, "No way. I'll not have my sons fighting each other like this. If there is going to be a fight it will remain in the family, with the gloves on in the back yard". So they never fought.

Freddie joined the Montreal Fire Department and that's where he stayed. Freddie was always on the go. Beside his job at the Fire Department, he also worked on the side driving a truck for the Montreal Star Newspaper. He used to joke that the Star job was for his beer money. He always said that he'd never spend a cent of his firefighter's salary on beer.

All his life Freddie was involved in one way or another in boxing. After he finished fighting in the ring, he became an outstanding boxing referee and he even refereed at the 1976 Olympics when they were here in Montreal. In fact, Freddie was supposed to go to the U.S. and turn pro as a referee right after he retired from the Fire Department, but it never happened. He died of a heart attack at a celebration of my father's 75th birthday. The party started in the evening and a big gang of people was at the tavern celebrating. There was supposed to be a gift presentation toward the end of the night. But, as it turned out, the night wore on and the gift was never given, so the crowd just agreed to regroup at the tavern early the next day. We all congregated the next day at the tavern and Freddie put up his hand to order a beer for the first round. Before his hand came down he was hit with the heart attack. It all happened very quickly. All his life, any chance Freddie got to help someone, he would. I remember one of the things he used to do all the time was help his friends move. In the Point, people were always moving from one flat to another. Freddie had a heart of gold. My father passed away five days after Freddie. I just heard quite recently that the person who gave Freddie mouth-to-mouth resuscitation in the tavern passed away himself.

My brother David worked at the Northern. He spent some time up north doing installations. He was very active in the Irish community as well and served for a term as a President of the United Irish Societies. Overall, though, David was a bit of a loner. Sadly, David was killed in a car crash. He was driving in from the Eastern Townships to attend Mass with us. The Sunday

St. Gabriel School in the St. Patrick's Day Parade. 2013.

before St. Patrick's Day we always have a Mass of Anticipation in the morning at St. Gabriel's. It's quite a big event really. After the Mass everyone gets together downstairs at the church for a meal and to talk to old friends. As David was driving in from the Eastern Townships to attend the Mass he got caught in a blizzard—it was a real whiteout. He crashed and was killed.

Like I said, I had four sisters: Margaret, Joan, Madeleine and Kathleen. Margaret was quite small but she was a real tomboy and a good athlete. When she was older she really enjoyed sitting with the kids in the family and telling them stories. The children absolutely loved it and they really liked having Margaret around. Unfortunately, she had a struggle with alcohol, too, and it lasted her whole life. She always worked though. She always found good jobs. Joan was the second oldest and she was very, very quiet. She lost a kidney when she was just a young child. All of us really tried to look after Joan. She had a good job too. She worked for the Federal government here in Montreal before she got married. Madeleine and Kathleen are my only sisters that are still with us and we get along very well. Both of them still help out in support of the needy here in Montreal. My mother had Kathleen when she was 43. Kathleen is the baby of the family. She is still working. She is a real estate agent in Montreal with Sutton and she does a lot of work around the Westmount area.

Brendan's father (fourth from left) and Brendan (third from right) with all of his siblings. 1977.

When we were growing up we used to have great house parties at my Grandmother Hayes' place. She lived on the other side of the canal on Quesnel Street. That area is called Little Burgundy now, but we just used to call it the West End. If you talk to people from the Point, that's what the older ones will call that area. Those parties at my grandmother's really stand out in my memory. She was a very good piano player and she knew a lot of entertainers. She used to bring some of them over to the house for the parties and some of them were black. In fact, her brother was a good friend of Oscar Peterson. I remember that some people from the Point were shocked when they would come over to a party and see black people there. In those days that wasn't very common. You didn't see much integration. Our family was different, and that's the way my wife and I always brought up our kids too—no discrimination! Those parties were special.

When we were growing up, that part of Montreal on the other side of the canal was where a good number of people from the black community lived. A great many worked at the CNR as what used to be called "red-caps" because of the uniforms they wore at that time. They worked on the passenger trains. Overall, like I said, there wasn't a lot of mixing, but on a Saturday you'd typically see some groups of the black kids come over to the Point to go the Centre Theatre. Later on, after the Vogue opened on Charlevoix, they'd come to movies there too.

All the boys in our family went to Canon O'Meara. We lived right across the street. And let me tell you, at Canon O'Meara, you learned. You learned because you either wanted to learn, or

Katie Deegan (front row, third from the right), in a class photo.1949.

you learned through fear! At Canon O'Meara you had no choice! The Presentation Brothers from Ireland were quite something. I can truthfully say that they were the first to bring real first rate education to the English Catholic kids in the Point. They started at the school in 1910. We didn't even have a Department of Education in Quebec until 1964 if you can believe that. The very young Brothers taught the youngest kids and the older Brothers taught the kids up until grade nine. They were great teachers.

They taught us our academics and they taught us values. They taught us to always love our families and love the church. They instilled in us the value of education and the love of sports. They organized a lot of different inter-parish sports for us and they used to teach us boxing. The main event when we had boxing match events at the school in my day was always between Cathal Duffy and my brother Freddie. The Brothers schooled us to always stand up for ourselves. They told us if we were knocked down to always get back up. They taught us the importance of a healthy mind in a healthy body. To this day I don't drink and I never have. I don't smoke, and every morning I am on the treadmill—without fail! Yes, the Brothers were tough, but they really cared. They helped us and they helped the poor people of the Point. They worked hard for the community. Every Christmas, the Brothers organized a turkey draw. Like magic, it was always the absolutely poorest families that won those draws! The Brothers brought a lot to the Point. I had the greatest respect for them.

Over the years our family became quite close to many of the Brothers. They used to walk across the street to our house on a Saturday night, sit down with my father, have a few drinks and watch the hockey game. And if there was a knock on the door early on a Sunday morning we knew what that meant. It meant that one of the altar boys hadn't shown up at St. Gabriel's for Mass and one of the five of us was going to fill in.

There are only three Presentation Brothers left alive in Canada. Brother Philip is one of them and he is living in a home in Scarborough, Ontario. I call him once a week to say hello and see how he is. He is 94 years old and still very sharp. I just recently went to Toronto and took the opportunity to go and see him. Katie and I took him out to lunch and he really enjoyed it. He has a little trouble walking, but other than that he's in good health. The Order in Ireland knows that I am very active in the Irish community and when another Brother was about to pass away here in Canada, they phoned me. They asked if I would look after his affairs. He was in Toronto, as well, and in the last stages of Alzheimer's. I still smile when I think that during his last days he was sharing a room with a nun! Brother Ivan and Brother Henry are still alive, as well. They're in Toronto too.

There was also Sarsfield School in the Point for the catholic boys and St. Gabriel's for the girls. My wife, Katie graduated from St. Gabriel's in 1956. The Protestants had Lorne School. It was mixed (boys and girls). On the Catholic side, things were pretty clear-cut. Canon O'Meara was the Irish boys' school. Sarsfield, more or less, handled the other Catholic boys in the Point, and we had pockets of other ethnic groups in the Point like Polish and Ukrainian. There were some Irish at Sarsfield too, though. Other than space at Canon O'Meara nothing would have stopped these kids from coming to our school. There weren't any strict boundaries or anything. It was just a combination of space and self-selection. They were lay teachers at Sarsfield.

Overall, I would have to say that the girls at St. Gabriel's probably got the best education of all the Catholic schools. The nuns were truly amazing. They were very good teachers. None of the St. Gabriel's girls ever had any trouble getting jobs. Eventually, as the population of the Point began to shrink, the Catholic schools merged into one—St. Gabriel's. It is on Wellington Street. It stands on the ground where Leber School once stood. As far as I can remember that was a Catholic girls' school. Today the public schools in Quebec aren't organized along religious lines. In the public system now you have the French schools and the English schools.

My twin brother and I were both pretty good in school. We got good grades at Canon O'Meara. The reality was that I just never found school that hard. I didn't find exams very difficult. I didn't study a lot in school in those days, but I have a great memory and when I was in class I listened. After I finished at Canon O'Meara I fell sick with osteomyolitis. I was in the hospital for a year. At first the doctors said I'd never walk again. They were wrong there. When I recovered I went on to Loyola High School and I was studying with the Jesuits. Father Flood was the priest at St. Gabriel's Church at that time and he was my uncle. He called Father Scott at Loyola and put in the word for me. That's how I got in. I learned the score about how things got done when I was quite young. Anyway, for the relatively short time I was there I learned a lot from the Jesuits but it didn't work out. Towards the end of the first year Father Scott called me in and just said it wasn't working out. He told me I was just far too street-oriented for Loyola. He was right. Although I wasn't trying to get into the taverns like some of my 15 and 16 year-old friends, I was just far more interested in the pool rooms and running around than I was in school.

St. Gabriel's Church on Centre Street in Point St. Charles. 2010.

I had a great time at that period of my life. It was a lot of fun. I had a number of different jobs. Some of them didn't last long and some were dangerous. I got a job in a turpentine factory, but I knew on the first day that breathing this stuff in all day could be very bad for your health and that was the end of that. Another job I had was working at Stelco. One of the things I had to do was hop over a conveyor belt while I was carrying things like cases of soft drinks. The conveyor belt was carrying red-hot coals. If I had ever tripped or just lost my balance on that thing it would have been very bad. In those days, there just wasn't the protection for workers that you have today. Eventually I went to work for the Northern. At that time I'd say about 70% of the people in the Point must have been working there. Others worked at places like Simmons, Redpath Sugar, Canada Packers, Stelco or Dominion Glass. Some went down to the docks and a few of them became racketeers. Most of the girls went to Northern, or to Insurance companies, or into other office jobs.

By the time I was twenty-six I decided I wanted to go to Teachers College. Kevin was already teaching by then. At the very same time that I came to that decision, a guy I knew at Northern was getting laid off. He was older than me and had eight kids. I went up to see my boss and said, "Look, lay me off and keep him on. He's got eight kids and I want to do something else anyway". It wasn't like I was trying to be a hero or something. It just seemed that since I was ready to move on and he was getting laid off, it was a good way to go. The people at Northern agreed and that was that.

The problem was that I didn't have all the qualifications I needed to get into St. Joseph Teachers College. At that time the college was up near McGill on Durocher Street. Father Hilton was running it, though, and I knew he owed my father a favour. I went to see him and tried to explain as nicely as I could that I was calling in the favour. After some discussion, he agreed that I could, as he put it, audit some courses. So, I got my foot in the door, worked hard, and before long my status was changed to regular student. I started at 'St. Joe's' in 1959 and I began teaching in 1961. I spent the next 50 years teaching. I worked hard and I studied hard. I taught English in the French system for 35 years and then after my retirement I taught as a substitute teacher at the Kahnawake Indian reserve for another 15 years.

I remember bumping into a buddy of mine once in the Point when I was teaching. He had been at Canon O'Meara with me and he had learned I was a teacher. "How the hell did you ever

St. Ann's Church in Griffintown before and during the 1970 demolition

decide to become a teacher", he asked, "you were never at school—you didn't give a shit!" I just looked at him and told him I didn't really know how it happened, but that I was glad it did. I have had a great life.

I taught during the day and went to school three nights a week at Loyola. Then, when Loyola merged with Sir George Williams University and formed Concordia, I kept on going there to upgrade my credentials. I studied at night for 20 years but it paid off. One of the happiest and proudest moments of my life was graduating from Concordia with my son, Brendan, in the same year—1987. We are on the same page of the Concordia Yearbook. Brendan was a teacher at first but moved to the private sector. He still does some substitute teaching. Shannon, my other son, graduated from the University of Vermont. Then he went on to get a Masters in peace studies and political science at Trinity College, Dublin, and a Masters in business administration at Yale. He works in the private sector too. Shannon is in the States and Brendan is here in Montreal. I see them both regularly.

Another guy bumped into me once and asked me, "How did you manage to get both your kids into university?" Not that many children from our area went on to university at the time. The answer was that we were so poor when they were young, one of the only things I could bring home were books from the library and from the schools where I was teaching, and that both boys would read them. I am very proud of both my sons.

Katie did a great job with the boys. I was away so much at night school, teaching, and doing community work that a lot fell on her shoulders. She spent a lot of time with the boys. After they both graduated from high school, Katie then went on to a 20-year career in the Bell System. Katie worked very hard. Sometimes I feel that she is the one that deserves the degree.

I still keep myself very busy. For a while after I retired I helped out with a well-known priest here in Montreal who ran an outreach program for street kids. He had a truck that he'd load up with food and coffee and stuff and we'd hit the streets to help feed the homeless kids. For the last 20 years over here on the South Shore, Katie and I have been helping with H.O.P.E.; that stands for "Helping Other People Effectively". It is a charitable organization that works out of St. Mary's Parish. We do our best to help in a variety of ways. It could be helping to feed or clothe families, counseling, or simply working with young people to help them pull together resumes or get ready for job interviews. When we receive a phone call from the dispatcher, we're ready to go.

I'm working on this year's "Walk to the Stone", and I'm also planning for the Mass in the park. This is an annual event that we hold at the site of the old St. Ann's Church in Griffintown. I'm looking forward to both of these events.

Future generations reading about the Point, Griffintown and Goose Village should understand that the Irish that lived there were very, very proud of their heritage and that St. Ann's Church in Griffintown and St. Gabriel's in the Point were very important to us.

Left: The past site of St. Ann's Church is now the Griffintown St. Ann Park. Surrounded by the foundation stones of the church the park benches reflect the position of the church pews. In recent years redevelopment such as the high rise pictured in the background is closing in on this storied location. 2013.
Right: a past parishioner of the church enjoys a warm Spring afternoon in the park. 2014.

The "Walk to the Stone". 2012.

St. Patrick's Day: Brendan Deegan (centre). On the right, Victor Boyle, National President of the Ancient Order of Hibernians. On the left, Victor's uncle, "Paddy" Boyle. 2014.

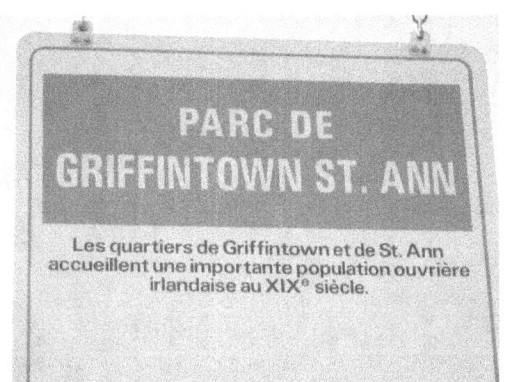

Beside the foundation stones of St. Ann's Church in Griffintown this sign recognizes the area's significant Irish population in the 19th century.

"Goose Village…

Well, it was a place where we all got along.

It was the kind of place where if someone baked a cake

they would invite a neighbor in to share some.

Goose Village was a sharing place.

We helped each other."

Rose Villeneuve

Rose Villeneuve
nee Tamburino

Rose grew up in Goose Village. Like many of her friends during the Second World War, Rose went to work in a Montreal ammunition factory. She was 17. By age 18 Rose was married and, for a while, lived in the Point. Rose and her husband went on to build a successful Montreal dry cleaning business. Rose currently lives across the Victoria Bridge on the south shore.

Photo: Rose at home. 2011.

"My husband and I moved to
Chateauguay Street in the Point,
then on to Verdun.
We got into the dry cleaning business
and built up a business from nothing
that eventually took up all three floors
of one side of a duplex
…we constantly expanded."

I was born on Conway Street in Goose Village in 1924. I lived in the Village for 20 years. My husband and I left the Village in 1944 when we moved to the Point.

Both my parents were from Italy. My father was born on March 7, 1885 in Gallucio, Calabria. His name was Pasquale Tamburino. My mother was born in Calabria. Her name was Angelina Palumbo. I had three brothers. Angelo was only nine months old when he died. I had two sisters. One died when she was 21 and the other when she was 89. I was only 12 when my first sister died. There is a bit of a story there. She became very sick and the doctors at the Royal Victoria Hospital had never seen anything like my sister's situation. Ultimately it was felt that she had a tumor on the brain and an operation was conducted to respond. Unfortunately, the operation was not successful and my sister passed away. It was determined at the autopsy that the tumor was actually at the nape of her neck. This came as a surprise to the people involved. Shortly after this, though, a young boy was brought up from America to the Royal Victoria, and the boy had exactly the same symptoms my sister had. This time the operation was a success, so I guess maybe the experience and knowledge gained by the doctors with my sister helped. The funeral for my sister was held at St. Ann's Church in Griffintown. The cars were lined up all the way back to and through Goose Village. People said they had never seen anything like it.

When my father first came from Italy to Canada he worked in Sudbury laying railway track. He was in some kind of industrial accident, though, and lost an eye. Then he moved to the Village and began working for Dominion Coal. The "Coal Pile" as Dominion Coal was referred to, was visible from our house. He became a foreman there. The flatbed rail cars with the

Dominion Coal Company docks. 1931.

wooden sides and open tops would come in loaded with coal. It was Welsh coal. My father had a whole team of men who would move from rail car to rail car, climb on and shovel the coal from the car onto the ground. Since my Dad was the foreman he didn't do any shoveling but he was right there with the men. He would have anywhere between 15 to 20 men on each car shoveling off the coal.

Then the coal delivery trucks would come and the coal would be loaded on the trucks. One truckload of coal would usually serve the needs of one house in the Village for a year. The trucks would roll up to your house, stick the long half-moon-shaped chute through the small bottom window at ground level and dump in the coal to the basement. In our house, we had to go out the back and then down to the basement to get the coal. You couldn't get to it from inside our house. When I think about where my friends' parents were working at that time, my recollection is that most of them, whether Irish or Italian, worked on the coal-pile. The vast majority I would say worked on the coal-pile.

My father was a very, very smart man. He did not know how to read or write but he had an amazing mind and memory. One of his jobs was to complete the men's time sheets every night and submit them to the company for their pay. When I was a young girl I'd watch as he sat down with my older sister every night and dictate to her that "so-and-so was off sick today, "so-and-so was required to leave for an emergency at 3:00", or "so-and-so didn't show up" etc. My sister

Canadian National Railway coal car. 1939.

would write up the time sheets as he spoke. He was amazing. When my sister died I was 12 and that became my job—doing the time sheets every night with my father.

My father worked from 7:00 in the morning until about 6:00 at night at the coal-pile. He worked six days a week and he worked very hard. He had an hour for lunch and he'd come home every day. He would be absolutely covered in coal dust. My mum would always have a full home-cooked meal ready for him at lunchtime. He would eat, then lie down on the floor and have a quick sleep. He couldn't lie down on the bed because of all the coal dust. I don't remember my dad eating breakfast, but he always had a full homemade meal at noon and at night. We'd have polenta, macaroni, or maybe Italian stew. The stew was always made with tomato sauce. My mother made everything from scratch.

My Dad kept a regular schedule in the Village, from the time he got up until he went to bed. He would come home at the end of the day and he would always have a cup of coffee with a shot of gin in it. Then he would have his bath and eat dinner. We would do the time sheets and then my father would go out. He would always dress up nicely. Every night he would put on a fresh, white shirt with an open collar and I remember he would always put a small piece of basil at the tip of his shirt pocket. Sometimes he would go out in his Buick to see his friends. Other times he would just go to one of the Blind Pigs [unlicensed premises] in the Village, play cards, chat, and have a couple of drinks. I also remember that on very special occasions my dad would wear a bowler hat. He would always come home around 9:00 or 10:00. Sometimes there would still be

Bundling cordite for naval shells at Defence Industries, Ltd. Montreal, 1944.

time to play cards with him for a while before bed. My mother didn't go out very much. She was almost always at home looking after the kids, the home and my father. She was a very loving mother.

I started out at St. Alphonsus and went on to St. Ann's (Griffintown). But my sister died just as I was finishing grade six. That was when my father took me out of school so that I could help

Working at a munitions factory. Montreal, 1943.

out at home—so that is what I did. By the time I was 16, I really wanted to go out and get a job. It was 1940 and the war was on. Most of my friends were working at the ammunition factory. It was on Vitre Street down near the old Montreal Gazette building. My father would not allow it. He was very protective and strict. I really wasn't allowed to do very much outside the house. Eventually, when I was 17 he agreed that I could go and work at the factory. My job was to pack artillery shells with black powder explosive sacks. As I said, all my friends were working there so I was happy to be there.

That is where I met my husband-to-be. His name was Lucien Villeneuve. He came from the plateau area in Montreal. He lived on St. Joseph Boulevard, which was a very nice area of Montreal. He was three years older than me. Anyway, I saw him washing his hands one day and thought he looked really nice, so one lunch hour I went over and stood beside him to wash my own hands and we started talking and in no time we were boyfriend and girlfriend. Well, my father would never have condoned me having a boyfriend at the time so I didn't tell him. And I could never have just brought him over to the house. So, the only time I could see him was at lunchtime. We'd spend all our lunch hours talking and talking. I ended up throwing out my lunches so I could spend more time talking and I lost a lot of weight; so much so that my parents took me to the doctor. The doctor actually figured out what was happening. My father talked to me when I got home. At first I denied having a boyfriend but he eventually learned the story. He said to me "OK, you bring him over here, but if I don't like him, and you marry him and it does not go well, don't come back here".

So, we set a time for Lucien to come over. The whole family was there: my parents, my uncles and my aunts. They were all peering out the shutters when he came down the street. He had on this beautiful brown suit with a lovely tie. He had a brown camel-hair coat over his arm and he had on green suede shoes. Some people were following him down the street. My parents loved him, but my father told him "No monkey business with my daughter!" We set an engagement date and then we could go out together, but only with a chaperone—my sister. Someone had to follow us on our dates. We set an early marriage date so that we could stop the chaperoning.

I was 18 when I got married. We lived with my parents in the Village for two years before we moved to the Point, then Verdun. I remember that one week after we got married Lucien took me uptown and we got back to the Village around 2:00 a.m. My father was sitting on the front step waiting for me and he said, "Lucien, I don't like you bringing my daughter home at this time of night". Lucien looked at my father and said "Pa, Rose is not 'your daughter' any more, she is my wife". That ended any problems we had right there.

Growing up in the Village was interesting. Overall I had a very quiet but memorable time in the Village. Some of the kids, particularly the Irish, were pretty wild, though.

Did you know that the Victoria Bridge was built so that the farmers on the south shore could bring all their produce to Montreal to the market? Well, it was. When I was in the Village they would still bring all their produce to market by horse and cart across the Victoria Bridge. When they came over the Bridge they were right in Goose Village. Kids would hide and wait until the cart passed by. Then they'd jump out, run up behind the cart and start unloading produce and running off with it.

When I was around six or seven I remember that every Saturday this big car would arrive at the Village. It would drive along Forfar Street very, very slowly and every few feet or so it would stop, the back window would come down slowly and a man would throw out money for the kids to pick up off the street. Most of it was coppers but there would be the odd piece of silver. No one ever found out who he was. At the time I felt as if he was some kind of fairy godmother or something, except he was a man. This went on for a good year or so, right on our street. I guess he just felt that this was a very poor area.

We had a children's club on Britannia Street at the time. It was before the Victoriatown Boys' Club was built and it wasn't very big. It was downstairs from Martoni's store. We'd have our Sunday school there. We'd play cards. It was a place you could meet and talk. We would also have street dances in the Village in my day. Victoria Day was always a big event as well. The fires were set everywhere: in the parks, the streets, everywhere.

Our house was on Forfar Street and it backed up against the stockyards. In fact, it looked right out on where they unloaded the animals to take them in to be slaughtered. We'd see the box-cars coming in with the cattle and pigs. The men would be there waiting with their big canes and they would hit the animals to move them along as they came out. You'd hear them squealing all the time.

Unloading the Cars.

Workmen unloading rail cars at the Montreal Abattoir Company, 1881.

You couldn't smell the stockyards all the time in the Village, but when the wind was blowing the wrong way at the wrong time, like when the animal skins were out, watch out! It was terrible. I remember that when I was a kid I used to wonder how the animals could live inside their own skins.

What do I remember about the Lachine Canal? I remember how cold it was in the winter. At the beginning of every winter the City used to bring barges down the canal and position them so that when everything froze over they would act as a footbridge for the Goose Villagers crossing over to Griffintown. I think they did this to make things easier for everyone to get to St. Ann's Church, but we also used to use it to go to St. Ann's Girls' School at that time. It was a bitterly cold crossing. The wind would whistle down the canal as we crossed this bridge. It was set up at the end of Riverside. Overall though, the canal wasn't really a part of my life.

Talking about winter, I remember, as well, that the sidewalks in the Village were cleaned at that time by horse and driver. The horse would pull this affair behind it down the sidewalk. This thing collected the snow and when it was full it would be dumped on the street. A truck would then come along and pick up the pile of snow and so on. We always had huge snow-banks at the side of the streets in the Village in the winter.

Most of my friends left the Village after they got married just like we did. They moved on to places like the Point, Verdun and LaSalle. My husband and I moved to Châteauguay Street in the Point, then on to Verdun. We got into the dry cleaning business and built up a business from nothing that eventually took up all three floors of one side of a duplex in Verdun. We built it up into a successful jobber and valet service. We'd pick up and deliver dry cleaning to and from various dry cleaning enterprises. Part of our business would involve picking up the cleaned clothes from the dry cleaners, but doing the ironing ourselves in the basement of the duplex. That way we made more money than if we just delivered. My husband was a real go-getter.

I think I knocked on every door in Verdun to drum up business. We constantly expanded. I even got my own truck for pick-ups and deliveries. I still remember having to take a run at the snowbanks on the side of the road when I got out of my truck to make a delivery. That's what I used to have to do to get over them. The snowbanks were always high in Verdun too.

We built that business up from scratch. We started the business off in the basement of the duplex and went on from there. Eventually we owned the whole Verdun duplex for the business and we built a house for ourselves in Brossard on the south shore. We eventually sold the business and duplex to Hong Kong investors after 39 years of hard work.

My father owned property too. Over the years he acquired a lot of holdings in the Village. He owned a corner store and several of the houses on each side of it. But I remember he said to me once when I was about ten years old, "Rose, eventually the City will tear down this Village".

Goose Village's St. Alphonsus School just prior to the demolition. 1964.

He saw it coming. He sold off his properties in the 'forties and the 'fifties; all except a butcher store he also owned in the Village, which he turned into a house. He always sold the various properties to the people who were renting from him.

As I said, I left the Village in 1944 after 20 years. My parents left before the demolition as well. What should future generations know about Goose Village if they are reading about it or studying it? Well, it was a place where we all got along. It was the kind of place where if someone baked a cake they would invite a neighbor in to share some. Goose Village was a sharing place. We helped each other.

"We were brought up to have integrity,

to respect others,

to have faith in yourself,

and to stand up for yourself.

We were taught

that people from the Point

don't back down.

We were taught this

from an early age."

Roger Agnessi

Roger Agnessi

Roger Agnessi was born in the Point in 1953. Other than the four years he served in the Royal Canadian Navy, Roger has lived in Point St. Charles all of his life. After serving in the Navy, Roger joined the Montreal Police at age 21. He served for 31 years, ten of which were as a Detective Sergeant in general investigations, and eight in homicide.

Roger is deeply loyal to the Point and has studied the history of the area in great detail. He regularly submits short historical summaries to the website thepoint.ca. Walking the streets of the area with Roger, he can point to houses, institutions, vacant lots, new condos, the canal banks or elsewhere and readily describe the history of the locations.

Roger's grandfather moved from Italy to Canada in 1912. Roger's mother was, he says, "French/Irish". Roger spoke English at home and went to St. Charles School where he studied in French. Roger is fluently bilingual and has a good grasp of Italian.

Photo: Boatswain and Ship's Diver, Roger Agnessi, Royal Canadian Navy. 1970.

"I worked hard. I have a good pension now and things worked out well. But I'll say this—if something happened and financially I found myself at the bottom of the ladder tomorrow, I could look after myself just fine, thank you, because in the beginning, that's where I came from. I'm from the Point! It may not have been the classiest place in town, but it was our home."

You see how narrow this street is? You see how close the doors are to each other? Well, in the summer down here it can get hot, very hot—high eighties—sometimes in the nineties. And when I was growing up there weren't the trees in the Point that you have now, so you didn't get the shade you see on some of the streets today. But back then it didn't matter. People still cooked. The stoves in these flats and houses would be going full blast on even the hottest days. So you'd walk down the street in the heat of the summer and the scents would be a combination of the smells from the factories, sometimes a whiff from the stockyards and Canada Packers, together with wafts of what the women of the Point were cooking. All the doors and windows would be wide open. You could look right through someone's house and see out the back. You'd see people sitting and eating at the table. That was the Point St. Charles I grew up in during the

Roger playing in the yard behind his home on Charlevoix Street. This yard is now the parking lot for Magnan's—a well-known Point St. Charles establishment located on the corner of St. Patrick and Charlevoix, just across the street from the Lachine Canal. 1959.

'fifties and early 'sixties. Yeah, we used to say that you'd go outside to cool down in the summer, or to warm up in the winter.

I loved growing up in the Point and I wouldn't change things if I had the chance. And after I finished my stint in the Navy and graduated from the Montreal Police Academy, I chose to stay in the Point, live here and raise my children here. I remember early in my police career I was assigned temporarily to some of the wealthy areas in Montreal, like Hampstead and the Town of Mount Royal. I was amazed at the opulence of some of these homes. I could have moved elsewhere over the years. But I didn't, and I'm still in the Point. And I can also tell you that, honestly, there are still people here that I have known since I was a kid, and the Point is basically all they know. They have just never left the Point, and in some cases, a particular area of the Point—from one corner to the next.

I was born in a flat on Charlevoix Street at the corner of St. Patrick. We lived there for ten years. Then we moved to Island and Châteauguay. I stayed there until I got married and moved out. I remember that when I was small there was so much traffic in the Point from people getting out of work from the factories that my mother didn't want me to play in the streets between 3:00 and 5:00 p.m. The place was always busy. Not any more. When I was young we had five or six butcher shops alone in the Point. The last time I tried to add the numbers up I figured out that we used to have 11 doctors and seven dentists in the Point. Everything you needed was right here. Everybody shopped at their local corner stores and all the owners gave credit. As well as the corner stores we had all kinds of Mom and Pop operations all over the Point. Like, for example, on the corner of Richardson and Shearer we had Andy's restaurant. It was always busy with Northern employees. I swear, not one piece of furniture, cutlery or glassware in that place matched, but it didn't matter. There was a little dry-goods store not too far away, as well, that catered to Northern Electric people. It was called Samuel's and Samuel's. They did sewing, darning and things like that. You can still see traces of what it was like. If you look in the window of the old Salon Laurette beauty parlor on Centre Street, you can see that the only thing missing is the people. It has been closed for a very long time, but it just sits there, empty. It still has the same 1950s-style counter tops, sinks and colors. Nothing has changed, not even the painted sign on the window.

When we lived on Charlevoix Street we were just about right across the street from where Frank Hanley's garage stood. Believe me, Frank Hanley did a lot for the Point. Sometimes my grandfather and I would go over to his office and talk to him. You know, he used to keep a supply of tinned sauces and pasta and things like that in his office. If someone came over to tell Frank he was going hungry, Frank would give the person some food. If someone lost their job and came to Frank, he'd say, "OK, come back and see me late tomorrow", and then he'd be on the phone finding a job. I can remember situations when I was with my mother and someone would say something bad about Frank Hanley. She'd just turn right around and tell them to shut-up, and that Frank had done a great deal for the people of the Point.

There was a pretty big open space behind our building on Charlevoix Street. It was all dirt—no grass. It was all boxed in with houses or flats. That was our play area. It's part of the

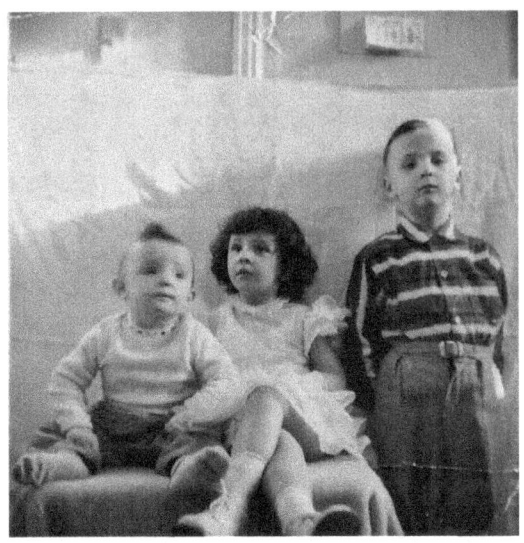

Brother Ronald, cousin Carole and Roger (age 5). 1958.

Magnan's Restaurant parking lot now. Even back then, cars used to park there. Magnan's was an old-style tavern in those days. I can remember when I was a kid that pretty regularly you'd see guys tumbling out of the place and into the street in a fight. I'll never forget these two Irish brothers that were there a lot. They were amazing. They were always fighting. I even remember them fighting more than once on the same night. They'd go in and drink, then come out and fight. Then they'd drink some more and come out and fight again. I was around eight or nine at the time. Sometimes we'd walk over to the old "Bucket of Blood" and sit up on the roof beside the tavern and just wait for a fight. You usually weren't disappointed. There were one or two other spots around the Point that you could do this too.

Yes, we had lots of taverns in the Point. My own favourite was Nap's tavern over on Mullins Street. Mullins is right beside the tracks that used to separate the English and French sides of the Point. The tavern was long and narrow on the inside. The French guys would sit at one end and the English guys at the other. There was a no-man's land in the middle where people that didn't know any better about the Point might stumble in and sit down. Since I was fluently bilingual I could go and aggravate people at both ends of the tavern! The joke about Nap's was that when you were there you didn't need to wear a watch. You could tell the time by who was sitting where; what size of beer bottle various well known patrons were ordering at a particular time of the day, or which group of people was coming or going from the different factories and businesses.

Canon O'Meara and Sarsfield were the big Irish schools. I went to the French boys' school, St. Charles, but we also had other schools in the Point and we had lots of different churches: Polish, Ukrainian—there was a good mix of people in the Point. To me, Richardson Street was the most multicultural, but I don't ever recall there being any "Little Ukraine"-type places or anything like that in the Point. The smaller ethnic groups like the Ukrainians were spread around

Richardson's on Charlevoix Street. 2011.

Roger on St. Patrick Street. 1959.

a bit. I didn't have much trouble with the French /English thing that people will talk about in the Point. I lived on the French side. I went to a French school and I spoke English at home. I was comfortable anywhere in the Point. I could go wherever I wanted, and I did. I can really only remember one situation in the Point where I was a target. I was walking alone in the English section of the Point when a group of guys passing me mumbled something at me in French. When I answered in fluent French that was their signal. They were all English. They started pushing me around a bit and they gave me a hard time. But what's interesting about this is that just a week or so after that I was walking alone in Verdun and something similar happened. A gang of Verdun guys that didn't recognize me started to move in on me. But as it happened, the very same English guys that had been pushing me around in the Point the week before were walking on the other side of the street and saw this. They immediately ran across the street and confronted the Verdun bunch. It didn't matter that they had been giving me a hard time the week before in the Point. What mattered was that someone from the Point was outnumbered and in trouble.

My father worked for the Canadian Pacific Railway (CPR), and my mother worked at Walker Papers over in Griffintown. Walker was very close to the CNR's old Wellington tower. After I was born my mother stayed at home. But when my father passed away at age 29, that changed everything. I was eight years old and my brother was three. My mother went back to work and she juggled several part-time jobs while raising us. She worked cleaning houses. She worked at Loiselle Grocery. Then, on the weekends my mother worked at a caterer's. She worked very hard to support us and she never remarried. And at the time my younger brother had some health challenges.

When I was growing up I did what I could to help out. I started delivering the <u>Montreal Matin</u> and the <u>Montreal Gazette</u> when I was quite young. I'd also take my wagon over to the A&P grocery store and stand outside and wait to help people carry their bags home. Later on, I worked in grocery stores and rode the big three-wheeler delivery bikes. I had several other part time jobs over the years. I remember when Chargex cards were becoming all the rage; I got a job delivering them door-to-door. You'd hand them over and have people sign for them. I was assigned to deliver them in Hampstead once and I was stopped and questioned by the Hampstead Police on three separate occasions. Here was this kid walking around in black and white sneakers carrying a bag and knocking on doors. I guess I looked quite out of place by Hampstead standards. Right from the beginning, whatever money I made I would turn it over to my mother and then she would give me some back for my pocket money. And when I joined the Navy, I sent money home every payday to my mother. We could buy cigarettes cheaply in the Navy so I used to buy some, package them up and send them home. I supported my mother and brother.

My mother had a pretty straightforward philosophy of life when it came to raising kids —"Don't make me ashamed of you!" I remember I came home after school one summer and said, "That's it, and I'm not going back to school any more. I'm finished!" My mother immediately went over to Steinberg's. I guess

Frank Hanley. (1909–2006). Date unknown.

she knew someone there. She came home and told me to report to Steinberg's the next morning for work. I did, and let me tell you, they worked me to the bone in that supermarket. Each time I finished something there was something else, and then something else. They kept me late and they never stopped. Looking back, I guess it was a set-up. I went back to school.

Mostly when we were young my crowd would stay in the Point, but sometimes we'd go over into Griffintown or neighboring areas like Saint-Henri or Old Montreal. Leo Leonard was a big name in Griffintown. He ran that Horse Palace for as long as I can remember and I used to hang around there from time to time. I'd get horses ready for Leo to groom. He'd just call over and say, "Go and get so-and-so". You know, Leo Leonard knew so much about horses that sometimes veterinarians would ask him for his opinion. A vet would be over at his place looking at a horse with some issue he couldn't figure out and he'd call Leo over and ask, "What do you think, Leo?" And the thing is, the veterinarian would listen. Leo Leonard knew a lot about horses. Just a little while ago I attended Leo's funeral.

Growing up in the Point, none of us had a lot of money, but we had other things. We had a lot of friends and we knew that the people of the area were looking out for us. When I was on Island and Châteauguay we lived in a typical Point St. Charles three-storey walk-up. Some of the

The derelict Wellington (railway) tower and adjacent swing bridge that served the Lachine Canal viewed from Griffintown's rapidly redeveloping Wellington Street. 2013.

places in the Point had staircases on the outside. Others had them on the inside. Ours were on the inside and the building housed a corner store. The store isn't there any more. It just got converted into living space. In that small tenement we had about 35 kids between the ages of 2 and 15. There was a good mix of people there too…Irish, Polish, French, Italian.

The kitchen was always the soul of the houses in the Point. Often, they'd be the biggest rooms in the flats, and they were always the warmest. We were lucky. The kitchens in both the flats I lived in were a good size. In our second place we had a wood stove that was converted to oil for heating, and we had an electric stove for cooking. The kitchen was big enough that if the weather was just too bad my friends and I could play there. I remember that one game we played was floor hockey with sawed-off hockey sticks. We'd play the game on our knees with very short hockey sticks that you'd hold with only one hand.

Behind the building of our second place there was also a patch of land—again, no grass, just dirt. It had three big sheds in the back that went from the ground to the third floor. There were little catwalks from the flats to the sheds where people stored wood and things like that. Anyway, that space in the back is where we played and we made our own fun. In the winter, in that little patch of land the kids from the tenement organized and looked after three small skating rinks. One guy on the main floor used to let us attach a hose to his kitchen sink and get water. Maybe he had a little more money than some others, but I think he was just content to see his kids happy and playing so he covered the water bill. One rink was for the tiny kids, another little square rink was for older kids and then we had one that stretched from the far corner of the back yard down the driveway to the sidewalk on Island. That's the one we called our speed rink. No one ever used

The Griffintown Horse Palace. 2010 and 2011.

the driveway so we took it over. We looked after it all ourselves. I remember I got my first pair of hockey gloves from my mother after she collected these little stamps you'd get when you bought groceries. They were called "Gold Star" stamps. After you collected enough of them you could trade them in for different articles. Well, she saved and saved these stamps until we had enough for her to order these hockey gloves for me. I was very proud of those gloves. They weren't professional gloves or anything. I think the wrist protectors were probably made of cardboard, but they were my own gloves and I appreciated and valued them.

In our tenement we had several extended families. I remember two different sets of brothers. Each brother had his own flat. In our building, if one of the mums had an appointment or something, the kids would always get looked after by someone else, whether family or not. You just added some more water to the soup and everyone had something to eat. Sometimes I'd find myself at one of the Polish family's flats. "Come on in", they'd say. "Sit down and eat!" You could say I became an epicurean growing up in the Point. But it wasn't because we were going out to fancy restaurants or anything. It was because there was a lot of sharing going on between the different families and cultures in the places I lived. I'll give you another example. I can remember going over to my Aunt Carmen's house to visit. She was my dad's sister. She and her neighbor were so close that they knocked a small hole in the adjoining kitchen walls between the two row houses they lived in. It was about shoulder height and small doors were installed on both sides. The two of them would pass food between the two houses. If one had sauce and one had pasta, both families had spaghetti. If one had peanut butter and the other family had lots of bread, you had peanut butter sandwiches.

Yvon Deschamps is a very well-known celebrity in Quebec. He talks about Saint-Henri and how families there shared yards just like we did. And as he says, if something goes wrong, 18 doors open and 36 sets of arms come out. Well, that about sums it up for the Point St. Charles where I grew up—very similar, same attitude, same very strong sense of community. At Christmas time it was quite something. Some of the streets around our place were so lit up with

Leo Leonard. 2010.

outside decorations and lights it was like daylight! We had a real sense of community in that place that people just don't seem to have now.

Delivery vans were always a target for kids all over the Point and we were no different. It didn't matter what kind. We were always on the lookout for soft drink delivery trucks for cases of empties that we could run off with and cash in. If you scraped up enough to buy a few of the big bottles of Royal Stewart Ginger Ale doing this, and also managed to raid a bakery truck for one of those big cakes, then the whole gang could go back to a shed in the back yard and have a feast. I remember that the guys who drove the Thibeault ice delivery trucks were always pretty good with the kids. During the summer they'd often purposely drop big blocks of ice on the road beside groups of kids. The ice would smash and we'd have our popsicles. One of our neighbors was a truck driver. He drove one of those big 40-foot trucks and he'd often deliver fruit to outlets in the area. Depending on the season it could be anything—watermelons, strawberries and sometimes apples. Sometimes the supplier would give him an extra pallet of fruit for himself and he'd bring the truck over to our building and back this thing up our narrow driveway and into the yard to share the fruit. All the kids would race out and help themselves to the fresh fruit. I remember that apples always seemed to be very plentiful.

We didn't have a lot of parks in the Point, but my favourite was what we used to call the Goose Village Park. It's at the corner of St. Patrick Street just over the bridge from Griffintown into the Point. They had things there you could climb on. But if we weren't at the park, we'd be busy with something else. We used to spend a lot of time in what our bunch called the "jungle". It was quite a big strip of bush land in between Wellington Street and Verdun near Butler. It was long, narrow and full of trees and marshy land. A branch of the St. Pierre River is underneath this area. We'd go there and stay practically all day. We'd vanish in there climbing and building things. There was a railway overpass right beside the jungle and we used to play on that a lot as well.

There was a car dealership not too far from where we lived, and on Sundays there was never anyone there. Those were the days when a lot of the cars had push button starters. We'd go over and jimmy our way into these cars and start playing with the starters to make the cars jump. You'd stick with one car until you ran the battery flat and then move over to another one. And whenever we'd hear the fire truck sirens or bells we'd either chase the fire trucks or run directly over to the fire station to see if it was empty. And if it was, we'd go inside and play. I remember once we were upstairs in one of the stations playing pool when some of the firefighters returned from a call and caught us. All they did was tell us to get out. Yeah, my mother used to say that she always knew where we were if she heard a siren—at the fire or at the fire station. Other times we'd go over to Verdun and fish in the Montreal Aqueduct. There are two big Montreal filtration plants drawing from the aqueduct. One is in Verdun and one is farther out west. We didn't ever swim in the aqueduct, though, because my mother had us terrified that there were huge pipes everywhere that would suck us away underwater if we went in.

Speaking of Verdun, that was another story. There was more money in Verdun than in the Point and the houses were nicer. One of my cousins lived there. We'd go over there we'd all go out and play and, of course, we'd get dirty. That's what kids do. Well, we'd go back to his place and his mother would give him a set of clean clothes before lunch and he'd even get a fresh pair of white sneakers. If we stayed over

Roger, pointing to his third-floor flat on Island Street. He and his friends in the building looked after their own skating rinks. 2012.

longer, like for dinner, he'd change again. This used to absolutely amaze me. That's not the way it worked in the Point. I joke with people that I was proud of the layers of dirt I developed when I was playing.

When I was growing up I was a big reader. Give me a good book and I was happy. I loved reading, and reading all kinds of stuff. When I was a kid I enjoyed what they used to call the "Classic" comic books. They were bigger than the regular books and they were actually summaries of good books like A Tale of Two Cities and things like that. I wasn't into the superhero stuff. Anyway, not too far away from our place there was a big recycling outfit and they used to get box upon box of old comic books to recycle. So we used to sneak in there when it was closed and go through all the boxes looking for these Classic comics.

When I was a teenager I guess you could say I was adventurous, and by sixteen I was looking for something else. This was at the height of the Vietnam war. My friend and I decided that we'd go and join the U.S. Marines. No one knew about it but us. We crossed the border and went to Plattsburgh where we sat down with a recruiter. In those days you were supposed to be 18, but you could get in with your parents' signature if you were 17. Like I said, we were 16. The recruiter had probably seen this all before. He talked to us for a while and he gave us each a form to take back to Canada. He told us to wait until we were 17, get our parents' approval and then come back and see him if we were still interested. Back we went and I showed it to my mother.

Roger near the train trestle that he and his friends played on as children. 2012.

To put it mildly, she went out of her mind. The result of it all was that, like I said before, I joined the Canadian Navy instead where I served for four years. I was a Boatswain and the Ship's Diver. You know, a lot of guys from the Point joined the services. The Navy was popular. The 79th Battery of the Royal Canadian Artillery was in the Point and a lot of young men also joined the Black Watch. On Remembrance Day down here, you can still hear the older guys refer to the Point as "Black Watch Country".

My service in the Navy taught me discipline and it served me very well. When I got out I joined the Montreal Police and served for 31 years. I was a detective for 18 of those years— ten in general investigations and eight in homicide. Throughout my career I always made sure to treat people with respect, regardless of the situation or where they came from. I can remember many instances in my police life where someone I might have arrested, but treated fairly and with respect would call me years later, sometimes out of the blue, to help me with a case. Other times I could call someone I had previously arrested and ask for some information. As often as not, I'd get it.

What were the values that were admired in the Point? We were brought up to have integrity, to respect others, to have faith in yourself, and to stand up for yourself. We were taught that people from the Point don't back down. We were taught this from an early age. We were brought up to have moxie, and if confronted we were fearsome. We learned in the Point to look after ourselves individually but also collectively. If you think about it, that Verdun situation where the guys that pushed me around the week before came to my aid in Verdun the next week sort of sums it up—it's an example of the sense of community—a sense of family in the Point. You can have lots of arguments and disagreements in the family, but if challenged as a family you pull together. In the Point, we were also taught never to look down on people.

When my mother passed away there were almost 500 people that came to pay their respects over a two-day period, either at the wake or at the funeral. That's because my mother grew up in, and committed herself to the area and to helping others. On numerous occasions, for example, I have seen her step in to help in tragic situations and organize funerals for neighbors. She'd take charge of all the work. I remember her calling people, including me and delegating tasks in order to make sure everything went well. There was never any question. That's just the way it was. Again, that was the sense of community—the idea of commitment. And when close to 500 people show up that tells you something about both the person's life and the community. In the Point, you committed and you gave—you didn't just take. In the Point, Goose Village and Griffintown you earned respect. You had to commit. My own take on things is that unfortunately, the sense of community in today's society is much weaker than when I was growing up in the Point.

We never had a lot of material possessions, but we had heart, respect and consideration for others. Let's face it, from a financial standpoint, people from the Point back when I was a kid were down near the bottom of the ladder. But the people from that area strived to better themselves. A lot of families arrived in the Point and were seen as a source of cheap labour—ditch diggers. Maybe so, but as the generations progressed, you could trace families going from ditch diggers, to factories and inside jobs, to public works, firefighters, police, then on to jobs like engineers and other professionals. I know families that go four generations back with the Canadian National Railway and other organizations and you can see the progression. In any community you'll always have the small minority that go the wrong way and get into trouble, and

Roger (right) at the Remembrance Day ceremony in Marguerite Bourgeoys Park. 2012.

we had our share. And yes, the area had a welfare challenge. In one case I know of, a family has been on welfare for four generations—but that's not the Point as a whole—that's the caricature of the Point. The truth is that 95% of the people in the Point just wanted to do the right things and build a better life for their families. I have known people from Griffintown and Village for my whole life and they'll tell you the same thing. If we wanted something we knew that the way to get it was by hard work and persistence. The Point and Griffintown and areas like what is now called Little Burgundy produced a good number of firefighters, policemen and lots of public works guys. When the people with money in places like Westmount and Mount Royal and Hampstead were home at night in bed, it was a lot of guys like us, usually from modest upbringings that were out there making sure the City was safe. I sometimes think about that.

I'm retired now but I am involved in various associations and clubs like the Erin Sports Club. We help sports organizations and we do community work. For example, we host an annual Christmas party for underprivileged children from the area. Usually, each child leaves with a gift that is worth at least $50. We try to help St. Gabriel's Church too. I'm pretty good with my hands, so I also keep busy doing some renovation work here and there, and I maintain my long-time interest in the history of Point St. Charles, the CNR, the old Montreal tramlines and things like that.

I worked hard. I have a good pension now and things worked out well. But I'll say this—if something happened and financially, I found myself at the bottom of the ladder tomorrow, I could look after myself just fine, thank you, because in the beginning, that's where I came from. I'm from the Point! It may not have been the classiest place in town, but it was our home.

"There are a lot of sights and sounds

from the Point

that anybody that lived there

back in the busy days

won't ever forget:

the sounds of the trains,

the kids all over the street,

the baseball games down at the park on Butler…

There was always the sound of people on the balconies

talking to each other

and calling out to others in the streets."

Eddy Nolan

Eddy Nolan

Eddy Nolan is a five-time Quebec *Golden Gloves* boxing champion, a marathon runner, and a nationally recognized fundraiser in the fight against cancer. He is also a symbol of courage and determination for the students of Roslyn School in Westmount where he is caretaker.

As a young man, Eddy was inspired deeply by Terry Fox's story. Eddy has run 31 Terry Fox marathons—every one held so far. Ten years ago, Eddy talked to the children at Roslyn School and asked them to join him in helping to raise money to fight cancer. After nine years they had raised just over $171,000. He then asked the kids if they could make it to $200,000 and they agreed.

Then, in early 2011 Eddy was diagnosed with stage four cancer—the most serious. Through his battle with cancer, now in remission, Eddy continued to run and raise funds. Eddy's goal of raising $200,000 with the children from Roslyn was recently surpassed. The money that is raised is donated to the Terry Fox Foundation.

"…growing up in the Point was tough. My father always said Never quit, but my mother always told me never to give up trying. I got the toughness and hardness from my father, but I got the love and compassion from my mother."

In honour of Eddy's accomplishments, he was inducted into the Point St. Charles Hall of Recognition in 2011. In addition to continued fund raising, Eddy is also pursuing the goal of having April 12th declared "Terry Fox Day" across Canada. That was the day Terry started his cross-country run. Says Eddy, "I would like to see that day in every Canadian school's calendar and every student's school agenda."

As of December 3, 2012 Eddy was once again working full time. When he returned to Roslyn School part time in September of 2012, the 2011–2012 graduating class presented Eddy with a large framed drawing of himself and Terry Fox. Beside the drawing are written comments from every graduating student. The messages outline how much of an inspiration Eddy has been to the students of Roslyn School. In November of 2012, Eddy was awarded the Queen Elizabeth II Diamond Jubilee Medal. It was presented to him at Roslyn School by Marc Garneau (MP Ville Marie), Eddy received the award in honor of his efforts in the fight against cancer. Eddy remains in good health, and is still running marathons. He continues to work with many across Canada in an effort to establish April 12th as National Terry Fox Day.

Although Eddy has lived in the West Island of Montreal for the last 17 years, he will tell you that he will always be a proud "Pointer". Eddy is a rapid-fire storyteller. He loves to laugh, and he loves the Point. This is Eddy's story.

Photo: Eddy leads a throng of runners to the start line of the 2013 Terry Fox run at the Old Port.

I was born in 1957. A year ago, I went to the doctor because my neck was sore. I thought it was muscular. The doctor scoped my nose and my throat and said, "No, it's not muscular.". He went to the phone and called emergency and said that he had a patient with him, Mr. Nolan, and that it looked like cancer and he needed some tests done—right away. Just like that! I was floored! My first thought was how could this be happening to me? I have been working for 30 years to raise money for the fight against cancer. I've been running marathons since I was 22. This can't happen to me! Then I settled down a bit and thought, that's crazy—of course it can happen to me. Why couldn't it? Let's see what the tests say.

I immediately underwent some tests and I was called in a few days later. Sure enough, it was cancer. The doctor said it was stage four—very serious—that it was in the lymph nodes and tonsils…no time to waste! And from that point on, no time was wasted—35 straight days of radiation on my neck, accompanied by chemotherapy. It was painful. My neck took a while to recover from the radiation burns. But I've been a fighter all my life. I started boxing when I was seven and I always fought as hard as I could. I didn't back down in the ring and I didn't back down in the streets. On the one hand, that approach has served me well. On the other, not pulling back on a few occasions did lead to some difficult situations for me later in life.

Well, I'm in a fight now. But I've just had tremendous support from people everywhere: my girlfriend Mary, my family, marathon runners I have met from all over the world, my friends in the Point, and the children at Roslyn School in Westmount. Those kids at the school are amazing. They all rallied behind me. They have been absolutely wonderful. I love working with them. They call me "Mr. Eddy". They have raised thousands of dollars that we've donated to the Terry Fox Foundation over the years, and since I got sick they haven't stopped. It has been ten years since I first asked the kids if they'd like to help raise money in the fight against cancer and they have worked hard ever since. So far we have raised over $228,000.

I'm on leave from the school now because the doctors said I'm not supposed to lift anything over 10 lbs. Can you believe that? Everything a caretaker touches weighs over ten lbs.! Also, I still have a feeding tube in my stomach. If one of the kids at school were to accidentally run into it I could be in trouble. I only have to use the tube at lunchtime. I get to eat breakfast and dinner normally, so I'm pretty fortunate there.

The cancer is in remission now. Seven months after the diagnosis I ran my first marathon—the Marine Corps Marathon in Washington DC. I wore a runner's shirt with the words "Seven months after cancer recovery" written on the back. Then, four months later I ran the Shamrock Marathon in Virginia. This time my shirt read "11 months after cancer treatment". Yeah…I'm still running. I improved my finishing time at the Shamrock marathon, as well, so I'm happy about that.

I am looking forward to getting back to work. I enjoy the school a lot. The staff at Roslyn usually has lunch together. Sometimes they'll ask me to tell them some stories about growing up in the Point, and, believe me, there are lots of stories. So I tell them some. They'll have a good laugh, then, in one form or another it will come around to the same question that I've been asked many, many times before—"how did you survive?" I just give my usual response, "Ah…it was easy!" I have already been asked by several writers to collaborate with them on a book.

I'm a very proud Pointer and I always will be. I grew up in a big Point St. Charles family. I had six sisters and four brothers—eleven of us. From one child to the next we were close in age. We lived on several different streets in the Point: Ash, Coleraine and Hibernia. We only ever had one bathroom in our flats, and we'd never have less than two sets of bunk beds in each bedroom, sometimes three. I remember that if the person on the bottom bunk kicked up hard enough you could launch the person in the top bunk right out of bed. My father had a carpenter friend of his build us a big, long bench so that we could all squeeze in for meals. Thinking back

Eddy (left) and his old friend and sparring partner Ian Clyde. 2013.

to those days, I can remember the harder times when all there was for a snack for us sometimes was some bread with butter with a little sugar sprinkled on it. I remember other times, although it wasn't all that often, that we wouldn't have milk for our cereal. We'd just use water.

In our house we always had pictures of the Pope on the wall, as well as paintings of the Virgin Mary and the Last Supper and things like that. I remember that, from time to time, my dad would ask one of us why the Apostles were all sitting on one side of the table. Then he'd laugh and say "it's because they all wanted to be in the picture!" We also always had a cross on the wall. It was my mother's. I have that cross now and it's on the wall of the bedroom that my daughter uses when she comes to visit.

There was never a lot of money in the house and my mum was very careful with what we had. My father was very careful too. For example, he was always after us about wasting water. He used to turn the faucets off so tightly that you could hardly open them. We all had to do the same thing. If he saw a faucet dripping, watch out! Even today, I still can't help myself. Sometimes my girlfriend has trouble opening a faucet that I've turned off.

When I was growing up in the Point most of the houses were heated by oil. You'd have these great big pipes running from the burner across the ceilings to the various rooms. I used to wake up in the morning with blinding headaches from the oil that was being burned. In those days they actually had oil-dispensing machines located around the Point. You'd put your money in the machine, then put a hose from the machine into a bucket and fill it with oil. The machine we used was near Kobelinski Cleaners. My father would always send me out with these two big buckets to get oil. They were the buckets with the wire handles across the top. They carried about five gallons each and when they were full these things were heavy. The wire handles would dig into your hands. So I'd have a bucket in each hand and I'd have to work my way home. I'd walk a bit, then stop, walk some more, then stop. Sometimes the oil would splash from the buckets onto my clothing.

One night after I went and got some oil, I was playing outside with my friends. There was some street work going on nearby. In those days when the workers finished their shift they'd leave some eternal flames burning to warn drivers and pedestrians during the night. These things were small steel balls with a flat bottom. They were a little smaller than a volleyball. They had a few holes in the top. They were filled with oil and had a wick or something inside that you could light. No matter what you did, these things would never go out. I guess that's why they were called eternal flames. Anyway, one of the guys starts kicking one around like a soccer ball and the fun starts, except when it got to me. I still had oil on my clothes from the trip to the oil-vending machine. The eternal flame hit my pant leg and I went up like a candle. I started running—and I was fast. That didn't help. By the time I hit the dirt and the guys started throwing things on me I already had first, second and third degree burns. Even some of my hair was burned off. I could actually hear the blisters popping on my skin. It was like bacon cooking. I had pieces of skin hanging off. It was quite a scene. One of the guys goes running through the streets to my place screaming "Eddy's dead…Eddy's dead…Eddy's dead". I healed up though. Now, you'd never know it happened. I was in the hospital for a week and the best part was getting all the chocolate and chips. I like to joke with people that it all worked out for the better. I tell them I had curly hair before I caught fire, but when it grew back in it was straight!

We all had jobs to do in the house. Going to the dispensing machine for oil was one of mine. One of my sisters had the laundry and there was lots of it with 13 people in the flat. Sometimes I thought my sister spent half her life at the Laundromat. I used to help her sometimes. In the winter we'd haul the clothing over to the Laundromat on a toboggan. I'd pull the toboggan with the big bags of laundry on it and she'd be in the back trying to make sure they were balanced on the toboggan. We'd have a pocketful of dimes and quarters for the machines. Some of the dryers would run longer than the others, so those were the ones you'd always try and get. It was cheaper that way. Yeah, it seemed sometimes like she was there every night!

When I was small we'd get our baths in a big metal tub that my father would put on the floor. My two younger brothers would go first, then me. I'd always tell them—"Don't pee in that water." I still remember that just before my brother would get out he'd often say, "Hey Eddy, look", and he'd stand up and pee in the water. Then I'd have to get in. My dad always made sure we were clean and he had this thing about checking our hair for bugs. We'd have to bend over a big piece of brown paper and he'd go through our hair with this special, fine comb. It was very small and sharp and he was pretty rough. But we never had bugs. He'd also line us up and clip our nails as well. In the Point when we got our report cards at school there was a section on cleanliness. That was a big deal in those days. People didn't have the facilities back then that we have now. I didn't really understand all this until I got a little older.

My father joined the military when he was very young. He spent around seven years in the army and he fought in places like Italy, Holland and Belgium during the Second World War. He was a Bren Gunner on tanks. He manned those machine guns on the top of the tanks. He didn't talk to me much about the war. I only ever heard him mention it when he was drunk. I do know that he was hit with shrapnel at some point during the war. After the war my father got a job working on the docks in Montreal and he stayed there until he retired. That was back when the Irish controlled the wharf. My dad was a hard man and he was very meticulous. He ran the house like an army unit. There was no hugging or kissing in our house. "Men don't hug and kiss", he'd say. "Men don't cry". Before bed every night, he'd line the boys up in their pajamas and shake hands with us.

My dad ran the Point St. Charles Boys' and Girls' Club for a year and one of his jobs was to empty the cash from the soft-drink machines and chocolate-bar machines and things like that at night, then tally the money. I remember him and my mum rolling the money until late at night, then my dad would take it to the bank the next day. He never took a cent of that money. He was always scrupulously honest.

My parents always did their best, and they tried to make sure that we were always properly dressed and fed. My mother used to go down to a clothing store on St. Lawrence Street because the owner gave my mother credit for our clothing. He did this all over the Point. I remember that the collector would come by the house every Thursday at exactly the same time to collect a two-dollar payment. He'd have this little pink book. If you paid him he'd sign it and you'd sign it. Well, sometimes we just didn't have the money. I'd go to the door while my mother hid. I'd tell him that my mother wasn't home, but that she'd pay him four dollars next week. All the time we're talking he's trying to look over my shoulders—first one shoulder, then the other. So, I'm bobbing right and left trying to block his view. It was like we were doing a dance at the front door. He was absolutely like clockwork on his pick-ups. Honest, a volcano could have erupted in the middle of the Point and he'd still be there! A hurricane could have hit and there he'd be at the door for his two dollars! He must have made a fortune in the Point charging interest to families on these loans.

I remember that my mother used to take onions and slice them up, then soak them in vinegar and put them in the fridge. One day, one of my brothers and I went to the fridge at the same time and there might have been one or two onion slices left sitting on a plate. We both wanted those onion slices. We ended up getting into a full on, toe-to-toe fight in the kitchen over those slices. Another time, when I was quite young I grabbed a sausage off one of my brothers' plates and swallowed it down when he was distracted over something. I got knocked around for it, sure, but at that time, I didn't care. There were lots of families in the Point in the same boat as us. The people in the Point would always share stuff, though. If you needed a couple of tea bags and a half a cup of sugar, your mum could send you over to a neighbor's house to borrow what you needed.

When I was growing up, five or six of my father's friends would come over to our house after dinner on payday. This was a regular thing. I think payday was Thursday. Some of them were from the docks. Others were just friends from the Point. They'd all sit around, tell stories, and drink beer. My father didn't go to the taverns. As the evening wore on they'd all start singing. Someone would break out an accordion. Someone else would sit down at my sister's small drum set. *Danny Boy* was always one of their favorites. This would go on until late in the morning. Then they'd go home, sleep for a while, get up and go back to the wharf. During those visits I'd sit and listen to all these stories until the early morning.

Other times my Dad would sit with me alone until late at night and tell me stories. We'd talk until the early morning. Then I'd go to school dead tired the next day. Sometimes I'd just fall asleep in class. As long as we were talking about boxing or the Montreal wharf everything was fine between us.

I never knew my grandparents. I know that my dad was originally from Goose Village but he moved to the Point. My mother was from Griffintown. My dad was a boxer when he was young, and a very good one. He and my uncle Pat were both boxers. My father won the *Golden Gloves* in 1936, '37 and '38. One time, when he won the *Golden Gloves* he was awarded a very small gold boxing glove that you could wear on a chain. It is inscribed with the date and the initials of the Griffintown Boys' Club. I wear that glove around my neck from time to time. When my father stopped boxing he got into coaching. Boxing was truly his passion. I got involved just like every one of my brothers. One of them won the city championship one year, but I stayed in the game the longest. Maybe I did it to win my father's approval because if you were boxing you were one of his favorites. I started when I was seven and didn't stop until my twenties. It wasn't something I desperately wanted to do when I was a kid. It wasn't my life or anything. But I got very good at it and started to like it. Many of the guys that fought in the Point also had fathers who were fighters before them. Back then, a lot of the guys boxed because it just seemed like it was the thing to do. Times were tough and the people were tough.

My father boxed out of Griffintown. I think when he started coaching it was at the 79th Battery. It wasn't exactly what you'd call a professional facility. Then he started the Shamrock Boxing Club in the Point. He did this with the help of Herman Halperin and Larry Sloan. It was on Sullivan Street, right behind the old Fiesta Club. It cost $75 a month for the rent. We used to put on boxing shows on Sundays for the Fiesta guys and anybody else that came around. Then we'd pass the hat to help cover the rent. My dad's right-hand man all during his coaching days in the Point was Stan Royston. Stan was everywhere in the gym. Whatever my father asked him to do, it was done in a heartbeat. It could range from coaching kids, to Vaselining gloves, to cleaning spit buckets, often with a lot of blood in them. Stan was one hell of a man! He'd be there six or seven days a week. He'd drive us to our fights too. Stan had two sons that were fairly accomplished boxers and they fought with us too. After a while, the club left that location and moved over to a building at the south end of Ash Street right beside where the Point St. Charles Boys' and Girls' Club was built. Finally, we moved into the Boys' and Girls' Club. When we made the move, they asked us to change our name to the Leo's Boys Shamrock Boxing Club. That was fine with us because we still got to keep Shamrock in our name.

One of my father's old friends from the docks was Mr. Jackie Matticks. His family owned a big canvas and rope company out in LaSalle. Mr. Matticks arranged to have the company refinish all our equipment with canvas, leather or rope as needed. All the bags were done with black leather. We had two top-grade boxing rings built. When it was all delivered it just came with a note indicating that it was compliments of the company. Another of my father's friends was a regular at the gym and he was a very proficient welder. His name was Jackie Hughes. He did a lot of work with big hydraulic machines. He had the four steel corner-posts made up for us. I can still remember the day I saw him carrying those posts into the gym. Our facilities and coaching were so good that by the mid-seventies the 1976 Canadian Olympic team even trained there. I was nineteen at the time and sparred with a lot of the guys on the team.

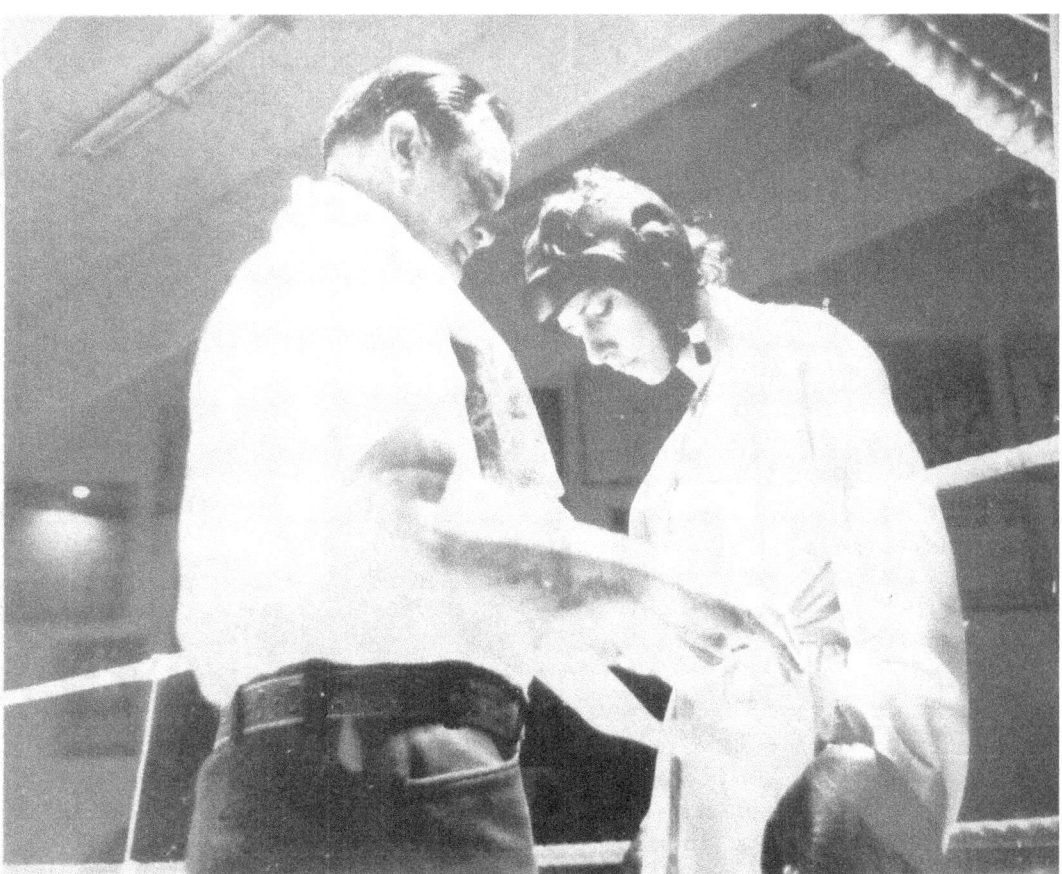

Mike "Sonny" Nolan and Eddy getting ready.

Back in the earlier days of boxing in Griffintown and the surrounding areas Cliff Sowery was the key guy. Let me tell you, this man was like a god in the Griff and the Point. He was just a great coach. He got countless kids off the streets. The guys that competed for Cliff were tough as hell. Cliff Sowery coached my dad when he won his *Golden Gloves* championships three times. My dad then coached me from the start. He was a level five coach. That's the highest level there is.

My father taught me to be a smart fighter. He told me to always keep my head, be smart, fight defensively, stay balanced, and he always emphasized to me that the shortest distance between someone else's face and my fist was a straight line. He taught me to look in the opponent's eyes but see the whole fighter—like for example being able to recognize a subtle shift in body position that meant a swing was coming from the side—or being able to capitalize immediately and attack if I saw a fighter begin to cross one leg over the other in a shuffle. He taught me never, ever to quit. He impressed on us the importance of this. He used to tell us that if you quit once, it will get easier to do it again and it will just keep getting easier. He'd say,

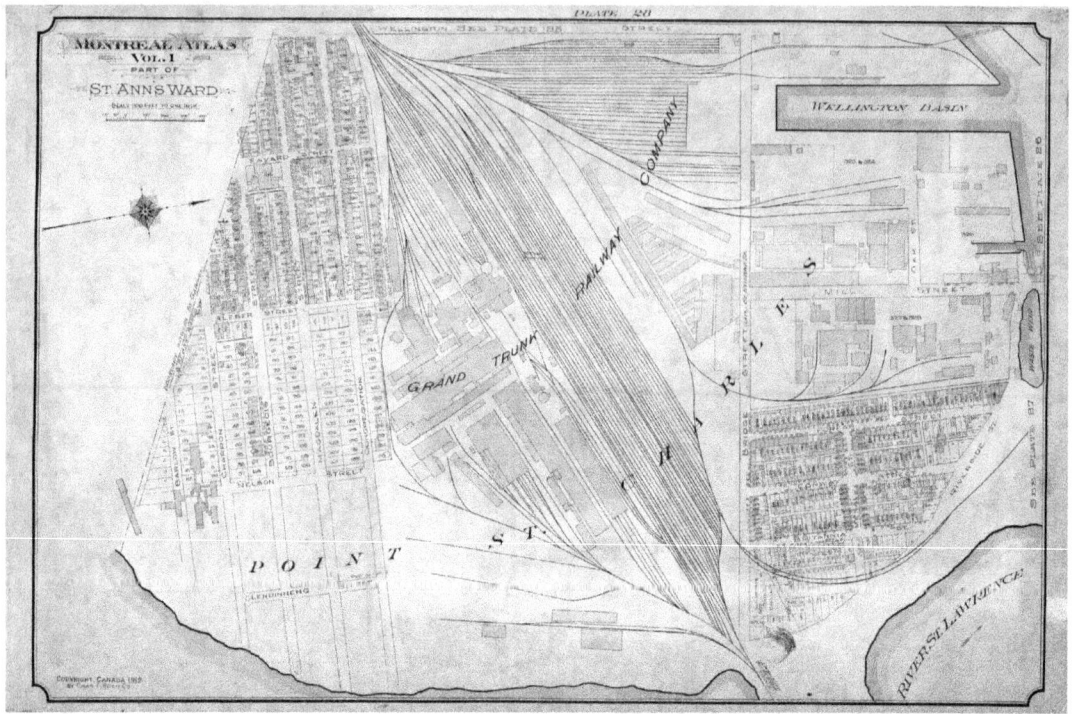

This Chas E. Goad Co. map centres on the Grand Trunk Railway yards (subsequently Canadian National Railway). It shows the relationship between the streets of the southeastern corner of Point St. Charles (top left) and the small community of Goose Village (bottom right), hemmed in by industry, rail yards and the St. Lawrence River. The rail lines converging at the bottom of the frame point to the north end of Victoria Bridge. 1912.

"Quitters never win and winners never quit". I didn't quit in the ring and I only came close to quitting once in a marathon. I was running this marathon in Burlington, Vermont and it was two or three weeks after I'd competed in the Boston marathon. I was exhausted, and I pulled up. I sat down and took my socks and shoes off and threw them in the middle of the street. I was completely frustrated. But my girlfriend was a spectator. When she saw me, she went over and got my shoes. She brought them over to me and just said, "What are you doing?" Thankfully, she talked me out of it and I finished. I had ten miles to go at the time.

By the time I finished fighting I had won five Golden Glove Championships and had fought some great boxers. I was a relatively small fighter—132 lbs. I often had to spar with guys above my own weight. It was hard, but it was good for me. Guys like the Hiltons were in our club for a while. Matthew Hilton was a very hard hitter. Ian Clyde was at our club too. He was a flyweight but he had a lot more experience than I did. Eventually, he went on to the pros under Angelo Dundee and his team. Ian and I used to really go at it sparring. The Boxing Club was in the basement of the Boys' and Girls' Club, and the older guys upstairs in the gym would ask to have someone tell them when Ian and I were putting on the gloves. They'd all come down to watch.

Looking across part of the Point St. Charles railyards toward the, as yet, undeveloped Nun's Island where Eddy and his friends played as children. The residential area of the Point is out of frame to the right. Date unknown

My dad coached Ian from the time he was a novice to being a great boxer. I don't think he ever got the credit he deserved for that. Others got the credit.

My father always looked out for me and for all of his boxers. People will sometimes ask me, "You were a boxer for a long time—how come your nose isn't broken?" I always tell them the same thing—"Because my father taught me how to fight properly". I was offered a pro contract at one point—$32,000 to start. I talked it over with my dad and he advised me against it. You take a lot of punishment in the pros. He had seen a lot of guys go that route and some of them were just never the same. I met my share of guys like that too. Like I said, my father looked after us. Anyway, it wouldn't have meant I was actually going to get $32,000, because you have to pay all your expenses out of that.

Looking back on boxing, I had some great experiences. I made some life-long friends. I fought at the nationals. I boxed on the Quebec team. I got to travel a lot. At one point I spent three weeks in France. We also had an exchange program in the Point with Irish boxers for a while so I spent some time in Ireland.

But even though I won those five Golden Gloves Championships, it just never seemed to be enough for my father. It just seemed like I was never good enough for him, no matter what I did. It was the same thing with running marathons. At one point my father was always talking about this young guy at the docks and how good a marathoner he was. Well, one time this guy was training for the same race as me. After the race I dropped over to see my dad. He didn't know I'd been in the race. When I told him I had just been in the marathon, he says to me, "Did you finish? So-and-so from the docks got a silver medal—his time was three hours and 20 minutes". I just reached into my pocket, pulled out a gold medal and said "three hours and four minutes". My father didn't say a word. He just got up and walked away. There were times over the years when I couldn't stand my dad and the feeling was probably mutual.

It wasn't until just before he died that my father ever told me he was proud of me. He was in a wheelchair at the time and I went over to see him. My girlfriend was with me. I took over my framed Terry Fox certificate. By that time I had accumulated 25 seals for the certificate. You get one every time you complete the Run. I have run every one so far. He looked at it for a bit and then said to me that doing something like that really took a lot of guts and determination. Then he told me something I had never heard—how proud he was of me for all of the things I had accomplished in life. I don't think I was ever as upset or angry in my life. I looked at him and said…"48 years you wait to tell me that! 48 years I have to wait to get your approval! I'm the guy you used to call a bum". He didn't say anything. He just turned the wheelchair around, went into another room for a few minutes and came back with a chequebook. He wrote out a cheque for $1000 for the Terry Fox Cancer Run and told me again how proud of me he was. He died not long after that.

But, you know, there was this thing about a lot of the fathers of that generation in the Point. It seemed like a lot of them just couldn't show any emotion at all. I don't remember my father even giving my mother a peck on the cheek more than a half a dozen times. I don't know why my father was like this. Maybe it was because he saw his own father die. When he was a little boy he used to carry lunch to his father at work. One day when he arrived at the bridge his father was helping build, it had just collapsed and killed his father. Maybe it was the experiences of the war that had an effect on my father. Like I said, I know that at one point he was wounded with shrapnel. Or maybe it was just because he couldn't give what he might never have received himself. All I know is that it was a very long and very hard wait to get his approval.

I remember when I was a kid sometimes just him and me would sit late at night and listen to some of the music that he liked. We'd just sit and listen. I can remember sometimes looking up at him and seeing the sadness in his eyes. I'd see them misting up a bit. You could see them change, but he never cried. You'd never see a tear. It couldn't have been easy for my father. When he lost his father, his mother remarried, but he never accepted the man. Then, after the war he spent his working life on the docks and came home every night to 11 kids. At the end of the week he'd give my mother his pay because she was the one that looked after all the bills and things like that. Then he'd get maybe twenty bucks back depending on the situation that week. That money was to get him through the week with cigarettes and other stuff. He always carried a lunch to the wharf. Sometimes he'd be working in twenty below zero weather and things like that. No, I'm sure it wasn't easy.

When I was growing up in the Point I was very close to three other guys. We were always together—one of them was originally from Goose Village. When the City demolished the Village

The stockyards. Date unknown

he moved over to the Point with his family. A lot of Italians from the Village moved over to the Point. The four of us all went to Canon O'Meara. By the time we got there, the Presentation Brothers had already left. I was pretty good in school and remember that once I came first in a spelling bee and won a Montreal Catholic School Commission medal. I got along well with the teachers. I found out later that one of my teachers even named one of their children after me. Another teacher that I had used to eat at her mother's place in the Point at lunch-time. On Fridays she'd sometimes take me with her. Her mother would make these really good grilled cheese sandwiches and there was always lots of milk. When we left, her father always gave me a quarter.

Yeah, I got along fine at school and I was always friendly with the girls that were there too. But in the Point, kids learned to fight. You had to. At school, things could start in a flash, and me and my three buddies were pretty much the tough guys of our age group. We knew how to mix it up. I remember one situation when I was quite young. This guy who was older and much bigger than me comes over and steals my bag of chips. I told him twice to give it back. The answer was the same both times—"F#:K-off Nolan!" I knew there was no way I could overpower this guy, and I didn't want to let this go. I didn't ask a third time. I walked away for a

The stockyards. Above, and facing page. Dates unknown.

few minutes, came back, tapped him on the shoulder and when he turned around I settled it—physically, and quickly, but not in a way that would be considered acceptable by today's standards, and certainly not in a way I would advocate to a child today. Back then, it was a different time and a much different place. Today, we take bullying very seriously in schools and there are many different and positive conflict resolution processes available. I know that when I'm at the school, any chance I get I speak to the children about the importance of respect for each other, and that bullying or violence is just unacceptable.

But like I said, in my old world it was a different place. I remember that my father used to tell me that if I was ever in a situation where I was getting taken advantage of by a much bigger kid or a bully, that I should just make sure that before things were over I got one really good shot in. He told me they'd never forget it and wouldn't bother me any more.

After Canon O'Meara I went to James Lyng High School in Saint-Henri. You'd get situations there too. Somebody would say something like, "You Point guys are nothing but a bunch of welfare bums and there are rats in your houses". Then the fight would be on. I got booted out of James Lyng. Like I said earlier, this type of attitude, not knowing when to back off, got me in some situations in life. I remember my mother would hear about things like this

and she used to always remind me that "It isn't where you live, it is how you live". Well, that may be true, but back in those days in the schoolyard when someone was saying things like that involving your neighborhood, your family and your friends, it was just a different story. Yeah…growing up in the Point was tough. My father always said, "Never quit", but my mother always told me never to give up trying. I got the toughness and hardness from my father, but I got the love and compassion from my mother.

The truth is that guys in the Point worked hard. We were brought up with the idea that if you did a job, you did it right. To me, it's a nice thing to know that when you go home you've done the job the best way you know how. You know, one of my very closest friends from the Point is a University Professor out west. He has written several books. He has a daughter and a son and they are both studying to be doctors. And, like a lot of other people from the point, he didn't have a particularly easy life when he was young. You don't accomplish what he has without hard work.

No, we never had all that much growing up in our family, and we weren't much different than anyone else in the Point. Things got handed down. If you got a bike it was likely your big brother's, but we grew up valuing what we had. Our parents would just tell us that "wants are many, needs are few". For a little while, when I was young, I have to say, that I was bit uneasy about being from the Point. But after I started boxing and got good at it, I'd look people right in the eye when they asked me where I was from, and I'd just say, "I'm from the Point". Sometimes they'd just say…"Oh".

Through it all I loved growing up in the Point. I wouldn't change it for the world. The stories could go on forever. In the summer we'd sleep on our balconies under a roof we'd make out of blankets that we'd pin around the railings and things. Our playgrounds were places like the Canada Packers Stockyards, the CN railway yards, the streets, the Lachine Canal, Nun's Island before any houses were built on it, and other similar places. We had freedom then as 11- and 12-year-olds that kids just don't have today.

We used to sneak into the Canada Packers Stockyards over by Goose Village a lot. The best way to get there was to work your way through the CN railyards from the Point St. Charles side. You had to avoid the CN Police when you were doing this. We'd get into the stockyards and ride anything that walked, you name it—sheep, cows, pigs, horses, anything! We'd build forts in the stockyard hay bales as well. We'd burrow in underneath. The guards at the stockyards were always on the lookout. They'd go around with pitchforks from time to time prodding around in the hay piles. I remember once I got caught, and when you did, the guards would throw you into this big pool of white stuff. I don't know what it was but it stained your clothes badly and you couldn't get it out. The guards knew that if they did that your parents would know you'd been caught in the stockyards. I got caught once and I begged the guard not to throw me in. At the last minute he asks me "What's your name?" I told him Eddy Nolan. He says, "Are you Sonny Nolan's kid?" I told him, no, my father's name was Mike. He whacks me in the head and says "That's Sonny, are you trying to be smart?" I didn't know at that time that Sonny was my father's nickname. Then the guard reaches in his pocket, takes out a quarter, gives it to me and says, "Now get the f@#k outta here!"

We were always building forts in the Point when we were kids. In the winter it was out of snow. In the summer you'd do it with bits and pieces of cardboard, wood, and anything you could find lying around. We'd spend hours building these things and then we'd attack each other's forts. If it wasn't forts it was pushcarts. We were always on the lookout for material to build home made pushcarts. One guy would push, the other would steer. The wheels and axles from baby carriages were always in high demand.

I learned how to swim when a bunch of guys—they were all brothers—just picked me up and threw me into the Lachine Canal. They all jumped in after me. They all gathered around me in the water and started yelling instructions to me, "Do this, do that, kick your feet" That's how I learned to swim. The water in that canal was black and when you got out you stunk.

And Nun's Island—well, that was great! It was like a huge campground for us. My mum used to buy me these little cans of Irish stew and a few other things to take with me on a Friday night. We would go over and camp for the weekend. We weren't supposed to. It was private property, but we didn't care and usually the guys who were responsible for the place would leave us alone. We'd start a fire, make beds out of tree branches, see who could spear the most field

Inside the railway shops, 1929

mice over the weekend, go fishing, and do other things like that. We used to catch these great big catfish. There was a guy in the Point who'd buy them for two bucks each.

We always used to dive for golf balls in the water hazards at the golf course on Nun's Island. You had to be careful doing this because the hazards were full of bloodsuckers and you couldn't see very well. We just used to wrap our arms in garbage bags when we were rooting around the bottom for balls. Sometimes we'd just wait near the hazards for someone to shoot their ball in. We'd dive it, get it, and sell it back to them. I remember I could make $30 in a weekend diving for golf balls. That was a lot of money. The thing was that we were supposed to give the balls to the pro shop instead of selling them directly to golfers. But we made more money selling to the golfers than the pro shop. One day the Pro caught us selling them on our own and banned us.

I also remember going with some pals from the Point to Morin Heights up in the Laurentians. We'd go down to the bus station at Berri Street and take the Provincial bus up to Morin Heights and camp there just the way we would on Nun's Island. I liked it up there. My

The snack bar where young Eddy worked when it was simply known as "Roy's". 2011.

Mum used to always try and scrape enough money together to rent a small cabin for the summer too. She didn't want us running the streets in the Point every day. She wanted us out in the fresh air in the country. She usually pulled it together. I was even a counselor up there for several summers with a couple of camps. To me it was like getting paid to play. I couldn't believe it when I got the offer via the Point St. Charles Boys' and Girls' Club. The Director of the Club at the time offered me the job at Camp Louis Voyageur. $250 bucks to go up to the Laurentians for the summer!

If you could make a buck in the Point, you would. I used to sell newspapers outside the Northern. Me and a few buddies used to go the various doors at the Northern and sell papers to the employees as they went to work. We were always on the go. A lot of the roofs in the Point were finished in copper. We'd climb up on the roofs all over the Point, pull off chunks of copper and carry them off in a hockey bag. You could make a fair amount of money selling the copper, and we knew the guys in the Point you could take it to that would pay you for it and then resell it.

In the winter we were always at the rink playing hockey. They were always packed. You'd have to wait your turn to get on and play a game. I would stay there and play game after game. Sometimes staying at the rink was just a happier environment than being at home. We had some good organized teams in the Point too. I remember playing on a district championship team once but I'm not sure if it was Pee Wee or Bantam. I do remember that we had a championship party and Frank Hanley showed up to congratulate us.

Different groups had their own hangouts in the Point too. We used to go to this little snack-bar-type place called Joe's. It was on Bourgeoys Street. The owner's nickname was "Three finger Joe". There was a jukebox and a couple of pinball machines. Joe was a really good guy. He used to make us these salami burgers and we loved them. First, he'd take a regular hamburger bun and put it face down to toast on the grill. At the same time he'd be warming up some salami slices on the grill. When it was all heated up he'd slap the salami on the burger bun, and smother the salami with mustard. Yeah…that was good. He'd sell us cigarettes too. One for five cents—three for a dime.

There was another snack bar I'd go to as well. It was on the corner of Coleraine and Charlevoix. It's called Paul Patates now, but I knew it when it was just Roy's. I think it's still the same family that owns it. There's a sign on the window that says it has been around since 1958. When I was a kid I used to take the garbage out every week. Every Thursday I'd hump out around 30 bags of garbage. My pay was two hot dogs, fries and a coke. I looked forward to that.

We'd go to Diorio's grocery store too. That's where you'd get cakes or bottles of coke or this type of thing. The owner, Frankie Diorio, was originally from Goose Village but he moved to the

L-R: Eddy, brother Mickey Nolan and David O'Neill, Montreal's 2004 "Irishman of the Year". 2012.

Point. He was always good to us. He used to give people in the Point credit at his store. I remember he always had sawdust on the floor. His store was on Charlevoix Street where Connie's Pizza is now.

There are a lot of sights and sounds from the Point that anybody that lived there back in the busy days won't ever forget: the sounds of the trains, the kids all over the street, the baseball games down at the park on Butler. The taverns all had teams. They'd get big turnouts for these games and we had some good ballplayers. One guy I remember very well is Abby Ryan. He was one of the heavy hitters and I've seen him hit the ball so hard it went over the tracks and into Verdun. There was always the sound of people on the balconies talking to each other and calling out to others in the streets. Some of the women on those balconies never missed a trick—24/7— and every now and then you'd get squealed on by one of them for something you did.

Apparently they have car thieves in New York that are supposed to be able to pull apart a stolen car for parts in no time flat. They call them "minute-men". Well, when we were kids in the Point you could have called us a different kind of minute-men. If a bakery truck ever got stranded in the snow, or broke down in the Point, it could take about a minute if the driver was gone and there wouldn't be a cake left in that truck! Another good target was the soft-drink trucks. They used to have the open cases stacked up on the sides of the trucks.

Eddy and Mary outside Roslyn School after Eddy received the QEII Diamond Jubilee medal, 2012.

You always had to be careful in the Point, though. One time we were being chased by another gang of guys and one of my friends jumped a fence into an electricity station. He fell the wrong way and got a very bad shock— 12,000 volts. Eventually, he was OK though. After fresh snowfalls we used to grab onto the bumpers of buses or trucks, hunch down and get dragged along behind like we were skiing. One day, one of the Point kids was doing this and the truck he was hooking stopped, then rolled backwards. He was crushed and killed. Sometimes we used to go to school at James Lyng by jumping the freight trains that were heading west from the railway yards Sometimes they'd pick up a lot of speed by the time we had to jump off. The Point could be a dangerous place.

I left school when I was fifteen. By the age of sixteen I was on my own in an apartment. I had a number of jobs that kept me going until I was eventually hired at the Canadian National Railway. One of these jobs was at King's Transfer Van Lines out of Griffintown. They had good contracts with Alcan and Air Canada and both of these companies had their offices at Place Ville Marie, downtown. But, one day, a friend who had come to see me boxing suggested that I should go and see a friend of his at CN for a job, so I did, and I got it. In those days, if you got a job at CN or the Northern you were set for life. I spent 14 years with the CN railway and I have been working for 20 years now with the School Board.

How did the marathon running start? Actually, I only started running longer distances after I hurt my hand boxing. I was 21. I hit a guy so hard in a boxing match that I fractured three fingers of my right hand—the index finger and the next two. The fractures stretched from the big knuckle down to the second knuckle of all three fingers. So, my father told me that until they healed completely I should just do more running. So I did. I started running five miles, then upped it to ten. One day I was running down at Ash Street Park and two of my friends in running gear came up to me. They asked if I'd like to run with them, and that they were training for the Montreal Marathon—"26 miles", they said. I just laughed, told them, "No thanks. I have a car!"

I saw them a couple of more times and eventually joined in. They asked me to run the marathon and I did. I had no idea what I was doing. I had the wrong shoes—big clunky things, no coaching, but I did it. They told me repeatedly, "Whatever you do, don't stop running!" They said this so often I figured I'd get disqualified if I did. I was so scared of stopping I remember jumping over this poor guy that collapsed in front of me about a mile from the finish line. That was my first race and I just kept going from there. It took me a while to learn the ropes. I remember one time this guy told me I would run better if I ran without socks on. I tried it and lost nine toenails.

One day I was training and it was brutally hot. When I got home I started complaining about the heat. Then I turned on the television and saw Terry Fox for the first time. Here is this young cancer survivor with one leg running across Canada to raise money to fight cancer. He's running a marathon a day on one leg and here I am complaining about the heat. He didn't have any big-name sponsors on his shirt, or any big backers. He just started running. This guy, I thought, is a real hero. He was a big influence on me and I started to raise money. I remember going into the taverns in the Point to get pledges. People like big Ricky McGurnaghan

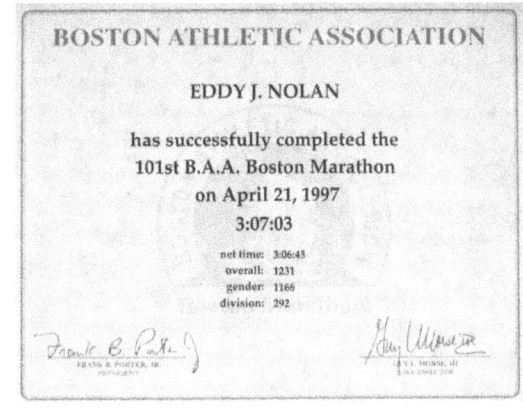

would help me. He ran the Olympic Tavern. He'd get everyone's attention and say "Eddy's raising money for Terry Fox. No more beer is getting served until all you guys ante up". Then I'd pass the hat. Things just built from there.

There was a lot of happiness in the Point, but there was sadness too. I have seen success and I have seen heartbreak. Personally, I had some real challenges in my earlier years. Looking back, I often think that if it weren't for my involvement in boxing and running I'd have ended up in some real trouble.

Like I also told you before, not knowing when to back off or let things go did get me in some situations. Just as an example, my friends used to like to eat at this place that had a real bully as an owner. One day I saw him at it and I'd just had enough. I told him to lay off, and that if he was looking for someone to push around, he should push around someone that could fight back, like me! He took me up on it and from that point, things deteriorated rapidly and dangerously. A long time ago I remember stepping into another similar situation and it could have easily cost me my life. I have definitely been in some scrapes. For a while, I guess you could say I was living a pretty fast life style and it took a serious toll on my health.

But, all of that is behind me now. It has been for many years. Today, I lead a quiet life. The cancer is in remission. I am established well at work. My focus now is wellness, getting back on the job, and continuing to raise money in the fight against cancer. I'm also working hard to establish a Terry Fox Day in Canada. I'm working with runners across Canada, Members of Parliament, and other interested groups to have April 12th designated as Terry Fox Day. That's the day that Terry started his run, so that's the day I'm shooting for. It wouldn't be a holiday or anything, just a day to commemorate a true Canadian hero and help raise funds.

I'm not that great on the computer, but I have a small set-up here at home and it's from here that I'm trying to spearhead the drive for a national Terry Fox Day. To help raise awareness for this initiative I organized the first Terry Fox Tribute Run on April 12, 2012 and it was very successful. I arranged to have a runner in every Province in Canada run a marathon downtown in their respective cities. They all carried flags. We were on Canada A.M. We had press reports in

Eddy completing the Terry Fox Run, 2013

various papers. Within the next three years, I'd really like to see April 12th declared Terry Fox Day, nationally.

I communicate with people all over Canada and the world. I know marathon runners from many countries. They know about my fund-raising work and my own challenges with cancer. I get a lot of moral support and notes of encouragement from these people. I have also received messages from Terry's parents over the years. The Calgary Stampeders sent me an official football sweater, number 31, for all the Terry Fox runs I have completed so far. All the players signed it. The Cheerleaders sent me a calendar that they all signed. I'm grateful for the support of some members of our Federal Parliament, and the media has shown a lot of interest. Since I was diagnosed with cancer several reporters have come to see me.

The kids and the staff at Roslyn have been just great. I love seeing the kids and they have sent me stacks of cards, projects, and photographs since I was diagnosed. When I visit, they run up to me in the halls and ask if they can help me. Back when I was working they would talk to me all the time. I talk to them about Terry, about respect for each other, and about things like never, ever being a bully. Sometimes when I visit the school parents will come over and talk to me and thank me for the time I spend talking to the kids about things like respect for each other. But they also thank me for my fund raising efforts. One of the parents of a student at Roslyn is affiliated with an organization that supports multiple charities. When he heard I was diagnosed with cancer he arranged for a donation of $10,000 to the cause. People are very supportive.

If I get a chance to help people in other ways, I do that too. A few years ago I was helping a young Irish boxer who was here on an exchange. He was around 21 at the time. He was, you know, a young tough guy. My girlfriend and I had him over to the house on a few occasions. He opened up to us and liked to talk about all sorts of different things. He went back to Ireland, but unfortunately he got in some serious trouble. He is in jail now, and he'll be there for a while. It is very sad. He calls us almost every Saturday from Ireland. We spend a few minutes on the phone. I try to help keep his spirits up. I encourage him to stay strong. I tell him we will see each other again either in Ireland or here. He always sends us cards. He never misses a birthday or Christmas or a St. Patrick's Day.

Through my work on the Internet I recently linked up with a well-known ex-professional boxer by the name of Donald "Donny" Poole. At one point he was the pro welterweight champion of Canada. During one period in his career, he lived in Quebec for over a year. He was very well liked. He was tough as nails. He became a firefighter and a paramedic. He has saved a lot of lives. Like me, he was recently diagnosed with cancer. He contacted me and we began to talk about what happened and how we are both adapting and moving ahead. Sometimes we'll spend hours

Eddy and Mary (holding flag) with the McGill University Faculty of Medicine contingent, Terry Fox Run. 2013.

on the phone. I was pleased to hear that Donny found that his discussions with me have helped him. I find that the discussions I have had with Donny and other people across the country and the world recently, whether they are marathoners, fund raisers, long-time friends, or simply new acquaintances has been very helpful to me as well.

When I moved out here a few years ago to my girlfriend's big house in the West Island of Montreal it felt very strange. I joke with people that my bedroom here is bigger than my apartment was in the Point—but it's true. I still spend some time in the Point and I'm deeply loyal to the area and the people there. Dominic the Barber's shop is still open but he's retiring. He's training someone to run the business so he comes in one or two days a week. For over 50 years I went to Dominic. I went to him from day one. I still check in now to find out when he'll be there so he can cut my hair. It was the same deal if I needed to have any work done on my clothing. I'd go and see Jerry the Cleaners in the Point. For as long as I remember, he'd be the guy we'd see to hem our jeans and things like that. He's gone now. But the thing is, you'd go to the people you knew all your life. It is about loyalty and respect. Look, there's never going to be another Point St. Charles. It can't happen. It's not the same now. Society has changed. When you go down there now, it's like big business has taken over. It's big-time gentrification now. The thing that really strikes me, though, is that there aren't as many kids running around as there was in our day.

Like I said before, it is a much quieter life for me out here on Ile Bizard with my girlfriend than it was growing up in the Point. It certainly isn't what I was used to for all those years, but that's fine. Working from here, trying to make a difference in the fight against cancer, preparing hard for the next marathon, and getting back to work as soon as I can is fine with me. It feels as

Eddy's parents, Audrey and Mike "Sonny" Nolan. Date unknown.

if I'm finally where I should be in life. I say a prayer every morning when I get up, and I say a prayer every night before I go to bed. It's kind of like for the first time in my life I'm truly happy.

When I am preparing for a marathon I do exactly the same thing now that I did when I was in training for boxing. I create a meticulous training plan just like my father taught me. I print everything out in columns. I go over each letter in ink, three times, just like he did. When I finish a training block, I write notes to myself on how I felt as I was training. I run 600-700 miles preparing for each race. I will run the Terry Fox marathon until the day I die. If I have to crawl, I will keep doing that marathon every year. Nothing will stop me!

My mother died in 1997 and my father passed away in 2006. We didn't take a lot of family photos when I was young. I really only have one photo that shows my mother and father together. It is a good photograph. I keep it in front of me at the computer when I do my fundraising and as I try to establish a Terry Fox Day. I was sitting here a few weeks ago looking at my mother in the photo. She was a very strong woman who cared deeply for us all. My mother didn't come to my fights. She just couldn't stand to see me get hit. I remember once they were showing one of my fights on TV. It was on the "Wide World of Sports" show. It was taped from a fight I had at the Verdun auditorium against a Belfast boxer. So we're all sitting at our place watching it—all except my mother. She had to leave the room. Even on television, she couldn't watch.

One night looking at her picture I decided to write her a note in the form of a poem and then I decided to share it on Facebook with my friends. I didn't know what to expect, but I received a lot of very nice messages. I do things in my life now that would have been unheard of back in the day in the Point. Imagine—a tough guy like me from Point St. Charles—writing poetry and showing emotion…!

For Mom—Missing You

Sometimes I look up and I ask why
So much pain in this world, I start to cry.
Mom and Dad are gone, but not far away
I feel her presence telling me son, it'll be O.K.
I hold on to dreams, that were once only mine
She tells me to follow them, and I will be fine.
Scared to move forward not knowing what's ahead
Again I hear her saying "Go for it Ed".
Mom seems to know when I am in pain.
She comes to me in dreams again and again
Telling me it will be alright.
I feel her arms, holding me tight.
I miss her so much, each and every day
I ask God at night, why'd she go away.
Her pain was greater than I could understand
I wish I would of just taken her hand
Rest easy dear Mom, for you've done your time
I will keep going till I cross that finish line.

Your son,
Eddy,

Feb. 17th, 2012

"I also really just looked up
to all of the neighbours in general.
They made you feel so secure.
You knew that you could knock
on any door for help
if you ever needed it
—and you wouldn't be imposing.
People respected each other
and looked out for each other."

Carol Bellware

Carol (Scott) Bellware

A major event took place in the Point on February 11, 1954. The Point St. Charles Boys' and Girls' Club opened the doors to its own state-of-the-art recreation facility for the children of the Point.

Photos of the event show dignitaries, invited guests and hundreds of kids packed into the gymnasium for the opening ceremony. At 13 years old, Carol was selected to thank the Club's benefactor, John W. McConnell for, as she said, "making the dreams of every boy and girl in the Point come true".

Over 50 years later Carol was invited back to the Point to pay homage when Mr. McConnell was inducted (posthumously) into the Point St. Charles Hall of Recognition.

Carol lived in the Point from the time she was born until she married. After her marriage she at first took up residence in LaSalle then Châteauguay and Pointe Claire. She now resides in Alexandria, Ontario, but remains in very close association with her Point St. Charles roots.

Over recent years, Carol co-authored *A Story In Each of Us—Memories of Glengarry Storytellers* (2011) and *Glengarry, My New Home—Immigration to Glengarry County 1945–2012* (2013). Profit from both of these publications benefit Glengarry Encore Education, a non-profit volunteer organization that conducts workshops for seniors in Glengarry.

"When the Boys' and Girls' Club opened in 1954 it really changed my life… The Club also offered occasions to do volunteer work as well. I was asked if I would help mentor a small group of younger girls. It was very rewarding and was my beginning of a lifetime of volunteerism."

Photo: Carol at Alexandria book launch. 2013.

I was born at the Royal Victoria Hospital in Montreal on January 2nd, 1941 and lived at 657 Hibernia Road in the Point until I was ten years old. In 1951 we moved to 529 Charon Street until 1960, the year I was married.

My paternal grandparents met and were married in March 1907 in Rugby, England. Later, due to a strike at the Sheffield Steel Mills, the family immigrated to Canada. They sailed from Liverpool on December 15, 1920 aboard the Empress of France, and during their crossing had

The corner of Menai and Forfar Streets in Goose Village. c. 1963.

529 Charon Street in Point St. Charles. 2014.

to bury their 11-month old infant daughter at sea. Their port of entry into Canada was Saint John, N.B. where they boarded the train that took them to their final destination, arriving in Montreal on Christmas Eve, 1920.

Their first Canadian home was a second floor flat on Church Avenue in Verdun and five years later they moved to 3 Forfar Street in Goose Village. My grandfather was employed with Peck's Rolling Mills as a steel worker; more specifically a "steel turner". During his employment he was involved in an industrial accident at the mill and lost some fingers.

My father's name is Philip Scott and my mother's name was Olive Bell.

Shortly after my father's family moved from Goose Village to Mullins Street in Point St. Charles, my parents met. They were both 12 years old at the time and married six years later at the age of 18. My only sibling is a younger brother, also named Philip Scott, (nicknamed "Junior"). His first after-school job was to deliver clothing, by bicycle, for Jerry Hewitt's Dry Cleaners on Wellington Street. When he left school, he worked at the Head Office of Seagram's Distillers and later on gained employment with the Canadian National Railway. He remained there until his retirement.

During WWII my father served with the Royal Canadian Army Service Corps. After the war he returned to civilian life and worked for Borden's Dairy on a Westmount route delivering milk by horse and wagon. A few years later he went to work for Northern Electric Company in the Point until he decided to go back into active service and signed up as a military policeman with

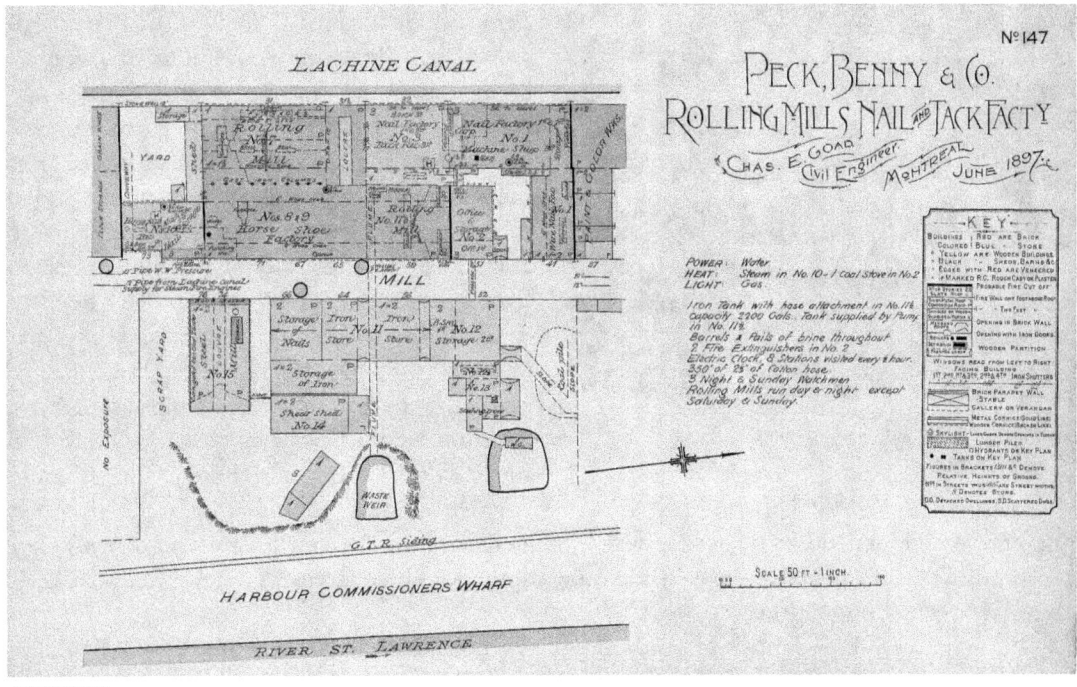

Fire Insurance Plan. Peck, Benny & Co. Chas. E Goad, Civil Engineer, Montreal. 1897.

the Canadian Provost Corps. In all his years as a career soldier we were extremely fortunate to have remained in Montreal. One year after my marriage, he was posted to Sainte-Foy and Camp Valcartier, near Quebec City. Shortly after he retired from military life he was offered and accepted the position as a private chauffeur to Westmount millionaire, Leonard Ellen.

My father recently turned 90 years old and still maintains his home in Verdun. He continues to be an active member of the Verdun and Point St. Charles Branch of the Royal Canadian Legion. This year he laid a wreath at the Remembrance Day services on behalf of the Veterans of WWII at the cenotaph in Marguerite Bourgeoys Park.

My mother stayed home until my brother and I were both in school and arrangements were made for us to go to a neighbour's house for lunch. In those days because we didn't have a car my parents travelled to work by streetcar. At first, she worked in the Stelco cafeteria along with my grandmother and aunt. She left there to accept a position at the cafeteria of the Royal Bank of Canada Head Office and in a very short time assumed the responsibilities of Pastry Chef. My mother was an excellent cook and made the most wonderful cream puffs and pies. She retired in 1961 when my father was posted to Sainte-Foy, Quebec.

Growing up, my parents were poor. My mother often talked about how difficult it was during the depression. She spoke of the many times of having to eat bread and "drippings" for a meal because food was scarce; how she shared clothing and a bed with two sisters; and at times had to

Philip Scott pinning a poppy on Carol's daughter, Kelly. 2013.

fight lice infestations. One of her favourite stories was about my grandmother's "Tomato Soup Cake". It was an economical dessert because it didn't need butter, which was rationed during the depression. After sharing the recipe with their neighbour, Mrs. Faubert called over the gallery to my grandmother to ask what she should do with the vegetables from the soup.

Wartime was tough on families. Food was rationed, but neighbours in the Point helped each other by trading ration stamps and tokens, depending on a particular need. A family with four or five younger children, for example, might need more milk than a family with only one or two children and so on. The owners of the corner stores (which were everywhere) were so supportive of the people, especially to young mothers with children, who never knew if they'd ever see their husbands again.

I don't have a lot of relatives in Montreal any more. During my childhood days I used to have quite a few in the Point and I never needed to call before visiting. I would just knock on the door, and be welcomed with a pot of tea and cake or scones on the table. Not any more, though.

My earliest memory is when I was about three years old. My brother and I shared a bedroom and our 3' x 3' bathroom only contained a toilet bowl. I vividly remember the hole at the bottom of the bathroom door and was later told that it was made by the sewer rats that came up the toilet pipes. Although there was talk about it, I never saw any rats in either of the houses that we lived in. Our weekly baths were taken in a galvanized washtub placed in the middle of the kitchen and filled with water that had been heated on the gas stove.

When we lived on Hibernia Road our days were spent outside, playing in the streets or at Marguerite Bourgeoys Park. On summer evenings all the kids in the neighbourhood congregated to play hide and seek, run-sheep-run or kick the can. Sometimes we'd share roller skates, play hopscotch or alleys (they call it marbles today). As a teenager, learning to jitterbug became an obsession.

Time spent with childhood friends, Maureen Bradley and Barbara Allen, and with a nickel in our pockets, we headed for the nickelodeon in the soda shop on our street. Because we played the same song over and over, practicing our new techniques, the store-owner pulled the plug and asked us to leave. That meant that we would end up in one of our bedrooms to play records or just talk. In the winter, we put on our skates and headed for the frozen roads in front of our house because the skating rinks were too far away.

When the Boys' and Girls' Club opened in 1954 it really changed my life. It had so much to offer: a gym with two basketball courts, an Olympic-sized swimming pool, gymnastics, floor hockey, boxing, woodworking, photography shop and a teenagers' room with a jukebox. Besides that, all kinds of opportunities were available to us like playing in organized sports leagues such

Now a YMCA, this building was originally the Point
St. Charles Boys' and Girls' Club. 2014.

Carol's father Philip (left) on Remembrance Day on
his way to help lay a wreath at the cenotaph in
Point St. Charles. 2013.

as baseball in the Summer and basketball in the
Winter. Our coaches were our neighbours and
they travelled with us on buses and streetcars to
compete in an inter-city league against teams
from Rosemount, Victoriatown (Goose Village) and Unity Boys' Club on Greene Avenue.

I was there the day the cornerstone was laid on the building for the Point St. Charles Boys'
and Girls' Club—and every day after school I rushed to the site to watch the construction
progress until it was completed. I couldn't wait for the doors to open.

Along with Cliff Sowery and Paddy Geary, Miss McCunn was a key player in setting up the
programs at the club. She was brought in from the Victoriatown Boys' Club and used her
experience from there to get things going at the Point Club. One evening after the doors were
opened, a bunch of us were in the gym throwing basketballs around while others were looking at
all the new equipment. Miss McCunn came into the gym and asked us to go into the teen-room.
Some sat on the floor, others on tables and we wondered why we were brought to that room.
She said "OK, you've got this building, now what do you want to do with it?" The ideas started
to fly. It was wonderful to have this opportunity to choose what we wanted to do. The Club also
offered occasions to do volunteer work as well. I was asked if I would help mentor a small group
of younger girls. It was very rewarding and was my beginning of a lifetime of volunteerism.

We were busy with other activities too. I remember being approached by coach Billy Killen,
with some of my friends, to form a cheerleading group for the Point St. Charles Eskies football
team. The players on the team would have been around 17-19 years old. I was 14 at the time.
What sticks out in my mind was the bitter cold weather and how we almost froze to death
sporting those little pleated skirts and bare legs, cheering for our Point guys.

In 1953 there was a fire in the Protestant elementary school in Goose Village. Arrangements
were made for the students to attend classes at Lorne School in the Point. One of these pupils
was named Malcolm (Mac) Vivian. He and I became friends and on occasion I would hop on the
Goose Village school bus and go to his house to spend time with him and his sister after school.
It didn't matter whether you lived in the Point or the Village—we always got along.

On behalf of the boys and girls of the Point, Carol was selected to give a speech thanking
Mr. W. J. McConnell for his support. 1954.

We never considered Goose Village to be a part of the Point proper, but I was disturbed and didn't think it was fair for the politicians to make all the decisions and not include the people who lived there, to be a part of the process when their community was destroyed to build the Autostade stadium. The residents should have been consulted.

Because our house on Charon Street had a big kitchen, Saturday nights usually brought family visitors who came to play cards. When I was too young to participate in these games, I played with my cousins in one of the bedrooms. It didn't take much to have a party. We had plenty of room and when there was a holiday or celebration of an anniversary or birthday, it would not be unusual for 30 people or more to enjoy a good old-fashioned kitchen party. This meant that my father would be playing his guitar, his best friend, Johnny Geary, played the mouth organ and everyone else sang our favourite rendition of Irish songs until the wee hours of the morning. When there was a large crowd, my father filled the bathtub with ice and beer and

The Point St. Charles "Rockettes". Carol is the first player on the right in the back row. 1956-57 season.

the women would be around the kitchen table making egg and onion sandwiches. I'll never forget the first time my future husband attended one of our parties, and even now, 60 years later, he still talks about the bathtub full of beer.

There is a legend about the fires on Victoria Day. For months in advance, the teenagers would gather and hide all kinds of flammable material in preparation for the bonfires. Fences were torn down and hidden in various sheds throughout the Point. The location of the stashes and the plans for the fires were always supposed to be kept secret, but typically, Knox Street always had the biggest and best fires in the middle of the street.

I went to Lorne School on Coleraine Street. That was the Protestant school for English kids. The classes were mixed but all the teachers except one were women. The only male teacher taught industrial arts to the boys but even the girls were taught safety in using tools and produced a simple wooden object. They were great days! The boys had a yard area at the back entrance of the school on Ryde Street. The girls played tag and skipping in the basement of the school, because there was no outside space on Coleraine Street.

Grade seven was the best year I had there. My teacher was Mrs. Marchment and at the beginning of the new year, I prayed that I would not have her as my seventh grade teacher. She was known to be very strict, knew how to keep the class under control and wouldn't hesitate to give the boys the strap when warranted. She was the best teacher of my life and even when I was

The old Lorne Street school, and books from Carol's student days. 2012.

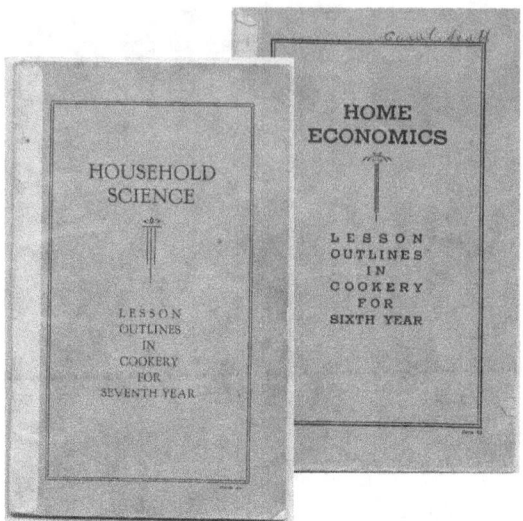

in high school I would go back to visit her. Mr. Kneeland was the principal at Lorne School at that time. He was really a nice man and he was strict also.

The people who chose teaching as a profession in those days were truly dedicated. None of them lived in our community: none of them owned cars so they travelled by bus and streetcar from various parts of Montreal. Miss Hunter was one of my teachers and she was there long enough to have taught my mother, father and one uncle and she was still travelling to the Point many years later. There is no doubt that Mrs. Marchment was a great influence in my life. She knew how to make kids feel proud of themselves and their accomplishments.

I have great memories of my days at Lorne School. I was a good student and enjoyed going to school. As I think back now, I believe I became a teacher's pet because I was asked fairly often to fill in for the grade-one or grade-two teachers if either one was absent. I am grateful to this day that in addition to academics, the school taught us leadership and home economics in grades six and seven. We learned a lot about housekeeping, cooking, food nutrients, carbohydrates, etc. To this day, I still refer to the Lorne School cooking books (that I was given in our home economics course almost 60 years ago). This training was important and remained with me through life.

We didn't have school lunch programs like the kids of today. We just all went home for lunch. I do remember so well, that every day we were given milk and cod liver oil pills that looked like miniature footballs. It was awful. The milk came in pint size bottles, delivered in a wooden crate to each classroom door and would sit there until recess break. The milk was always warm and I can still taste cod liver oil. Did they think we needed this because we were from the Point? Did other schools under the jurisdiction of the Protestant School Board of Greater Montreal have this program? To this day I cannot drink milk.

From the standpoint of the larger community, I really admired Frank Hanley when I was growing up. We used to call him the "poor man's Robin Hood". There were all sorts of stories

Saint Columba House. "...a community ministry of the United Church of Canada..." 2010.

The old Grace Church on Wellington Street. 2014.

of how Frank fixed things for people in the Point. When I was really young, I remember making placards and parading up and down Hibernia Road promoting Frank in the elections. He organized outdoor movies and band concerts at Marguerite Bourgeoys Park during summer months. He was also our neighbour and was really in tune with the people of the Point. Reverend Brown at Columba House was like an icon for us as well. He was a mentor and always looked out for the Point kids. But, I also really just looked up to all of the neighbours in general. They made you feel so secure. You knew that you could knock on any door for help if you ever needed it—and you wouldn't be imposing. People respected each other and looked out for each other. I didn't know of one person who took drugs. Sure, I knew boys who liked to fight, but I never heard of anyone getting raped. We were never scared to walk home at night, our doors were always left unlocked and being safe was not a concern.

As a child, church was very important to me. My brother and I attended Sunday School and church services regularly. I was confirmed at 13 as an Anglican at Grace Church. After Sunday school, Phil and I would go to the candy store on Wellington Street and buy one-cent bags of potato chips with the money we were supposed to put into the collection plate in church. After a while the wardens who were making the collection didn't even bother to come to our pew. When we bought the chips we would scrunch them into little pieces. That way they seemed to last longer—but what a mess we made on the floor in front of our pew.

When I was 13, education became a complete new adventure at Montreal High School For Girls. It was a big school located across the street from McGill University. The building was divided with the boys attending Montreal High School and they had their own entrances, classrooms and gymnasium. A schedule was set up so that both sexes used the swimming pool facilities at separate times. The school was a melting pot for kids from affluent areas of Montreal. Some of their families owned businesses in the clothing industry and I was very thankful that there was a school uniform policy in place because we all looked the same. There was some class-consciousness and often someone would say "Oh, you're from the Point". I didn't quite

In a Point St. Charles family get-together, Carol is the young girl in the print dress sitting just behind her grandmother (left). 1946.

understand the comments. I would never be ashamed to say "I'm from the Point", and I believe that the vast majority of people from the Point would say the same thing today.

I didn't like the teachers at Montreal High and I hated the travelling involved in going uptown to school. I simply did not feel like I belonged at that school and I failed grade eight. I went to grade nine but then I packed it in and went to work for The Bell Telephone Company in their Revenue Accounting Department. I stayed there until I got married.

For the most part, my cohort group all were married young and went to work in places like the Banks, Northern Electric, Redpath Sugar, Bell Telephone, Sun Life Insurance, and Canadian National or Canadian Pacific Railways. A few went on to college and I can only remember one instance of someone getting pregnant before they were married. The majority of my friends ended up moving out of the Point to places like Verdun or LaSalle if they had good jobs. Those that were taking the next step to buy a house would often go to places like Châteauguay across the river because housing prices were affordable.

In 1991 I organized a reunion for people who went to the Point St. Charles Boys' and Girls' Club. It took me quite a while to decide to do it and after I made the decision, it took over two years to track people down, send out letters and advertise in the papers across Canada. It was a big undertaking but I organized committees to look after the various events of the weekend. We had a very successful, "Once in a lifetime reunion of Point kids". The building was no longer

Carol (seated, second from right) and the rest of the team at the launch of their book, 'Glengarry, My New Home: Immigration to Glengarry County 1945–2012.' (Alexandria, Ontario) 2013.

"The Club" as it had been taken over by the YMCA. We held the reunion at the "Y" but it was understood by everyone involved that it was a Point Boys' and Girls' Club reunion.

About 600 people attended and I'd say approximately 80% or so were from the greater Montreal area with the rest of the attendees coming from across Canada and the United States. It was held on a Victoria Day weekend beginning on Friday night with registration and "meet and greet". People change in 50 years but we all had name-tags. There was a lot of laughing, reminiscing and, at times, tears. The old billiards room was set up with displays of photos, videos and other memorabilia.

Saturday was the big day. We organized an old-fashioned Point Club Dance and even brought CJAD' s Mike Stevens host of "Club 800 of the 50's" back on stage. We were instantly transported back to our youth! He didn't stay long but it was the highlight of the evening to have him there. I can tell you this, we sold a lot of beer and liquor that night.

Sunday morning people attended services and mass at their childhood churches in the Point then came back to The Club for brunch. The closing event was a formal catered dinner with Mr. McConnell's daughter in attendance. By this time, Mr. McConnell had passed away but we needed to express our gratitude for this great building and the effect it had on our lives. I presented her with a scroll containing all the signatures of the people that attended the reunion.

What else can I say to help future generations understand the Point back then? Well, there were a lot of poor people in the Point, but you know, we made do. In those days we didn't waste anything. We did not go out to restaurants like people do today and people cared for each other. I think that things are made too easy for people now. The Point was about simple people, living simple lives and being brought up that way. We learned on our own. We had few expectations. Point St. Charles was, and remains a big part of my life: the people, connections, the memories.

To add to this, my cousin, Lynn Bell Griffin did some genealogical research and recently discovered that our great, great grandparents were from County Cork, Ireland! All this time, I believed that my background was exclusively from England. When you think of it, what could be a happier surprise than to have grown up in Point St. Charles and then find out much later that you actually have some Irish background. Somehow, I always knew.

I am also enjoying writing. Here in Alexandria I am involved with a book entitled: *A Story In Each of Us—Memories of Glengarry Storytellers*. This book contains a collection of short stories by authors of this area and was published in 2011, and has sold well.

I still keep very much in touch with my Point roots. I also offer my assistance to other Point St. Charles projects that crop up from time to time like this book on oral histories. I check into the website "thepoint.ca" on a regular basis to catch up and I remain in contact with many of my old friends who live in the Montreal area—and will always be *A Point Girl*.

Songs we used to sing:

We don't care for all the rest of Canada,

All the rest of Canada, All the rest of Canada

We don't care for all the rest of Canada

We're from Point St. Charles

~~~

Point St. Charles, Point St. Charles

That's where I long to be

Where my friends are good to me

Hogan's Bath on Wellington Street

Where the "Griff" bums wash their feet

Where I can swear, I don't care anywhere—for

It's Point St. Charles for me.

Point St. Charles: updated, multiple dwellings on Bourgeoys Street. 2014.

"A lot of our parents and grandparents

came to Griffintown

from Ireland and other places

with very little.

But with two or three generations

of hard work

many of us moved a long way.

We worked hard.

We educated our kids."

Terry McCarthy

Terry McCarthy

Terry lived in Griffintown from age five until 16. He attended St. Ann's Boys' School, then trade school in Montreal. Terry worked for the Steel Company of Canada (Stelco) for 32 years. At that time, Stelco operated two plants on the banks of the Lachine Canal. The installation closest to Griffintown is now an attractive condominium project that retains much of the original architecture. Terry enjoyed a long and varied career with Stelco ranging from apprentice machinist to president of the company's credit union. Terry now lives in Ottawa.

Photo: 2013.

I was born on March 30, 1937. Until I was five we lived near the corner of St. Antoine and Calumet up near Atwater Street in the West End. Then the family moved to Griffintown. We lived at 798 William, between Duke and Prince Street. That's on the eastern side of Griffintown. It was

"In my own extended family we have children who grew up to be doctors and lawyers, as well as presidents and vice-presidents of companies. We didn't do too badly for ourselves in life."

a standard row house. The front door was right at the sidewalk and it had two floors. We had one bathroom upstairs. I had one brother and three sisters. My twin sisters were the oldest. I was the fourth born. I lived there until I was 16. That was when we moved to Outremont. I left home when I was 24.

I'm not sure of the exact place, but I know my grandparents came from the south of Ireland. When they moved here my grandfather got a job as a janitor with Ayers McKenna Pharmaceutical. I travelled to the Republic of Ireland once with my brother. We went all over the south, but I remember that my brother would have nothing to do with going to Northern Ireland at the time. That was during the troubles and he was very concerned about the volatility of that era. He just refused to visit the north.

My father was an educated man, and when I was very young he worked for several years in taxation for the government. I'm not sure if it was provincial or federal. He was involved in some kind of audit work, but he didn't make a career out of it. Instead, he moved over to the docks and was hired as a checker. He worked very hard on the docks and did a lot of overtime. For those days he made a lot of money. By that, I mean he was clearing about three times the wage of an average working man. And just to put that in perspective, our rent was around $7 a month.

Young Terry in Griffintown.

That was a time when some of the workplace benefits that we take for granted now were really just beginning to kick in. So, on Sundays, for example, he'd get double time and a half. I don't really remember my father being around for dinner all that much because of all the overtime he'd work. Many times he wouldn't get home from work until about 8:00 or 9:00 p.m. Other times, he'd finish a long day and go over to one of the taverns like Joe Beef for a few beers with his friends. I remember that I was often the one to run over to pick up the envelope on payday. In those days the men were paid in cash. My father would usually tell me in advance to meet him at a particular shed on the wharf.

Like I said, we lived in the eastern end of Griffintown. When you think about it, as I was growing up it was sort of like, in some ways there were two Griffintowns. The western side was centered closer to St. Ann's Church and it was very Irish. It stretched from around Colborne Street (now Peel Street) over to Guy. Our end went from Colborne over to McGill Street in the east. My end of Griffintown was quite heavily industrialized—more so than over towards St. Ann's. The kids from both ends all went to school together and played on the same teams, but we each had clusters of friends on our own sides. We didn't move much out of Griffintown either when we were kids. Until I was about fifteen I didn't really venture north of Notre Dame and out of Griffintown often unless it was to go to the Montreal Forum to play in a hockey tournament or watch a game.

Our play area when I was a kid was a small patch of land behind our house and our neighbors' houses. We used to call it the "big yard", but it wasn't that big. We didn't have much open space. The big yard was all dirt—no grass. Across the street from Darling Brothers' Foundry there was one very small patch of grass that we could play on. We called that area the "green grass". If we wanted to try and play football or something, we'd say, "Let's go over to the green grass". Half of the families around us were French and half the kids playing in the big yard were French. We all grew up together and played together. In my family alone, all my siblings married into French families from Griffintown and I married an English Protestant from Westmount. I don't remember any real trouble between the French and English that lived in Griffintown. It wasn't like the Point where you had a distinct English side and a French side.

Now an arts centre, the old Darling Brothers Foundry building was close to Terry's childhood home in the eastern end of Griffintown. 2010.

Another thing is that in Griffintown the French and English schools were separated. In the Point, Canon O'Meara and St. Charles were back-to-back.

I went to St. Ann's Boys' School in Griffintown. To be honest, I didn't really like school all that much. But when I think back to all the teachers we had, I'd say Mike McNamara was the best. He was my grade seven teacher and he was very demanding. He was a very good teacher. I don't ever remember anyone failing his class. I did enjoy the sports at St. Ann's and we always had a hockey team. We played in a church league and it was very competitive. When I was in school I always had part-time jobs like delivering newspapers, or working in grocery stores. At Gantis Grocery on the corner of Ottawa and Duke, I used to make $4 for delivering groceries on Friday night and all day Saturday.

After St. Ann's I enrolled in a trade school over on Notre Dame and St. Remi. The building is still there, but it isn't a trade school any more. At first I was going to be an electrician, but after I got started I decided to shift over and study to be a machinist. You can't see electricity when you're working with it, but you can see your product when you're a machinist. That's probably what was the deciding factor in my final choice of trades.

So, after eight years at St. Ann's, then two years of trade school, I was working as a machinist when I was 17. My first job was at Dominion Oilcloth. Oilcloth was essentially another name for linoleum at the time. Huge rolls of base-layer would travel through a very large machine for stamping. As it moved along, it was imprinted with various designs, one color and aspect of the design at a time. It was really just a 50-foot printing press. It was a wet process—sort of like silk screening. After all the stamping was completed the oilcloth was sent through a furnace for drying. I was expected to repair and make parts for any of the machines in the plant if they broke down. The difficulty when I first went to work was that in trade school you always worked with miniatures. For example, if you were learning to make a cam for a machine you'd produce a small model to scale. But you never had a chance to produce full-size industrial machinery of the sort that confronted us on the factory floor at a place like Dominion Oilcloth. There was no apprenticeship at Dominion. But, you adjust. You went downstairs, requisitioned the raw material you needed and got busy. I was there for three and a half years. I left and took a job for less than a year on one of the oil tankers that sailed back and forth from Thunder Bay to Toronto. That wasn't for me, so I got back to work as a machinist. I joined the Steel Company of Canada—Stelco—and worked there for 32 years.

In the downtown area, Stelco had two Montreal plants on the north side of the Lachine Canal—one in Saint-Henri and one nearer Griffintown where I worked. A third plant was out in Lachine. It was on the canal-bank as well. Stelco's main plant was the Hilton Works in Hamilton where they actually made the steel. It employed thousands of people. The only day it was ever closed down was Christmas. In that business, you don't stop the furnaces. There were two more plants in that area as well. One was for making basic steel and the other produced wire. Other plants were located in Ganonoque and Toronto, Ontario. The Montreal plants were 24-hour operations. Where I worked, we'd receive the steel that was manufactured in Hamilton and then we rolled it out into various products. The steel that was shipped to us was shaped in the form of what we called billets—long, solid bars about 20 feet long and four inches square. That is what we'd fire up to red-hot and reshape into product for industry. That's called the reduction process. These billets travelled along a series of conveyor belts and rollers that shaped the red-hot steel. At various stages in the process, men would use large tongs and physically lift and move the red-hot steel to the next phase. Because of the extreme heat they could only work 20 minutes at a time. They wore heavy clothing and long underwear to try and protect themselves and these men were constantly bathed in sweat. The saying goes that you need a ton of water to turn out a ton of steel product. That's where the Lachine Canal came in. We diverted water from the canal to cool the red-hot steel. The water was then directed back into the canal downstream. The water flowed in and out of the plant via large grates located underwater on the side of the canal.

We made products like reinforcing bars for concrete, nuts, bolts, wire, nails, as well as many other items. In the Stelco nail shop alone we had between 70 and 100 machines, and each one punched out about 600 nails a minute. You cannot imagine the noise from that shop.

This building once housed the Steel Company of Canada where Terry worked. It is a short distance west from Griffintown and just across the canal from Point St. Charles. It is now a stylish condo. 2011.

Door to an old factory on King Street in the eastern end of Griffintown. (painting by D. Flavell, 2010)

Steel plants will typically send steel product over to the nail shop if it doesn't quite meet specifications. I remember that we used to ship to Canadian and American clients. One of our big customers was always Hydro Québec—a huge operation. When I joined Stelco as a machinist the shop floor was a broad mix of French, English and a few other nationalities. It was a very positive environment. The social package was top-notch. There was just nothing better than Stelco in those days and I am still benefitting from the heath-care support. The attitude in the company was very good and nobody ever had to push us to get to work. We started at 7:00 a.m. and we worked hard. We also worked a lot of overtime.

I was 21 when I started at Stelco and the company really gave me the structure and direction I needed at that point in my life. They told me when I joined the company that I was qualified to begin as a "Class One Apprentice". The apprenticeship had 18 levels and, give or take a few weeks, each level took somewhere in the range of five or six months to complete. Each step required a certain amount of hours on various machines, so the length of time at each step could vary based on overtime. It was a very rigorous and well-structured environment. Highly experienced machinists that were hired from the outside were not permitted to join Stelco as class one machinists. There was no lateral entry to the top level. If they were considered qualified, they could potentially come in up to level 14—max., then they'd have to take tests and prove themselves to get to the top level. Stelco had the best team of machinists in Quebec, but each person had to prove it—on lathes, milling machines, benchwork, everything!

I remember that until I completed my 18-level apprenticeship I had to submit a weekly report. The report involved drawing a colored diagram of the particular machine I had been working on for the week. I had to label every part. I also had to include a summary of all the work I had done for the week and outline what new knowledge I had learned. I remember once I handed in a typed version of my weekly report. My girlfriend had typed it up for me. I was called in to my supervisor. "I didn't know you could type", he said. I told him the story and he made it perfectly clear that he expected my work to be my own and if I couldn't type, that meant hand-written. Another time I wrote in my report that I hadn't really learned anything new that week. That was a mistake. My foreman was called on the carpet for not teaching me anything new. The senior management of Stelco, as I remember it, was largely old-school Scots, but like I said, the shop floor was a broad mix. Ninety percent of the machinists that worked with me were from Griffintown, Goose Village or the Point. In Lachine, it was the same idea—they all lived in Lachine. And I'll tell you this, you didn't see a lot of people leaving Stelco if they got in. They didn't quit. The money was there. It was a good workplace. Even the men in the hard labour jobs like the guys moving around the red-hot steel billets by hand—they stayed!

Back in those days, you could pretty much step outside your door all around the east end of the canal and get a job. In the eastern end of Griffintown where I lived it was very busy with industry. Mayer Shoes was across the street from our house. Kraft Foods was in the Griff before they and some others moved farther north toward the border of Montreal and St. Laurent. Darling Brothers' Foundry and Elevators, Liberty Smelting, Hydro Québec, and lots of others provided opportunities for people. We all worked. When I finished my Stelco shift at 4:00 p.m., if I wasn't working overtime I'd very often walk over to Saint-Henri and work at Talerico's until around 8:00 p.m. Talerico made heating ducts and things like that.

As I got a bit older I started going to McGill at night. I spent a lot of time studying management and most of my classes were at the Bronfman building. When I moved into management at Stelco I saw my share of challenges there, just like anywhere else. We were very supportive of our staff at the company, though. When people had problems, personal or other- wise, Stelco did what was necessary to assist their employees. People were not usually fired at Stelco. They were helped with their problems.

At Stelco we had our own Credit Union. It was in operation before I started at the company. A gentleman by the name of A. Scott started the Credit Union and it worked out very well. Loan payments were deducted directly from people's paychecks and the vast majority of loans were for cars or houses. You could usually arrange your loan with a phone call. It was nothing like today. When I bought my first house in 1972 I needed a loan of $500 for a down payment. It was done with a quick phone call to our credit union. I served as President of this credit union for a while.

Looking back, it may sound funny to hear people from my era talking about the great quality of life they had in such a heavily industrialized area as Griffintown. But for me, it was always about the people. On the material side we didn't have a lot, but the people were special. I'm not aware of any other place like it. You can bump into someone from Griffintown that you haven't seen for 50 years and just take up like it was yesterday. I'm not really sure that anyone 30 or 40 years in the future reading about Griffintown will, or could ever really understand what life was like, or what we had down in that area. I don't think they could really grasp the feeling. I remember when I was in my teens, there were about 30-35 people in our crowd. We used to have new jackets made up every year with the word "Griffintown" embroidered on the front— nothing else—just "Griffintown". They were made of a blue and white silky material like the team jackets you'd see in the 'fifties. Sometimes there would be 15 or 20 of us going out together at night or going up north to one of the resorts all dressed in these jackets. We didn't look for trouble, but and no one ever gave us any.

You know, if you mention the Point or Griffintown, a lot of people will immediately jump to a negative stereotype of the people that lived there—but it's not accurate. A lot of our parents and grandparents came to Griffintown from Ireland and other places with very little. But with two or three generations of hard work many of us moved a long way. We worked hard. We educated our kids. In my own extended family we have children who grew up to be doctors and lawyers, as well as presidents and vice presidents of companies. We didn't do too badly for ourselves in life.

When we were children we didn't really know we were poor compared to the people in Westmount or Côte St. Luc or places like that. We didn't know about life on the other side and I'm sure they had no idea of life, as we knew it, in Griffintown. You had to live it to really understand it.

We knew that Griffintown was a good place—but it's hard to put into words.

Lachine Canal, Charlevoix Bridge and the building that was once occupied by Stelco. 2014.
See facing page for the location of the St. Henri Stelco site a few blocks west.

Top: The modern building at left sits on part of the venue that once housed the St. Henri Stelco installation. The brick building immediately to the right with the chimney housed Dominion Textile. Both were major employers for decades. Now condos, they are only a short walk from Point St. Charles. The downtown Montreal skyline stands in the background.

Bottom left: Skaters pass the corner of the former site of Simmons Ltd. (mattress manufacturing), another important employer on the Lachine Canal. This architectural style is commonplace across the area.

Right: The derelict Canada Malting Company Ltd. site—west of the Point on the north side of the Lachine Canal.

All photos 2014.

"In a nutshell,

the Village was a world onto its own.

People worked hard, lived hard, and played hard.

They were decent people

who truly enjoyed their homes,

their neighbourhood,

and their way of life.

It was a 'Village',

in all senses of the word."

Theresa Norris

Theresa Norris
nee Shanahan

Theresa is retired and lives just outside Ottawa in Kanata. Theresa was 15 when the Village was torn down in 1964. She and her friends were among the last group of teenagers to live in the Village just before the demolition. After graduating from high school in Verdun Theresa went to work in the private sector—first with Greenshields Investments in Montreal, and subsequently with Digital Equipment Corporation in Kanata. Theresa still keeps in close contact with several of her childhood friends from Goose Village.

Photo: 2013.

"I lost touch with most of the Goose Villagers, although I do still keep in touch with some very close friends. I can tell you, though, that at the reunions that Linda Frainetti organized, you can still truly feel the love."

The City of Montreal recently organized an exhibition at the Montreal History Centre down in Old Montreal called *Quartiers Disparu* (Neighbourhoods that Disappeared). One of the areas they focus on is Goose Village. A few months ago, my daughter and her family went to see it. When she saw me for the first time after her Montreal visit, she said, "Mum, you grew up in a slum!" I was shocked! That really hurt me. To me, as I was growing up, Goose Village wasn't a slum at all—it was my home and it was a very loving and positive place to grow up.

Every day I would see mothers cleaning the sidewalks in front of their homes. The Villagers were a very proud people. When you walked down the street, you could smell all the different kinds of food that were being prepared and cooked.

In the Village, my brother and I were simply referred to by everyone as "the twins". The Village was a very social place. If you were walking around the Village, the whole journey could take you seven hours! Everyone knew everyone else and you'd stop to talk (and sometimes share their food, but mostly, their drinks).

The people who lived in the Village worked very hard, and my father was an example of this. He never missed a day at work. He drove his Canadian Pacific truck in the downtown area of Montreal and never had an accident. He was very meticulous. He was very proud of what he did. Every year for as long as he worked, he would receive commendations for his excellent performance. On the weekends, he would drive a Diamond taxi cab to help supplement his week-day truck job.

The Shanahan twins with grandmother Giovanetti. 1949.

Theresa with Dad on St. Patrick's Day. 1953

He worked all the time. I don't remember him being around our home a lot because he was trying, as best as he could, to provide for his family.

My mother and father were both born in the Village. My mother was of Italian descent and my father was of Irish descent. My father read all the time. He was very well informed. He followed politics very, very closely. He would always be reading the newspapers—as many as he could get his hands on. He also listened very carefully to the news on the radio and he loved all the heated discussions that followed. He often offered us his opinions on the politics and the politicians of the day.

Both my parents were very religious. They observed every single Catholic rite. They always attended the weekly Sunday Mass, either at St. Ann's Church in Griffintown or in the gym at the Boys' and Girls' Club. My mother and her sister Laura always attended the Tuesday devotions (Our Lady of Perpetual Help) at St. Ann's Church. These Tuesday devotions were so famous that they were even broadcasted via radio throughout the City of Montreal.

The Sunday Masses were held in the Boys' and Girls' Club gym. My father regularly acted as the altar boy at these Masses. I can still see him, with his little green felt money deposit box, giving change to the adults who, in those days, had to "pay" for their seats. He also liked to sample the wine just before Mass—to make sure that it was good enough for the presiding priest!

I remember what a sad day it was when my family attended the very last Christmas midnight mass at St. Ann's Church before it was torn down. It was a special but sad evening for all of us.

Occasionally, we marched in the St. Patrick's Day Parade with the St. Ann's Church contingent. My brother and I were always covered with shamrocks and I don't mean the imitation shamrocks you see today. With us, back then, it was the real thing—from head to toe. All the kids had real shamrocks. My snowsuit always had to be green for the parade. I remember one snowsuit in particular—it was made of green velvet.

And it wasn't just the St. Patrick's Day Parade that we'd walk in either. We had other events of this nature too, like Corpus Christi and other parish-related celebrations. Easter was always a very important time for us. Every Easter, we would get new clothes. I would get a new coat, a dress, an Easter hat, and shoes. It was

Theresa at St. Ann's Girls' School, Griffintown. 1957.

a real tradition. And it didn't matter if it was still snowing on that particular Easter Sunday, we had to wear our new spring clothes! After mass, dressed in our Sunday best, we would go to our maternal grandparents' house for an Easter feast! Meat, pasta, salads, soups, desserts, etc. One such Easter, my grandmother told me that our pet rabbit had run away. Sure enough, I'm almost positive that he was part of our Easter meal that particular Sunday. And, of course, there always was my grandfather's delicious home-made wine, made in his cellar.

When my brother and I were youngsters, my father would sometimes take us for walks in Griffintown. He would take us to the candy store and give us some money. He'd say, "Here, go and pick some stuff and wait here a few minutes, I have a quick errand to run". Later on, he told us what he was really doing was slipping in for a quick beer with his friends in one of Griffintown's many taverns. We had several "Blind Pigs" in the area and my father knew where they were all located.

The Victoriatown Boys' and Girls' Club was important to us. There were lots of activities. We had great dances at the club and we'd have dance contests. Linda Frainetti was amazing. She was a really good dancer. I used to love dancing with her. Every Friday night in the summer, the club sponsored outdoor movies in the park directly across the street. In one sense, the Village was a closed environment, but we had lots of opportunities to move outside it. The excursions from the Victoriatown Boys' and Girls' Club served us well. They were a lot of fun. Joe Berlettano

Theresa and husband Doug. 2012.

took us out of the Village often and exposed us to many other places and things that we may not have had the opportunity to experience.

At school, I always studied very hard. I was a real bookworm, and I guess you could say I strived to be the teacher's pet. I guess I would be classified as a nerd today. I did very well and could have gone to university but I decided that I wanted to follow the commercial route in high school. I knew fairly early on that I wanted to be a secretary. It was a white collar job and that is what I wanted. The nuns at St. Ann's Girls' School put me in the high achievers class because I had good grades and they didn't listen to my request for the commercial course. Well, I went home, complaining to my father, who, the very next day, marched to the school, asked to speak to the principal, and demanded that his daughter be put in the commercial stream as per her wishes. While I was in school, I took many supplemental courses on my own and I usually got high marks. I had a job waiting for me after high school with Greenshields Investment at Place Ville Marie as a secretary.

When I started to work, I was living at home because that's what good Italian/Irish young women did back then—until you married. I was very well looked after and I was very fortunate. I could afford the best in clothes and I could save money as well. My parents asked me to pay a modest room and board. I didn't know it at the time, but they were saving all of the money I gave them. When I married and moved to the United States and started life as a young bride, my parents gave all my "room and board" money back to me so that we could purchase furniture for our new apartment. That was the way my parents lived. They sacrificed and went without for my brother and me. I really looked up to my parents. They were kind and very generous. They were role models that I still, to this day, strive to follow.

When I heard the Village was going to be torn down, I found the news quite sad and I remember wondering why it was happening. But, once it was decided, I began to look forward to going to Verdun Catholic High School. My parents had chosen a very nice place to live in Verdun. I was still going to be with some of my friends because a lot of the Villagers moved to Verdun after the demolition. In Verdun, I even had my own bedroom. I was happy for my parents as well.

Over the years, I lost touch with most of the Goose Villagers, although I do still keep in touch with some very dear friends. I can tell you, though, that at the reunions that Linda Frainetti organized, you can still truly feel the love.

In a nutshell, the Village was a world onto its own. People worked hard, lived hard, and played hard. They were decent people who truly enjoyed their homes, their neighbourhood, and their way of life. It was a "village", in all senses of the word. Everyone knew you, your parents, and your parents' parents.

I would hope that in 50 years from now, people reading about the Village would have some appreciation for a different but wonderful way of life back then and how it was a shame and a mini tragedy that such an environment had to be demolished—for what?—a parking lot!!

Goose Village housing. c. 1963.

"The Italians transformed

their small backyards

—just patches of bare earth to start with—

into a metamorphosis of vines,

tomatoes, chicken coops.

A lush garden of Eden.

The coops would have three or four levels.

The doors were always open

and you'd see the chickens

running up and down the various levels laying eggs.

They were like little miniature apartment buildings

in these small back yards."

Tom Shanahan

Tom Shanahan

Tom Shanahan was born in 1948. He and his twin sister Theresa (Norris) lived in the Village until just before it was demolished in 1964. Tom graduated from Loyola College in Montreal with a B.A. in History and Literature. He subsequently attended McGill University where he earned a teaching certificate. He taught grades Three, Four, Five and Nine in Montreal. By 1981, Tom and his family had moved to Toronto where he taught grades 1-8 and enjoyed a fulfilling and highly rewarding teaching

"Sometimes I wonder… will Goose Village ever be remembered?"

career. He is now happily retired along with his wife, Michele, who is from northern France. She too, is a retired teacher. Tom is a history buff and a voracious reader. Tom now lives in Pickering, just east of Toronto and drives a school bus part time. "I just love the kids", says Tom.

From time to time, Tom visits the southwest area of Montreal where Goose Village once stood. Although there is no trace whatsoever of the buildings, he still conceptualizes the exact location of the streets by virtue of a tall, straight stand of trees that stood beside the stockyard and remain standing almost 50 years later.

Photo: Tom atop Mount Royal overlooking downtown Montreal and on to the St. Lawrence River. 2010.

My father was Irish and my mother is Italian. They were both born in Montreal. My mother's maiden name is Giovanetti. My Italian grandparents came from Italy, just east of Florence. When the Village was demolished my Italian grandparents moved to Ville St. Michel in the east end of Montreal. All my grandparents, both Irish and Italian, are buried in the Côte-des-Neiges cemetery in Montreal.

Originally, my Italian grandparents were going to move from Italy to Connecticut. That was what my grandfather wanted but my grandmother decided otherwise. She said they should go to Montreal and that is what they did. My grandfather worked at Dominion Coal in the Village. He shoveled coal from the railway cars onto the dock.

I remember my Irish grandmother very well. She was a very social person in the Village. She had five or six collapsible card tables and she would regularly pull them all out and fill her parlour with her friends. Her level of social interaction with people in the Village was really incredible. That was the case with most families. Entertainment in the Village for adults was almost always in the home. There were a few families that were a bit more distant, but that was the exception.

I can tell you that my twin sister and I were very fortunate in the Village. We wanted for nothing really. We ate well. We had good clothes. We were even one of the first to get a television

Theresa Flora and Thomas James
July 16, 1948

The "twins". 1948.

set, and we sensed that our parents wanted more for us than they had had. My mother never actually sat us down, as such, and said that, but you could tell by what they did that my mom and dad wanted us to climb the social ladder so to speak. They envisioned a prosperous future for us. Every once in a while, my mom would express a desire to move out of the Village. This, a few years before the demolition of the area was on the radar. She had an optimistic vision for the future, and this drive in her was embedded in me and my sister. This ambition would later propel Michele and me to move our family to progressive, dynamic and prosperous Toronto.

When we were growing up, my father drove a CP Express delivery truck following his career as a Staff Sergeant in the Royal Canadian Air Force. He did so for 25 years. Then on the weekends he drove a taxi. He was very, very hard working. He retired in 1975. I still wear the gold watch he was presented with on his retirement. As a young man he was also a merchant mariner. He travelled all over the world and he really stimulated my interest in geography, which, in later years, nurtured within me an equally profound interest in history. He instilled within me an insatiable desire to learn, explore and discover. My mother was a devoted homemaker, and she later worked as an elevator operator at the Montreal General Hospital. She has always been an eternal beacon of optimism whose favourite expression was, especially during the cold winter months, "Spring is just around the corner". Her optimistic attitude remains with me to this very day. It is because of her positive outlook that I believe in people. My mom and dad have been the unsung heroes in my life.

When I was a child my father used to take me around on Sunday all over the area. He loved ships. He'd take me to the docks, the grain elevators…all over Montreal harbour just at the foot of Forfar St. We would go to see the huge ocean going ships and the Great Lakes freighters. He would take me on board and introduce me to the captains of the ships. I always enjoyed watching them transfer the coal onto the ships. I think I have visited just about every kind of military ship imaginable with my father: submarines, helicopter aircraft carriers, you name it.

We didn't have a car and that was fine. My mother used to take us all over Montreal and the surrounding area by train and by bus. She used to take us on the train to Quebec City every fall. In doing this, my mom literally showed us how wonderful the world is and how it contained a limitless number of fascinating places to visit and explore. She planted within me an endless sense of adventure and discovery.

A lot of ex-Villagers still live in Montreal, and I know that a lot of others who don't, have said

The Shanahan family in Goose Village. 1950.

they'd move back if they could. I would not. I love it here in Toronto. I am very happy here That is, indeed, an understatement. I embraced the city. Some Villagers who moved here did not. I think Toronto is one of the most liberal-minded, dynamic, vibrant and cosmopolitan cities on the planet. I put it on the very same level as London, Paris and New York all of which I have visited. When I first moved to Toronto and would go back to Montreal to visit, I would sometimes feel myself getting a bit unsettled, because at that time (1981) I was never really sure where I belonged. Goose Village really hits to the heart. As time progressed, however, I adapted very well because my attitude was that I would accept Toronto under its terms and not under mine. Consequently, I consider myself to be a loyal Torontonian.

I lived in the Village until I was 14, and I lived in a boy's world. It was a wonderful place for boys, but you really had to have your wits about you. There is the viewpoint of Goose Village that you get from some of the girls who grew up there and then there are different memories that you'll get from the boys. The boys and girls did some of the activities together, like at the Boys' Club, but in other areas the boys and girls typically had different experiences. I lived in a boy's world. It was fantastic. It was a very dynamic and very bustling place. You almost forgot you were part of Montreal, or to be more precise, Point St. Charles. We lived in a bubble, but we were never bored. We created our own entertainment.

The Village was an industry-intensive place and it had its own particular sights and sounds that we all knew. I lived very close to an old church, for example, and it had been turned into some kind of metalworking shop. The doors were always open and when I'd walk past it you could see the streams of flying sparks. It seemed as well that there was a constant noise from the big shovel that was used to load and unload coal over at Dominion Coal. It was the kind that hung from a crane by a single steel cable and it had two huge jaws that would open, drop down and bite into the coal, rise up, then move sideways, and drop a big load of coal.

You'd also hear the noises coming from the big tubes that went from the grain elevators into the bellies of ships. Goose Village was right beside the CNR marshalling yard for the trains, so you'd constantly hear the trains hustling back and forth moving cars. When I was young they were still using steam engines and they made their own sounds. There were lots of whistles and horns in the Village and each had its special sound and its own purpose. One of my favourites was the slaughterhouse whistle announcing the noon lunch-break. You always knew what time it was in Goose Village. There was also the clop, clop, clop of the ice-man who, when I was very young, still delivered the ice by horse.

The tram also used to run close to the Village after crossing the Victoria Bridge from the South Shore. It was a single-car tram of The Montreal and Southern Counties Railway Company. They had bells that would clang loudly as they approached Riverside St. and then went down Mill Street. The Canada Packers trucks running back and forth also had their own sound as they moved around the area, and after a run of delivering carcasses, the workers would clean the trucks out with fire hoses so you'd hear that. They were amazingly clean. Absolutely spotless.

The fog horns of the big ocean-going ships also contributed their sounds to Goose Village and the rag man was often heard moving slowly up and down the streets and lanes saying, "Rags…rags…rags…rags…".

As far as Village smells go, there was always the smell of what people were cooking and that was fine. The slaughterhouse had its moments, though. At the corner of Forfar and Riverside was the tannery. It was a one-storey brick building if I recall correctly. They used to stack the hides on top of one another like pancakes and if you were close enough, the stench was terrible and overwhelming. Walking past it, you had to cross the street holding your nose. I was always amazed that even though we were so close to a stockyard in general, you did not really smell the manure or other things. You had to be really close to notice. Overall, Goose Village wasn't a neighborhood you'd remember by its smell, but by the never-ending activity, vehicles, and sounds. For a young boy like me…all of this was truly a world of wonder.

I had a great childhood growing up in Goose Village but I don't hold any overwhelmingly sentimental notions about going back if that were possible. Goose Village was, in essence, a microcosm of society. There was such a wide spectrum of characters and individuals…from the hard-working labourers to the highly educated intellectuals. Many of the residents

Tommy and his father on St. Patrick's Day. 1953.

worked all around the perimeter in places like the stockyards, the coal yards, Northern Electric in the Point, the railroad or the docks. They were labourers or truck drivers, things like that, although some managed to get better jobs, like with the Montreal Transit Company. Goose Village was a self-sufficient, and self-contained society; but, in any society there is always good and bad. Some people ended up going to university. Others landed in jail. It was not all just nice-nice in the Village. However, the vast majority of residents were decent and law-abiding who encouraged their children to prosper in life.

I know people from the Village who ended up in very serious trouble such as drug trafficking. I remember one day coming home from school and stopping to watch the police move in on someone with guns drawn. I remember people whose main interest growing up was trying to be the toughest person in the area. I knew bullies who would come after you. They were very tough SOBs and they would hurt you—maim you if they had the chance. These were the people we just stayed away from. I have nice things to say about the Village, but the presence of ruffians also made me somewhat of a cautious, defensive person. I witnessed both the positive and the negative aspects of human nature. I chose my friends carefully.

Children playing outside a Goose Village scrap yard. c. 1963.

Some of my friends were poor and destitute. I remember sometimes all they had to eat for dinner would be a slice of white bread with mustard on it. "Look", they'd say, "this is my dinner". Sometimes you could feel a real sense of shame among the people who were in difficult situations like this.

The Irish and Italian kids in the Village got along just great. You could say that my parents' generation sort of were polite to each other. The Irish more or less stuck together among the older generations and so did the Italians. I know that if an Italian was marrying an Irish person sometimes that could cause a little friction in the family among the older generations.

The Village could be a dangerous place in different ways. We were right beside the Point St. Charles railyards, and there were no fences. We'd walk on the tracks. The train yards were big and it was very dangerous. The bridge I often used to cross to go to St. Ann's Boys' School, for example, was a train bridge. I wasn't supposed to cross it but I did. One of the people in the Village had a really nice big dog, a St. Bernard named Pal. It made a dash at the tracks one day and it was cut completely in half by a train locomotive. That was a shock as it was my first experience with death.

Between St. Alphonsus and high school, Tom attended St. Ann's Boys' School in Griffintown. This is Tom's grade IV class. Tom is seated (first on the left) in the fourth row. 1958.

We also used to spend hours at the scrap yard beside the Village and that was a challenging environment. We used to go inside these massive rusted-out old industrial boilers and crawl around. If you cut yourself inside those with all the rust and stuff you were running a real risk of infection. You were getting a tetanus shot real quick.

What really used to scare me as a child were the wild dogs that intermittently would run down the streets of the Village. They were all big, about the size of German Shepherds although they were not purebred. They were raggedy, mangy–looking, vicious creatures. They would run in packs of about 6-10 dogs. You did not see them very often. I'd say I saw them racing down our street (Conway) maybe once a year or so. As they ran they would always be nipping at each other. This was truly a horrific sight for a ten–year-old to witness.

Then there were the stockyards on Bridge Street. That was a different world all together. We knew exactly what was going on in there (the cattle to be slaughtered), but we tried not to think about it too much. One day I turned a corner in the Village and right in front of me was a longhorn bull—a true Texas longhorn bull, about 15 steps away. It had those wide horns and I was terrified of getting gored. It was pawing the ground, snorting and I had no idea what to do. He looked right at me…I was his target. Right at that point, around five men came racing out of the stockyard, yelling and swinging their big canes. I turned and ran as fast as I could in the opposite direction. There were no fences surrounding the stockyard either. We'd just go in and wander around. It was like being on a big ranch. It was a huge network of aisles. There was always that low and constant sound the cows made. Some of the guys would climb the fences and ride the cows, not the bulls, though. The cows would start jumping around and bucking a bit…like in a rodeo.

The Lachine Canal was a danger zone as well. Coming home from school one day I saw a lot of police lights and fire trucks etc. so I ran over. They were pulling a dead body from the canal, near St. Ann's Church. I was in grade six when I saw this. Not something kids in more "affluent" areas would see. There were also what was called basins along the side of the Canal where large boats from various places used to moor. One was set aside to dump all the huge, old discarded canal lock doors. They were just left to rot in the water on Bridge St. They were slimy. If you slipped into the water among these, at night when it was difficult to see, it could be really dangerous. There were no fences or anything around the canal and the ground would get very wet and slippery at the lip of these basins.

The biggest fire I ever saw was also in the Village. It was a wooden factory, a paper factory actually. It was about three stories high and it really went up.

Yeah…the Village was a place where you had to be careful. A young boy had to use his common sense to avoid danger which lurked, sometimes, just around the corner.

The Village boys and girls all went to St. Alphonsus School right in Victoriatown and I loved it. The nuns were great teachers. I am a retired teacher myself. I spent over 35 years teaching in Montreal and Toronto and I can tell you that the nuns in Goose Village were way ahead of their time. They created a really inviting and stimulating environment for us in grades one to three. They set up the classrooms beautifully with hanging plants, posters etc. It really was a very warm and welcoming environment and they were so devoted. They used to take us out to events too. The first three-ring circus I ever saw was when the nuns took us to one at the old Montreal Forum. They would show up and meet us all for Sunday Mass as well.

The first high school I attended was D'Arcy McGee. I felt like I was in college. I loved D'Arcy McGee. I enjoyed it for a year and then we moved to Verdun, so I switched over to Verdun Catholic High School. I really loved Verdun as well.

At the Boys' Cub on Sundays in the Village we used to set up the gym for Mass. I was an altar boy. Although a lot of people went to St. Ann's Church in Griffintown on Sundays, a lot used to just attend mass at the Boys' Club. We had a portable altar on wheels that would be set up, and we would line up chairs for parishioners.

Talking about St. Ann's Church in Griffintown…it was incredibly beautiful. The pillars inside were a purple marble and you could see the veins throughout. The stained glass, the marble and the massive organ—it was absolutely drop-dead gorgeous! When they tore it down, for me, it was as if they demolished the Louvre. The altar railing was marble…white marble with inset branches and leaves fashioned out of iron. The craftsmanship was outstanding. The stained glass windows encircling the white marble altar were exquisite…on the same level as you find in the great Gothic medieval cathedrals of Europe. The boys' choir sang the Latin Masses exactly like the Vienna Boys' choir. I was very upset when I learned that St. Ann's Church was being destroyed. A remarkable work of art gone forever.

There were a lot of very positive things about Goose Village. The vast majority of Goose Villagers really cared about their area. A lot of the brick row-housing was painted over a kind of dark maroon color, and it seemed like all the doors and shutters would be dark green. I can't say for sure, but I'd estimate that about 60% of the properties were owner-occupied and most of them were well kept. The women of the Village used to polish the outside stone steps. I'm not kidding, polish the steps! And they'd polish the small gold mailboxes until they absolutely shone.

Tom and his mother, 2011.

On the inside, the Village houses were very simple, but very clean. The floors were usually linoleum with some of the hardwood showing around the outside edges. The old Irish women used to like to show off their multi-colored China tea-sets displayed in glass enclosed cabinets. One of my cousin's parents also had these glass display boxes above the four interior doors of their flat and in each one was a beautiful hand-crafted 19th century sailing ship model complete with all the rigging. The detail displayed in these models was amazing for a young boy to marvel at. You could just feel the sense of pride that many of the Villagers had in their homes.

You'd often see people just sitting around on chairs on the sidewalk, the cars slowing down, people leaning out of windows chatting with the people on the street. Each one of the six streets in the Village had its own particular character. I remember when we moved within the Village. Going just from one street to another I found myself making a whole new group of close friends. A new world lay just around the corner. It was very tight-knit.

A lot of the Italians used to make their own red wine, and it was very good. Superior quality, actually. My own Italian grandfather used to have a full professional set-up for wine making in the basement. In those days we called it the "cellar". Every Sunday, my sister and I would get a small glass of watered down wine. To this day, if I even smell a cork I think of my grandfather's basement; and, that was not the only thing. The Italians transformed their small backyards—just patches of bare earth to start with—into a metamorphosis of vines, tomatoes, chicken coops. A lush garden of Eden. The coops would have three or four levels. The doors were always open and you'd see the chickens running up and down the various levels laying eggs. They were like little miniature apartment buildings in these small back yards.

Some of the people in Goose Village also kept very small fishing boats. For a long time they moored them in a very secluded spot near the Montreal end of the Victoria Bridge. They were not much more than rowboats with motors. But that is all they needed to go out fishing in the St. Lawrence. Eventually, the city closed off access to where they all kept their boats.

Like everyone, various people in my life influenced me. Ed DiZazzo was one such person. He was a couple of years ahead of me in school. I remember once going over to his place in Verdun and seeing all kinds of books. As I said, my parents wanted us to do well but we really were not a reading family. The Village had no library as such. All these books absolutely fascinated me. Other times I would go out with Ed and his friend, Kenny, and we'd go for long walks and talk about things like Greek and Roman history and mythology. I did not know at the time that I was being influenced, but I was. Years later, I studied these Ancient Classics at Loyola. Nowadays I am an avid reader of various histories. History is my passion, among other things.

I still remember sitting at home when I was in my second year at Verdun Catholic High School when I saw a CBC TV news report on the Village and the scene was one of those great big wrecking balls destroying Ed DiZazzo's grandmother's store. It shocked me. Maybe it was the time, but there was no visible dissent. You certainly wouldn't see that today. There was always a very strong work ethic in the Village and people saved their money. So, a lot did move on to nicer neighbourhoods...more affluent areas shall we say.

Like I mentioned, I ended up going to Loyola College (University of Montreal) after high

A view of part of the Point St. Charles railway yards across the street from Goose Village. 1964.

school. Looking back I can say that about 60% of the people I knew at Verdun Catholic High went on to university somewhere: Loyola, Sir George Williams (Concordia), McGill. A few of us from the Village went to Loyola, but I don't actually recall hearing of very many from the Village moving on to post-secondary. I heard that a lot of them went to work for employers like the railway or the City of Montreal.

Leonard Pacelli was from the Village and he went to Loyola. He was a couple of years older than me. As a child Leonard used to take his wagon over to the train tracks near the Victoria Bridge. He'd collect scrap metal and sell it at the nearby scrap yard – an entrepreneur in the making! His family moved from the Village to the Point before the demolition, but he used to come back and visit relatives right up until Goose Village was torn down. When I was at Loyola it was Leonard that introduced me to my wife, Michele. He went on to a successful teaching career and real estate developer. He's retired now but continues his business interests.

Summing up, I'd say that some of the most important and memorable aspects of life in Goose Village were being in a small community where you knew so many people, you knew every street, and you had a group of loyal friends. It was a "community" in the real sense of the word. There was a tremendous devotion to family and a determination among the residents to improve their position in life. Joe Berlettano played a big role for us in nurturing and enhancing this sense of community. He lived right across the street from us and he really cared for the people and children. He was an excellent role model as to what one could accomplish in life. Stemming from all of this you had a sense that you had friends for life—very rare today! It was a very conservative, yet stimulating, place. With all the trains going to different places and the harbour literally at our doorsteps, Goose Village catapulted me into a wonderful world of learning and discovery and I am still enjoying the ride.

All of this is primarily due to the fact that my wonderful parents decided to raise me and my sister up in a very special place called Goose Village. Thank you, mom and dad.

"Back in the Village
music was a way
of bringing people together.
Someone would step outside
with a big bottle of wine
and an accordion
and start playing.
Someone else would come by
with another instrument,
have a glass of wine and join in.
People would have a great time."

Joe Berlettano

Joe Berlettano

After the third or fourth interview that I conducted in developing this book, a few names, such as that of Joe Berlettano kept resurfacing. Early in the project it was clear that the story of the life and times of Goose Village during the period targeted by this work wouldn't be complete without documenting Joe's story. I located Joe in Mississauga, Ontario.

Joe was born in the village in 1936. He lived there until he was 25. Joe was a community organizer in the Village from a very young age. As a pre-teen, he would raise money and organize silent movie showings for the children of Goose Village. By age 17, his already-strong record of community involvement led to the offer of a full-time job as a boys' worker at the Victoriatown Boys' Club. By age 18 he was the director of the Club. His responsibilities grew to include managing several summer camps under the auspices of Montreal's Catholic Community Services. He was the youngest camp Director in Canada when he first took over Trail's End Camp in

"It is important and appropriate that people hear the story of Goose Village and the 300 families that lived there."

the Laurentians. By age 22 Joe was responsible for all five of Montreal's Catholic Community Services' Boys' Clubs. Joe is remembered fondly and respected greatly by the people he helped during Goose Village's final 20 years.

Following 18½ years with Catholic Community Services, Joe moved on to the United Way (Centraide) in Montreal, then to Concordia University. Subsequently, Joe purchased and directed a successful travel agency.

Joe now lives in Mississauga Ontario with his spouse Civita who grew up in Point St. Charles. From time to time, more as a hobby than anything else, Joe still organizes and leads tours to various places across the globe. He also remains active as a member of the Rotary Club of Mississauga City Centre and continues his involvement with the Knights of Columbus. Joe was recently awarded honourary lifelong membership after 50 years with the organization.

Photo: 2014.

Joe's mother, Maria (centre) helping a Goose Village young person learn a trade. c. 1955.

I was born in our house in Goose Village on January 7, 1936. At first, the family lived on Menai Street. We moved over to Britannia for a while, then back to Menai where my father bought two cottages side-by-side. We lived at 175. I stayed at home in the Village until I was 25 and married Civita. After our marriage we moved to LaSalle. Civita was born in Gaeta Italy and came to Canada as a young child. Civita grew up in Point St. Charles and attended St. Ann's Girls' School in Griffintown.

My father came to Canada from Italy around 1909 as a very young boy. His name was Nascenzio Berlettano. Like some others from Goose Village, my father came from the Galluccio Caserta area of Italy. When he came to Canada with my grandfather they immediately took up residence in the Village. My mother's name was Maria, but people called her Mariette. She was from the north end of Montreal. When my parents got married my father convinced my mother to move to the Village. He told her it would only be for a short time, but they stayed in the Village until the expropriation.

In their own way my mother and father really were pioneers. They worked very closely together to support the family through some very difficult financial times. The depression was very hard on my parents and to get through it they really worked as a team.

My father completed a mechanic's apprenticeship with the Canadian National Railway and he worked there for over 50 years. He started work every morning at 8:00 o'clock. In those days they locked the gates to the Point St. Charles yards at 8:00 and if you weren't already inside you were locked out and lost a day's pay. He was always very punctual. Back then if you worked 50 years with the CNR you got a free pass on the railway for the rest of your life and a lifetime pass on Trans Canada Airways, the predecessor to Air Canada. My father was very proud of that pass. He would show it to people and talk about taking some trips, but he never used it.

My mother was an outstanding seamstress and she was very industrious. During the depression she opened up a small dry-goods store in the Village called Mariette's. She hand-made all kinds of clothing and was very well known. People would routinely ask her to create complete ensembles of wedding and bridesmaids' dresses for Village weddings. She was constantly sewing clothing and selling various types of dry goods from the store. My mother also taught sewing to the girls at the Victoriatown Boys' Club. The classes were very popular and my mother prepared many Village girls for careers as seamstresses. At that time there was always a demand for skilled seamstresses in factories in various locations in Montreal.

My mother was up early every morning. She made us our breakfast and helped get us out. Then she'd get busy at her work. She would stop for a while to make us our lunch and then get back to her sewing. Then she would make dinner. The days were very busy for her.

As a family, we were very close and music was always central to our lives. My father played many stringed instruments such as the mandolin, violin, guitar and the banjo. He taught me how to play the guitar. One of my sisters sang opera and the other played the piano. Yes, music was a very significant part of our family's life and I am very happy to say that my children and grand-children are also very interested in music. My own children play the piano and my grandchildren play piano and various other instruments. Back in the Village music was a way of bringing people together. Someone would step outside with a big bottle of wine and an accordion and start playing. Someone else would come by with another instrument, have a glass of wine and join in. People would have a great time.

Joe Berlettano (second from left) and friends on St. Patrick's Day. c. 1956.

In my early childhood days in the Village we had no television. Our time was filled with such activities as playing outside, music, sports or board games. I also sang in the school choir. I was a cantor. I was regularly up at about 6:00 a.m. so that I could take the bus over to St. Ann's Church in Griffintown and sing the morning Mass in Latin. The church often called on the school choir. Brother Norbert was in charge of the choir at St. Ann's Boys' School and he had a unique way of selecting children for the choir. He would visit each class at the beginning of school and ask each child to sing a scale. I remember so clearly that one year a boy refused to stand and he covered his mouth. He wouldn't sing. Brother Norbert gave him a couple of chances, but to no avail. He then looked at him and said… "You have been selected for the choir". I can tell you that Brother Norbert was an outstanding person in my life and that he had a very positive influence on many of the Griffintown and Goose Village children.

Mike McNamara was another teacher I admired very much at St. Ann's Boys' School. He was the only lay teacher on staff and he had a great influence on me. He was a really loveable guy but he was also very tough. You had to work very hard for him. It was only later in life, though, that I came to appreciate what he really meant to me.

I began volunteering in the Village at a very young age. Even before I was a teenager I was organizing various events for the kids of the Village, like silent movies or helping with field days and things like that. We also had a lot of sports teams in the Village. The older kids and men were involved in various sports like baseball, softball, football, boxing and hockey. I used to go to the senior teams and ask them if they would pass on things like bats, balls and gloves for the younger kids in the village. They were always very generous. I really looked up to these senior people in the community—people like Terry Furlong, who was a key organizer, Ron Baxter, who was very big in baseball, and Domenic Santori, who did a lot of fundraising for special education

Victoriatown (Goose Village) Boys' Club. c. 1963.

programs at St. Ann's. These were just three of the many that were very generous with their support for the children of the Village.

After St. Ann's Boys' School I went on to graduate from Cardinal Newman high school. Before my time in secondary school most of the Catholic kids from Griffintown and the Village moved on to D'Arcy McGee. But when I finished at St. Ann's demand was really increasing and D'Arcy McGee was at capacity. Brother Norbert spoke to us and suggested that we consider Cardinal Newman instead. The same congregation of Brothers that taught at St. Ann's, the Christian Brothers, was just in the process of taking over responsibility for Cardinal Newman at that time. Many of us decided to follow Brother Norbert's advice. When I was finishing high school only two people from my graduating class put up their hands when asked by one of our teachers who was interested in moving on to more studies. If I recall correctly, one wanted to go to teacher's college and the other to McGill.

After I graduated I was offered a job at Canadian Car. It was in Personnel. It wasn't as if I knew anything about the discipline at the time. It was a trainee position. It didn't last long,

Goose Village's park and skating rink. The Victoriatown Boys' Club is located across the park at the centre-left. c. 1963.

though, because Jack Dalton offered me a job as a boys' worker at the Victoriatown Boys' Club. I was 17. Jack was instrumental in getting the Boys' Club built and off the ground in the first place. He was also aware of my keen interest in community work and he knew that I had received some recognition for the work I had already done over the years. So, I left Canadian Car and began the journey with the Victoriatown Boys' Club.

As it turned out, things moved along very quickly. Henry McKewon was the Director of the Boys' Club at that time and a little over a year after I started working there he stepped down. He already had a full time job at the time and he was also very active in the Irish community. So, Jack Dalton asked me to take over as Director and I accepted. I was only 18 years old but I welcomed the challenge. My whole life I have always tried to approach things from an optimistic point of view. Thankfully, Henry McKewon remained active on a smaller scale as both an organizer and a boxing coach. I really looked up to Henry and I will always remember that it was on the morning of a St. Patrick's Day Parade in Montreal that he passed away.

We organized many different kinds of activities and special events for the children of the Village —things like dances, field days, talent parades and bus tours. We used to hold weekly movie events for the kids of the Village and they were very popular. We'd rent the movies and pack the place. After showing the movies to the kids I used to take the equipment over to the rectory at

Roller skating at the Victoriatown Boys' Club Gym. 1956.

St. Ann's Church and show the movies to the priests. They really enjoyed this and were very appreciative.

One summer event the kids really liked was our soapbox derby. In those days soapbox derbies were very popular. We organized our own in the Village, but we also used to compete in the more formal derbies where people took part from all over Montreal and elsewhere. At the Village level, we didn't race the carts on hills; one person pushed and the other steered. All the carts had to be hand-made. At the more competitive level, we would enter a more sophisticated cart. One year Marcel Bellefeuille was our representative. Marcel was a very nice boy and we had a very good entry.

Although it was called the Victoriatown Boys' Club, it was more than that. It was a larger community resource. For example, the facilities in the Village were not like today. A lot of the houses didn't have baths. We used to make the club available to people for showers. Often, you'd see the men of the Village taking advantage of this after a day's work at Dominion Coal. The men would arrive and they were covered so completely in coal dust all you could see really clearly were their eyes.

Field days in the Village. 1956.

Some of the services offered by the Victoriatown Boys' Club

SPORTS: Football, baseball, softball, ice hockey, floor hockey, badminton, bowling, soccer, volleyball, boxing, ping pong, track and field, handball, broomball, volleyball.

COURSES/HOBBIES/CRAFTS: Leather crafts, woodworking, sewing, knitting, fancy needle work, wood burning, art classes, airplane modeling, photography, dance, wire craft and jewelry, plaster molding.

SPECIAL EVENTS: Field days, soap box derbies, St Patrick's Day / Christmas / Easter parties etc., sports banquets, talent parades, Friday-night movies, regular weekend indoor teen dances, special street dances, Barn dances, children's bus tours to various cultural and entertainment venues, plays, outdoor movies in the park, boat rides.

CLUBS/COUNCILS ETC. Junior council, jazz club, drama club, bugle band.

A variety of other services were offered at the club to adults such as kindergarten, parent's time, as well as the use of the clubs broad range of facilities.

People in Goose Village were also constantly in need of clothing and a lot of them needed food as well. So we started a food and clothing distribution service at the Boys' Club. But the Villagers were also fiercely proud and did not want to be seen as relying on charity. So, the approach we took here was to engage the people by asking them to help us. We'd say "Look, the Club is overloaded with clothing, and it is taking up valuable space that we need, so could people please come and help us get this moved on?" We encouraged people to help us, and it worked.

Talking about this brings to mind so many different situations we saw. Sometimes it was the kind of thing you just didn't expect. I remember two young children from the Village. They were from very beautiful and caring families, but both of the children were a little slow. We wanted to see them active in the club. Very early in their involvement they were taking a shower with the other kids. After all the other children were finished we found the two of them still in the shower and both of them were crying. When we talked to them and asked what was wrong they said they didn't know what to do. They had never dressed themselves alone. So we started to work with them and taught them how to get things done.

Over the years in the Village I saw a lot of things that you wouldn't see in other areas of Montreal. Part of it was because of my job and part of it was just because I lived in the Village for 25 years. The Village was a caring place but we knew that it had a reputation. I knew that people from outside Victoriatown were afraid of the Village. For example, I know for a fact that sometimes taxi drivers simply refused to enter Goose Village. You'd get in the cab and give a

The "Suitmaker Black Hawks" softball team. Joe is in the back row, first on the right. 1956.

Goose Village address and sometimes the cabbie would just say, "That's in Goose Village. I'm not going down there".

We really tried to ensure that the young people of the Village stayed on the right path, but a lot of our kids ended up in juvenile court. Most of the time it would be for stealing. Often, it was stealing because of need. I frequently found myself involved with the courts and with caseworkers. I don't have the statistics, but I do know from discussions I had with people back then that they saw a significant drop in delinquency after the Boys' Club was opened. I also remember reading some newspaper articles to that effect as well. Once the Boys' Club was built the Village kids had a destination. They had things to do. It made a big difference for them. It gave them different options and added more of a structure to their lives.

My work with the young people of the Village certainly led to some challenging situations. I remember that one night a very upset teenager came to my office at the Boys' Club. He told me

VICTORIATOWN CHAMPS
1957-58
SPONSORED BY SUIT MAKERS LTD.

Victoriatown (Goose Village) softball team. 1957–1958 season.

that several of his friends were on their way to Canada Packers to steal a refrigerated truck full of beef. The truck had been readied to go on the road for deliveries the next morning. He was sure that all his friends would get caught and go to jail. He was probably right. I hurried over to Canada Packers and found the group of young men. I asked them to follow me to the Boys' Club for a sit-down to talk things over. At the time I wasn't much older than them. Eventually, cooler heads prevailed and they called off the theft. People in Goose Village tried to protect each other. That was precisely what that young man was doing when he came to see me. It wasn't necessarily the case with people from outside, but if you were from the Village you would get protected in various ways.

When it came to club activities I always made it a point to follow up with children on things if I saw them going in the wrong direction. It could be simple things, but I followed up as soon as I could. For example, we used to have a lot of things like board games at the club. The games were supposed to stay there for everyone. Sometimes you'd see kids playing with them and when

Victoriatown (Goose Village) soccer team. c. 1956.

they left the club the board game they were using would be gone. Right away, I would go to their houses to find them and talk to them. Sometimes you'd arrive and find them sitting outside playing the game on the street. I wouldn't scold them or lecture them. I'd simply say "Could you please bring the board game back just as soon as you finish playing?" Then they'd say, "Yes Joe", and they'd bring it back.

Things could flare up quickly in the Village. For example, once I remember hearing a great commotion in the street. I opened the shutters, looked out the window and saw two men just going at each other, fighting in the middle of the street. The next day I saw the same two men hugging each other. I remember another situation where a chap from the Village who had a lazy eye was at one of our street dances. His impediment gave the impression that he was looking in another direction. Another Villager mistook this impediment to mean that this individual was staring at his wife. He pulled a knife and slashed the man across the face. As you might imagine, things at the dance degenerated from there.

The Village was right beside the railway yards and that leads to a couple of other stories that stand out in my memory. There was this one fellow that wanted to build a country place. He told some of the younger guys in the village that he wanted lumber and that he'd pay them for it. So what these kids did was go over to the railyards and look for piles of long planks of wood left behind for pickup after the grain cars were opened and emptied. The grain car doors opened

A Goose Village football team. 1955.

from the side, but while in transit they were reinforced from the inside by several large planks that covered the full length of the door. For a period of time when this group of kids found any of these piles they would carry some of the planks back to the Village and sell them to the fellow who wanted the country house. He would then store the planks in his shed in the back. Well, after a while the shed was full, so these kids would just go inside the shed, take out some pieces that they had already sold to this fellow and resell them to him. He never knew.

One lady I remember well had the reputation as the toughest woman in the Village. I wouldn't argue with that description. If she needed wood for her stove, she'd collect up the nine or ten dogs she always kept and head off into the railway yards. She'd look for some of these planks as well. If she found any, she'd sling two or three across each shoulder—and these planks were heavy—and march right through the Village to her house, the nine or ten dogs in tow. She'd take a similar approach if she needed coal. Off she'd go with the dogs over to Dominion Coal after closing time. She'd fill a couple of buckets and come home. She was never without her dogs.

I remember one family in the Village that used to take clothing from other people's clotheslines. People would come to me in tears saying that they had just bought a really nice piece of clothing—what you might call today, designer clothing. They'd tell me that it had been lifted from their clothesline. I'd calm them down and suggest that they go and knock on so-and-so's

National Boys' Club Week in Goose Village. Crowning of the "king" and "queen". 1959.

door and ask if they might know anything about this certain piece of clothing. Typically, when they went to this house they would be asked in and shown several boxes of clothing. They would be invited to look for the lost piece. The person that lost the clothing would rifle through the boxes until they found the missing piece, then leave. Nothing else would be said, then or later. That's just the way it was in Goose Village.

Trucks full of livestock and chickens and such would often pass through the village on the way to the slaughterhouse. I can remember times when a truckload of chickens would be coming through for processing and someone would jump on the truck from the back, flip the catch and open the door. There would be chickens all over the street. People would grab a chicken, take it home and that was that. I have actually seen the same thing happen with pigs.

In the Village, you'd sometimes see groups of men standing around in the alleys drinking beer and rolling dice. The money would be on the ground. I remember once seeing a policeman come across one of the games. He tried to put a stop to it but he wasn't successful. People from the Village did sometimes get in trouble and some got arrested. But a lot of the people did things down there and weren't disturbed by anyone. It was a very unique place.

On the girls' side the issues were different. I would say that my biggest challenge was with Italian families that hadn't been in Canada for very long. In these families, in the mid–'fifties and early 'sixties, Italian girls from the old country were expected to stay home and help mother.

Children's parties. c. 1956.

Soap Box Derby races in Goose Village. c. 1955.

Going to street dances or Boys' Club dances, for example was just not on. As the Italian population grew and the Irish population of the Village diminished, there was a real drop-off in attendance at our dances. At one time they were hugely successful, but much less so towards the end. It was a very interesting transition to see. Nevertheless, we really tried hard to integrate these young Italian women into Club activities. Our big breakthrough came with the sewing classes. They began to participate in these and as I said, they became very popular. My mother played a big part in this success.

We did see a difference in the latitude that some of the Italian girls were given over the years though. You could even see it in a single family. As a younger sister grew up you could see that she was given more freedom than the older sister had been given. It was something that you could see as the Italian families became a little more accustomed to Canada and to the Village.

Christmas, for me, always brought with it the prospect of families in the Village going without —not having enough food for Christmas day and the rest of the holiday. This really bothered me.

Soap Box Derby races in Goose Village. c. 1955.

One of the strategies we developed at the Club was to issue vouchers redeemable at the corner stores. The understanding was, however, that the vouchers couldn't be used for liquor of any sort or for cigarettes. As well, every year I would talk to my mother about the most needy people in the Village and suggest that, as a family, we prepare a little something for these families and deliver it just before Christmas. I can tell you that the reception we received was quite something.

Throughout my association with the Club we always received a lot of requests for counseling. People came to us, for example, for marriage counseling, delinquency counseling, money problems, and a variety of other issues. Never once did we turn anyone away. We treated every person that came to see us as if they were family.

Like others, I was shocked and disappointed when I heard that the City was going to expropriate the Village. The decisions and processes were not handled well. The people of the Village needed guidance and support from the City and they didn't really get it. We made the Boys' Club

Soap Box Derby races in Goose Village—a very popular event. c. 1955.

available to the City as a centre for support and administration during the expropriation—a place to help Villagers with housing needs, but the people they sent weren't trained professionals.

People were told to just go ahead and buy a place somewhere else even though they hadn't received the expropriation money for their Village properties. I know that some people also had only recently bought their properties. With the expropriation and the loss of value in their investment it was very hard on some people, especially the new immigrants who had settled in the Village. I vividly remember one old gentleman standing in the middle of the street at the corner of Menai and Forfar yelling as loudly as he could; "I am not moving...I am not moving..."

Looking back on the whole experience of the Village, the Boys' Club and the summer camps, it was a truly fabulous time. Things were happening very quickly in Montreal in the 'fifties and 'sixties. The baby boomers were packing the schools and there was a huge demand for the services that Catholic Communities Services provided. As I said earlier, I was put in charge of

Joe Berlettano, back row, first on the right, and team at the Victoriatown Boys' Club. c. 1956–1959.

the Victoriatown Boys' Club at 18 and my responsibilities grew continually with the changing times. Things just kept growing and growing. In addition to the Victoriatown Boys' Club, Catholic Communities Services ran five other boys' clubs and for a period I was put in charge of overseeing them all. Each one had its own Director. We opened them in schools, parish halls— anywhere we needed to and from anywhere we got the call.

Catholic Community Services ran several summer camps. Not too long after I became director of the Boys' Club Jack Dalton expanded my responsibilities to include managing Trail's End Camp. It was located north of Joliette in the municipalities of Saint-Alphonse-Rodriguez and Sainte-Béatrix. I was the youngest camp director in Canada at the time and it didn't stop there. Several years after I took over Trail's End I was asked to take over two more camps: Camp Orelda Marion and Camp Kinkora. Orelda Marion was named after three priests by combining the first two letters of each man's name—O'Rourke, Elliott and Dawson. When I took over Trail's End we had 80 campers. By 1967, we had 192 campers and much improved facilities. We worked very hard to improve these camps and volunteers did a lot of the work. The people that worked and volunteered at the Boys' Clubs and elsewhere with Catholic community Services were wonderful to work with. It truly was a remarkable time in my life. I will be forever grateful to the team of hard-working, dedicated staff at the Boys' Club and the hundreds of

Four: Goose Village street scenes shortly before the demolition in 1964. See also p. 18-19.

volunteers that made it possible to carry out such an ambitious program of activities with very limited financial resources. After 18½ years with Catholic Community Services I moved on to United Way, or Centraide as it is called in Quebec. I was a social planner for five years and the Assistant Campaign Director for five. During my time there I worked almost completely in French.

I'd say about 90% of my work, both oral and written was in French. I wasn't able to do this at the beginning, but I had a very supportive manager. I took courses and practiced diligently. It all worked out well.

When I left Centraide, Dr. John O'Brien, the Rector of Concordia University, invited me to become the Capital Campaign Director for the University. While there, I helped raise part of the money to build the new library on boulevard De Maisonneuve. It is in downtown Montreal at what is now called the Sir George Williams Campus of Concordia.

After four years at Concordia I decided to buy a travel business on Mansfield Street in Montreal. It was called Kelen Travel and it was an early pioneer in bringing Eastern Block immigrants to Canada. It acted as a trading company as well. We were also in the position to help send gifts and money back home to Eastern-Block countries. Eventually I sold the company to House of Travel but continued to work for them. I always enjoyed working with people. That's just who I am. The travel business was something new for me and I enjoyed it very much. Even now, although I am essentially retired, I still organize one or two tours a year just by word of mouth. Civita and I lead the tours.

Goose Village was demolished in 1964. But even now, long after I stopped working for Catholic Community Services, from time to time I still hear from some of the Villagers. People still write to me, and every now and then someone will call for help or advice. Other times I'll just bump into someone from the Goose Village days and we'll start talking about something that is important to them. Then they'll say something like "What do you think I should do?"

We never turned anyone away 50 years ago and that holds just as true for me today as it did back then—always has. I remember when I was running the travel agency I had occasion at one point to help a young man I met in the travel industry. He had some good ideas. He was making headway but his successes outpaced his licensing rights in the Province of Quebec. I offered to bring his business under mine until he successfully completed all his courses and the licensing required for what he was doing. It was a rewarding experience for both of us as I had the opportunity to act as a mentor in some ways. He later acquired all his licenses and went back out on his own. He now has a very successful business in Montreal. I bumped into him in Montreal a few years later when I was visiting and he invited me over to see his operation, so I agreed. When I arrived he had all his staff lined up. He introduced me to each of them and then made a very nice speech saying that "This business wouldn't be here today if weren't for this gentleman!" I was really floored.

What should future generations understand about Goose Village? Well, my community, charitable and business involvement over the years has brought me in contact with many, many groups and communities, but I can say this. There was a sense of community among the people from Victoriatown that I have never, ever seen elsewhere. Goose Villagers built incredibly deep bonds. They were very close. Today it wouldn't matter where you might be in the world. If you are from the Village and someone else from the Village were to recognize you, you'd be approached like it was yesterday. It was truly a very unique place.

I knew almost every family in the Village, and I knew all the children. It is important and appropriate that people hear the story of Goose Village and the 300 families that lived there.

Joe and Civita at their 50th wedding anniversary. 2011

"What values

did growing up in the Point

help develop and reinforce in my life?…

The three values

that come to mind

are loyalty,

respect for others

and the importance

of self-confidence."

Robert Côté

Robert "Bob" Côté

In 1959, shortly after his release from the Army where he served in the Royal 22nd Regiment, Bob joined the ranks of the Montreal Police Department as a Constable. He was assigned to the neighborhood where he was born and grew up: Pointe-Saint-Charles, in the southwest sector of the city.

In 1963, with the advent of homegrown terrorism in the form of the Front de Libération du Québec, Bob volunteered and was selected to be part of the newly formed Montreal Police Bomb Squad, of which he later became Commanding Officer, with the rank of Lieutenant. During the 'sixties and 'seventies, Bob was Montreal's primary resource person in numerous tense and dramatic incidents involving homemade bombs. He received numerous honours and decorations, including the Police Medal of Bravery. In 1972, he was made an Officer of the Order of Canada. Promoted to the rank of Inspector in 1980, Bob commanded number 24 District, which

"My beloved Pointe-Saint-Charles. I left the Point but it is still with me."

includes Pointe-Saint-Charles, Griffintown, parts of Old Montreal, as well as parts of Saint-Henri and the area where Victoriatown (Goose Village) once stood. Later on Bob took charge of Montreal Police Telecommunications with the mission of implementing the Montreal 9-1-1 Emergency Telephone Service, inaugurated in 1985.

Bob retired from the Montreal Police Department in 1990, with the rank of Chief Inspector. In 1994, he made a foray into municipal politics, joining Vision Montreal, the political party of his old friend, Mayor Pierre Bourque. Bob was elected City Councilor for the district of Rosemont and became the first City Mediator, or Ombudsman, for a four-year term. In 1998, he served as Deputy Mayor of Montreal.

Bob, a widower, is now an occasional lecturer and full-time grandfather. He still lives in Montreal and is a volunteer writer for local police publications.

Photo: Chief Inspector R. Côté, Montreal Police Department. 1990.

Robert (right) with brother Claude on Centre Street in the Point. 1949.

I was born in 1936 on Knox Street in Pointe-Saint-Charles. I have two brothers and one sister. I am the youngest. I currently belong to the Pointe-Saint-Charles Historical Society and four other similar societies. I still visit the Point and I enjoy riding my bicycle along the bike paths of the Lachine Canal.

My father's name was Arthur. He was a mechanic and I am told he was a very popular man in the neighborhood. Unfortunately, I never knew my father. He died just five months after I was born. It was due to a complication after an appendix operation.

My mother's name was Marie-Anne Marleau, but she was always known as Marianna. Shortly after my father passed away, we moved from Knox Street to Centre Street in the Point. My mother took over at a difficult financial time in the country and at a time when there was little in the way of support for families in need.

I first went to school at St. Gabriel's School on Centre Street in the Point. I was only there for a year. The family continued to experience financial difficulties and my mother's brother, who was a member of the clergy in the Beauharnois Parish of St. Clement, exercised some influence to have the two youngest children of the family attend a Hospice run by the Grey

Then and now: Robert outside the childhood home on Centre Street. Left 1948; Right, 2011.

Nuns. It served several functions: an orphanage, a senior's home and a residential school for children whose parents could afford to pay all the costs. In the fall of 1942 the two youngest of the family, myself and my sister began our stay at Beauharnois.

I lived there for three years, virtually all year round except for times like Christmas and Easter. Overall, it remains a bad memory. There was very strict discipline, as well as considerable corporal punishment, some of which was humiliating and unpleasant to be forced to watch. Children were targeted for different transgressions. Mine was that I was left-handed. I was forced to change and to this day writing is the only thing I do right-handed. Perhaps that is why I am still teased from time to time about my hieroglyphics! I was there for three very difficult years, but I don't hold any grudges and I won't.

When I came back to the Point in the summer of my tenth year the family had moved to 2749 Centre Street. You could say it was the beginning of the golden years of Pointe-Saint-Charles. The men had returned from the war and things were looking up economically for the country. By that time my mother was working night shifts at Montreal's Juvenile Court, leaving home at 10:30 at night and finishing at 8:00 in the morning. She had Fridays off, but often worked at a local store on that day. I was attending St. Charles School in the Point.

Our house was located very near the Sherwin Williams paint factory at the western end of the Point. It was a big employer in Pointe-Saint-Charles. It is now a condo complex called Les Lofts Sherwill. I remember once waking up to a gigantic explosion on the Canal side of Sherwin

This now derelict swing bridge from Griffintown to the Point stands a short walk from the corner of de la Montagne & Wellington streets in Griffintown. 2011.

St. Gabriel (foreground) and St. Charles churches on Centre Street. 2011.

Williams. It caused a great deal of damage. Until recently, you could still see traces of the explosion on neighboring buildings, but they have all been demolished. Lives were lost in that explosion.

Growing up in Pointe-Saint-Charles, the French and English districts were pretty much divided by the railroad tracks running parallel to Mullins Street. Knox Street, where I was born, is also parallel to the tracks in Pointe-Saint-Charles. To this day I am still nostalgic about trains. South of the tracks it was mostly English, while north of the tracks it was mostly French. We just called the Irish "blokes" because that is how we referred to all the English. They called us the "Pea Soups". Every now and then we'd bump into the Irish and there would be a fight. Well, we kind of looked at it as what you'd call a "cultural exchange". I never really saw anyone get seriously hurt in these fights. They were almost more like wrestling matches.

After school sometimes we would swim in the Lachine Canal to cool off. In those days, we were not really concerned about the water. Given what we know now about pollution though, I must be immune to every ailment known to man because I have never been sick in my life. Some other times we would go to Hogan baths and pay five cents to rent a standard bathing suit and go swimming. In the earlier days in the Point, a lot of the houses didn't have baths. You couldn't dive in the public baths like Hogan because they were only a few feet deep, but you could swim. The Point baths got their name from a very influential Irish City Councilor by the name of Frank Hogan.

As kids we'd also go for what we called a "tour de pont". Most of the bridges across the Lachine Canal were swing bridges. They would swing open sideways so that the ships could pass by. The operator would sit in a little cabin on the top of the bridge, but he had a blind spot underneath where he sat. We would hide so that he could not see us and when he swung the bridge we'd go for a ride—a "tour de pont". We always knew when ships were coming down the canal because the bridge operators had to ring a bell to signal their approach to the various bridges before closing the gates to vehicles.

Back in the 1800s, French and English Roman Catholics in Pointe-Saint-Charles mostly all attended St. Gabriel's Church on Centre Street, but by 1874 it was getting very overcrowded. That

The Sherwin Williams Paint building (left) and the Hogan Bath building, both now condos. 2011.

was the year the Curé of the day recommended building a separate church for French Catholics. The new church opened in 1884 right next door to St. Gabriel's. That is why, to this day, there are two big Roman Catholic churches side by side on Centre Street in the Point. This is probably unique. Both churches are almost deserted now though, since so few people go to church.

My mother remarried in 1950—the same year I finished grade nine. This brought about a move to Verdun and it meant I could not attend school in Saint-Henri with my friends. I was required to attend school in Verdun. The transition did not really work out for me and when I was sixteen I decided that I would join the Army.

I was reading a lot at this time and I was very aware of what was going on in the world. I was interested in adventure and travel. I knew of the situation in Korea at the time and the Army seemed like a logical choice for me. Accordingly, I developed a successful strategy to acquire an official (but incorrectly dated) birth certificate indicating I was 18 and I joined the Royal 22nd Regiment (the "Vandoos"). I became a paratrooper by age 17 and spent six productive and very enjoyable years in the Army. I did a tour in Germany, traveled and participated in exercises all over Canada.

Coordinating my departure date from the Army with future employment, I applied to the Montreal Police, the Harbour Board Police, the Quebec Provincial Police (now the Sureté du Québec) and the RCMP. My brother was already a member of the Montreal Police at that time. The City of Montreal contacted me quickly, as did the Harbour Board and the RCMP. I decided to join Montreal. I don't know why the Sureté didn't call me, but if they ever do I'm going to have to tell them they are too late—I'm retired!

When I finished training with the City of Montreal I was immediately assigned back to where I grew up: Pointe-Saint-Charles. Station 11 was located at the corner of Grand Trunk and Shearer at that time. It was demolished some time ago. Charles-Lemoyne Polyvalent School is there now. The instructions I received from my sergeant upon arrival were clear: "Catch thieves, give out tickets and keep your mouth shut!"

Robert in Europe while serving with the Royal 22nd Regiment. 1954.

This advice served me well, at least in the early years, although I thought the ticket aspect might have backfired on me once. Early on in my career I was walking on Centre Street in the Point and saw a large white Cadillac parked in a bus stop. I handed out the appropriate ticket unaware that it was owned by the long-time Point legend and local City Councilor—Frank Hanley. The storekeeper in front of the bus stop waved me frantically into the store after I wrote the ticket and gave me the bad news. In those days, City Councilors like Frank had a say in who went where, and who got promoted to what in the police. I thought my future might well be in for a few bumps. However, Frank walked in, congratulated me and told me he'd "take care of it". I joked with Frank about this later in life. He said he remembered the day. I don't know if he did. After I retired from the police and moved on to the position of City Councilor I would call and ask to meet Frank. He would always ask if we could meet at his "office". His "office", as he called it, was the Capri Barserie on St. Patrick Street in the Point—one of the few old time Point taverns remaining!

But, back to my days in the Point. When I was walking the beat, typically, those with less seniority spent more time on night shifts. That was fine with me. Things were usually busier in the Point at night.

I was often assigned to foot patrol in Goose Village. In those days, to us, Goose Village was just considered part of Pointe-Saint-Charles since it was in the Station 11 patrol area. About 1500

One of the very few remaining indicators of Victoriatown (Goose Village). 2011.

people lived in the Village. The only physical reminder now of the name Victoriatown is a commemorative stone honouring the men and women from the area who lost their lives serving during the Second World War. At the bottom of the stone it indicates that it was erected by the citizens of Victoriatown. The Village was largely Irish at first, but over the years there was a gradual transition to a majority Italian area. You can see the traces of this by looking at the names on the commemorative Stone. The stone was recently moved farther down Bridge Street and closer to the "Black Rock" which commemorates the people who died of typhus coming to Montreal from Ireland in the mid 1800s.

Robert Côté early in his career with the Montreal Police. 1960.

I have many good memories of my time walking the beat in the Village. I was treated kindly when I worked there. Many of the small business owners would greet us as we came down the street, invite us in for some "grappa" and ask us if we'd like to come through to the back and watch them play bocce. They would call us "Mr. Policeman".

There were lots and lots of kids around the Village at the time. There wasn't any more crime in Goose Village than there was in other parts of Montreal. Back then, we didn't have the drug problems that we have today. At that time it was beer and wine. Also, the patrol priority in those days was certain areas in the Point. Centre Street and Charlevoix Street, for example, contributed to busy times. The Village, on the other hand, was typically quite quiet.

Jean Drapeau was the mayor of Montreal in the early 'sixties and it was just a few years before Montreal was to host the World's fair— Expo 67. The City's position was that Goose Village was a slum and that it should be demolished. That viewpoint prevailed and the land was expropriated. In 1964 the Village was razed. I believe that the real reason for this expropriation was that the City wanted the land to build an entrance to Expo 67 and a stadium. At the time there were other areas in the city that were in the same condition as Goose Village but they were not considered slums and razed. The Autostade and Place d'Accueil, the main welcoming area to Expo 67, were built right where Goose Village stood.

When it was there, though, Victoriatown truly was a "village". There were lots of events. Victoria Day, the Monday closest to May 24th, for example, was still celebrated in Quebec at that time. This was a big one in the Village. It was a huge party, even though it had really lost its historical meaning by that time. There was always a lot of drinking and the tradition on Victoria Day in that part of town was to set bonfires up and down the area. We would station policemen and firefighters at the various alarm boxes to prevent false alarms. Many years later as the Police Director for the Point as a whole, I would be confronted with this problem again.

The Village's location next to the meat processing plant led to some really ridiculous situations for the Police. Sometimes a cow or bull being led for processing at the plant would escape. We'd get the message that one of the animals was loose. That meant that we were about to go on what we called an "urban safari". All the police in the area would immediately rush in. Of course, to us, it was always a "bull" that was loose because a bull is far more impressive than

The old Pall Mall Tavern, now the Pub St. Charles. 2011.

a cow when you are on an urban safari! And after a few days, it became a "Toro". Fifty years ago we did not have the complex police procedures for something like this that we have today. And I can tell you that whatever the bull weighed when it got out, it weighed considerably more when it was returned to Canada Packers counting in the lead we sent its way.

Until 1966 there was a dumpsite located between Pointe-Saint-Charles and the St. Lawrence River. It was covered over to help in providing the land for a parking lot for the 1967 World's Fair. The Bonaventure Expressway into downtown Montreal was built over it as well. Then in the 1970s a short take-off and landing facility was built over the top of this land but it never worked out very well. The gasses emitted from the old dump kept pushing up and causing problems with the runway. That area is now called Le Technoparc.

But I can remember back to the days when I was a young constable and the dump was still there. It was a time when the rules on waste management, as well as the Montreal sewer system weren't as sophisticated as they are today. If you were patrolling by car down at the city dump at night and shone your headlights in you'd see rats foraging around for food. And in some areas of

Robert at the site of his first arrest as a police officer. The opening for the delivery chute has since been cemented over, 2011.

the Point back then when I was on foot patrol at night I'd sometimes run into them if I shone my flashlight down an alley.

I remember one instance when I was relatively new to the department. I received a call to go to a house in the Village. Upon arrival I found that several dresser drawers had been set up as cribs on the floor. The empty dresser was off to one side. Each night the drawers were removed to form these children's cribs. While asleep in one these drawers on the floor, one of the children had been bitten. Some calls stay with you over the years.

Typically, the stores in the Point and many of the houses opened directly onto the sidewalk. They had no front yard. I have visited Belfast and the row housing architecture of the living accommodation, common in the Point, is very similar. A lot of the stores at the time also had small chutes at ground level that opened directly onto the sidewalk. This facilitated the delivery of goods from the suppliers to the stores. I was walking along early one morning and saw a person beginning to crawl out of one of the chutes. Of course, it was a burglary in progress. I was as surprised to see him as he was to see me. In those days, we had no radios, nor did we have handcuffs. He was very cooperative however and we were not too far from the police station. I took him by the arm and started to walk him over. A local taxi driver had seen what was going on. He pulled over and asked if I'd like a lift so we jumped in. That's the way it was back then.

The first time I attended a suicide was also in the Point. Early one Sunday morning near the end of a night shift on foot patrol, I was walking beside Marguerite Bourgeoys Park. That morning I found a gentleman hanging from one of the trees in the park. He had obviously used a clothesline, because I was struck by the fact that the pulley, used to affix the lines to their houses or poles and move the clothing along the line, was still attached. It was dangling from the rope.

Fifty years ago people knew that in the Point we worked full shifts on foot patrol. We were required to phone in to the station at regular intervals to let the supervisors know we were OK and on schedule, so you were always on the move. We had specific beats to walk. Depending on the different beats, you'd call in either every half hour or hour from call-boxes located along the route of your beat.

In Montreal, in the winter, walking a full nightshift with everything closed down can get very, very cold. Unlike some other areas of the city, nothing was open after midnight in Pointe-Saint-Charles. Thankfully, some of the businesses, like one of the local gas stations, and the barbershop, secreted keys for us so that we could access the premises to warm up for short periods of time during our beat. One of the restaurants on Centre Street at the corner of Charelvoix also opened very early in the morning and that was always a most welcome sight.

There weren't a lot of murders in the Point, but on the weekends we had a lot of fights, drunk driving and break-ins to deal with. From Sunday to Friday, the Point was usually pretty quiet, but not on the weekends. We had 17 taverns in the Point. They had names like the Regal, the Palomino, and the Pall Mall. One we just called the "Bucket of Blood". It no longer exists.

The Point is located right next door to Verdun, and back then Verdun was a "dry" town. You could buy beer in local groceries in Verdun, but the *Scott Law* in Verdun dictated that restaurants could not serve any alcohol and there were no taverns allowed in Verdun. Verdun chose to apply this law in exchange for a Curé's commitment to build a school. So, on weekends a lot of the Verdun people came to our taverns in the Point.

A couple of them, like the old Pall Mall on Wellington and Butler, were just a few feet from Verdun. There were frequent fights in these taverns. It was not uncommon for three or four Montreal Police cars to arrive to break things up at tavern fights. Sometimes we'd arrive at fights just as things were ending and we'd help settle things down. Other times, we'd arrive and that would just start things up again.

Magnan's opened in 1932 during the Great Depression. At first it was just a small place. Now it is really a large and popular restaurant with an outdoor patio [On October 8, 2014 a Montreal Gazette writer, François Shalom, reported that Magnanès would close on December 21, 2014]. The only food that taverns were supposed to serve in the early days was pickled eggs and pickled tongue. But Madame Magnan used to cook in the house that was attached to the tavern and pass food through an opening for customers. This was back in the days when taverns were for men only. The Point also had lots of Blind Pigs and Social Clubs like the Arrawana and the Coronation. The Coronation was so named because it opened the same year Queen Elizabeth II was crowned.

Based on my experience, both as a constable on the beat and later in life as a senior officer in the department, my view that a lot of crime in the Point, as well as elsewhere in Montreal was driven by alcohol consumption. And sometimes things would spill over into the home and we'd get calls from neighbours about domestic disturbances. Arriving at the scene it was difficult for us to do anything because we had not been witness to any act. Although long since changed and improved, the legislation of the 1950s and 1960s didn't support the sorts of interventions available today.

Years ago we also had a lot of problems with illegal lotteries. The number you bought, often in the taverns, was really a time, down to the second, reflecting the length of a Montreal Canadiens hockey game at the Forum. If your ticket corresponded to the time of, for example, the first goal, you won. We found out once that the clock at the Forum had been rigged not to stop at certain numbers, though. I remember going around the bars in the Point, purposely dressed poorly, buying tickets. When successful, we would arrest the numbers vendor and try to bargain with him to turn over his supplier up the line. We made a very big seizure of a supplier once who was working out of Dominion Glass right in the Point. The illegal lottery problem lasted for many, many years until the introduction of Lotto Québec stopped it.

The Lachine Canal? That was a real dumping ground. We'd find stolen cars, safes (recovered after break-ins), occasionally murder victims, and suicides at the canal. When we'd find a body it was the Fire Department's job to get it out. I remember one body in particular that we found. It had obviously been in the canal for a very long time. It was hunched over, floating face down, and it was extremely inflated.

At about the same time as I was finishing my first four years at Station 11, we were beginning to experience some real trouble in Montreal with home-grown terrorism. The FLQ (Front de Libération du Québec) were starting to plant homemade bombs. It was a big surprise to the people of Montreal and to the Montreal Police. We only had one person assigned to bomb disposal on the Police Force at the time and his name was Leo Plouffe. The call went out for volunteers. The Department said they were looking for people preferably with a military background for the assignment. I successfully applied after some arm-twisting from lieutenant "Moe" Plante. I was sent for bomb disposal training with other police officers that also had military experience including my good friend Elmo Trepanier. I did the job for many years and eventually wrote a book <u>Ma Guerre Contre le FLQ</u> (My War Against the FLQ) chronicling my experiences.

It was a very difficult and stressful time, but as we built the team and I was placed in charge as a sergeant I had the great fortune to work with an outstanding group of people. Together, we saw the power of the home-made bombs increase considerably from the first bombs that exploded in Westmount mailboxes in 1963 to the 150 lb. *megabomb* we dismantled in 1970. Defusing a bomb is a very scary exercise and ultimately, in my view, it is as much art as science. And you can't call the police or a specialist, because you and your team serve both roles. We did not have some of the tools in those days that police departments routinely have at their disposal now, such as water cannons, and robots. In those days, we were the robots. The most valuable tool I ever had was a $4 set of nail clippers that I bought at a local department store in order to cut the wires and neutralize the bombs. I still have those clippers. As called for by tradition and as head of the team, I was the one who dismantled the bombs. That was my role—my responsibility.

My time on the Bomb Squad also coincided with what is known as the "October Crisis" when the FLQ kidnapped Pierre Laporte and Richard Cross. This affair did not require the services of my team to deactivate any bombs. However, towards the *denouement* of this sad event I was able to make what I felt to be a meaningful contribution. Then, in the following month of July when my son was born we named him "Pierre-Richard" after Mr. Laporte and Mr. Cross.

I left the Bomb squad and went on to several other interesting assignments, one of which revitalized my association with Pointe-Saint-Charles. In 1980 I was promoted to the position of Inspector in charge of District 24. The boundaries were Atwater Street, Saint Antoine Street, the St. Lawrence River and Old Montreal. This district included the Point and Griffintown.

By that time I had already had some very responsible positions, but I really had no background running a big operation like that. Fortunately my boss, Marcel Allard was a good mentor and supporter. He simply said to me, "Bob, you're in charge of operations and so you're steering. But, if I think I see you steering too far one way, I'll tell you. Or, if I think I see you steering too far another way, I'll tell you then, too". I was fortunate to have such a supportive boss. I had great respect for Marcel.

By then, however times had certainly changed in many ways in my old area. The golden years of the Point that I knew as a boy and young adult were definitely over. In the 1950s there were

30,000 people living in the Point. By the 1980s the number had shrunk to around 13,000—for obvious reasons such as opening of the St. Lawrence Seaway and the closure of the Lachine Canal to shipping. The canal closure really hurt the industries along the canal. We had some big employers in the Point such as Northern Electric (Nortel), Dominion Glass and, of course, Sherwin Williams, but by this time a lot of businesses had downsized or closed altogether.

The Village was long gone by then, as well. All of the families in the Village were displaced by virtue of the 1964 expropriation and many of them moved to the Point and Verdun. This helped prolong the tradition of Victoria Day fires in the Point. It was a problem for a long time and it could lead to real trouble.

The corner of Coleraine and Charlevoix, as well as elsewhere in the Point, were primary targets for these fires. They were serious. These fires were so big the city would have to re-asphalt the bonfire sites after the fires were extinguished. One of the tasks I was specifically assigned when I was sent in as District Chief was to clean this up. So, for several years around Victoria Day we tried to make sure in advance that there was as little scrap lying around Pointe-Saint-Charles as possible, like old mattresses that people could burn. We stationed a lot of police and firefighters throughout the area during the holiday and we infiltrated the crowds. Between 1982 and 1985 the tradition gradually slowed down and now it is just forgotten.

I mentioned earlier that my first arrest in the Point as a young police officer was for breaking and entering. Well, it was a problem then and it was a problem when I returned in 1980. When I took over the District I was somewhat surprised to see that the break-in rate in the Point was relatively high compared to some other areas of Montreal. A lot of the residents in the Point were low-income families, often living in low-rental housing. Unemployment was high. I didn't think the houses in the area would present a particularly interesting target for burglars relative to other areas. I was wrong. There were 908 cases the year I took over, compared with 745 in 1979. We conducted a complete study of all these break-ins. Not one work of art was stolen, but in a lot of cases, food was taken and in two cases I remember, children's toys were the reason for the burglaries.

Overall, I felt that the increase at the time was attributable to a variety of reasons including unemployment, inflation, more and more children being raised in single parent homes, the need to finance drug habits, etc. Juveniles accounted for at least 50% of all suspects arrested in my area, and given the laws that had recently been passed at the time, they were all back on the street within hours or days. This was a real source of frustration for our troops.

We did the best we could to respond. We believed in prevention and the value of police presence. In situations where a civilian could replace a police job we made the change, thereby freeing up a police officer for street duty.

At that time foot patrol in the Point had pretty much been abandoned. We reactivated it, as we found we had unwittingly lost contact with the people we were there to serve and protect. We tried to become more visible in other ways as well, like using marked cars over unmarked vehicles whenever we could. We made sure our members wore their uniforms unless specifically required to work in plain clothes.

We paid close attention to the findings of studies from reputable sources like the Rand Corporation where their research pointed to successful initiatives like ensuring to link detectives to groups of patrolmen. The results were encouraging at the time and community policing ideas like this have proven to be the way to go in many places across Canada today.

There were, to be sure, the light-hearted times as well. In my early days as a cop in the Point we'd often play tricks on the new constables as they arrived—sort of an initiation for them. For example, one was to tell a young constable that if he wanted to make some extra money working his day off that week, that the people over at the Maple Leaf meat packing plant phoned the station saying they needed some help slaughtering the cows. We'd tell the constable that if he was interested he should go over on his day off and ask for "Mr. Leboeuf" (a French surname that literally translated means "Mr. Beef"). We always knew if anyone actually fell for the prank because the people at Maple Leaf were in on the joke. If a constable went to the meatpacking plant he would be told that "Mr. Leboeuf" was not around but that they'd give him the message. Then they'd call us at the station and let us know.

Other times we would tell a young constable that there was a problem reported with the rotating spotlight on the top of the Place Ville Marie and that the people in charge of it were looking for some off-duty help. We'd tell the constable that if he was interested he should report to "Mr. Lalumière" (a French surname that literally translated means Mr. "Light") on his day off.

A third common initiation in the Point revolved around the railway tracks that cut through the middle of Pointe-Saint-Charles. At the end of one street near the station, there was a foot tunnel that went under the tracks. An hour or so before dusk we'd explain to a young cadet that one of our jobs every night was to turn on the lights in the tunnel and we'd send him off. There was no light switch. The lights were timed to go on automatically. We would then wait for the constable to finish his futile search and come back. He would explain to the Sergeant that he could not find the light switch and the Sergeant would then go into a well-practiced lecture about the quality of the new cadets and how they could not even find a light switch. He would then send the constable back to find the switch, ensuring to wait until the light switch was scheduled to go on automatically. We would then all have a laugh with the constable when he returned.

What values did growing up in the Point help develop and reinforce in my life? It was not something I ever really reflected upon, but the Point did have a big impact on me. The three values that come to mind are loyalty, respect for others and the importance of self-confidence.

Loyalty would be first on my list. Loyalty means every thing to me. As long as I can recall, I have always respected my word—whether I was a kid in the Point, later in the military, in the Montreal Police, or in politics. I was always a strong defender of the group that I was part of and in every function I held. My Superiors, my colleagues or later my subordinates, knew that I could always be relied upon. I expected the same in return. Still today, I cannot accept that the various organizations to which I have been part are criticized in bad faith. I have always been loyal to my country and have transmitted that value to my descendants.

Respect for others is very important to me. In my younger years at the Point, we were all on the same level: we were not rich but we lived honestly and in harmony with others. I respected others for who they were and I was respected for the same reason. It has become an important part of my adult life. At a young age the Point helped show us the importance of respect for others.

I have no doubt, as well, that my experiences in Pointe-Saint-Charles as I grew up contributed to the development of self-confidence. And as far as I can recall, I have always had confidence in what I was capable of achieving. In class at St. Charles School on Island Street I had difficulty with mathematics, but I was confident that I could compensate by being the best in other subjects, resulting in excellent grades at the end of the year. When I joined the Army, I became a para-trooper at age 17, although I had never set foot in an aircraft. I never doubted that I would jump from that aircraft, and I did—many times. Later in life, as a policeman, I was exposed to some of the most dangerous situations you can think of—from dismantling home-made bombs to taking part in shoot-outs. I never hesitated because I was confident that I could do the job. And I did. Still later, without any experience in municipal politics, I ran for a seat at City Council, confident that I could win, and I did!

What does the future hold for Pointe-Saint-Charles? I think the future looks promising. Today, the Point has a wonderful opportunity given its location in comparison to many other communities in greater Montreal. I think that there are already plans on the table to transform the old Northern Electric building into a combination of commercial and residential. The Point is close to downtown. It is on the Metro and gentrification is underway already in some areas. Much work is being done in and around the east end of the Lachine Canal. Instead of heavy industry and pollution around the downtown end of the canal, we are seeing decontamination, condos, parks and pleasure craft. Griffintown is farther ahead in all of this than the Point, but Griffintown had a lot more vacant land to offer from an infill perspective. As of yet, the old Goose Village is not residential at all due perhaps to contamination concerns. But I think all of that will change. All three areas will attract people who wish to live closer to the heart of Montreal. Of course, I do not expect to see the camaraderie and feeling that we had in the Point 50 years ago when we lived in row houses and knew all our neighbors. Many of the new inhabitants will be living in condos.

Now, at this stage in my life I devote much of my time to family, which includes my three beautiful grandchildren. They live close enough for me to see them almost every day and it gives me great pleasure. I help out at the Montreal Police Museum, as well as some other museums. I am involved in speaking engagements from time to time, and I also enjoy my association with several historical Societies, including the Pointe-Saint-Charles Historical Society. I am involved in some writing projects of my own and I have had several occasions over recent years to help out writers with their projects. I continue to do so now. This oral history collection of life and times in the Point, Goose Village, and Griffintown is an example.

Pointe-Saint-Charles will always mean a lot to me. My beloved Pointe-Saint-Charles. I left the Point, but it is still with me.

"To us,

growing up,

it was our world

and it seemed quite big.

When we lived in Griffintown

you never had to lock your door.

No one did.

The people were the best.

You always had lots of friends."

Thomas Patwell

Thomas "Tommy" Patwell

Tommy Patwell spent over 20 years in the neighborhood and began working at age 15. By 20, he secured a position on the Montreal waterfront and went on to spend 44 years on the wharf. Tommy was very active in the union movement for many years, rising to the position of President of the Checkers' Union, and subsequently serving as Business Agent. Tommy witnessed many changes on the docks over the years including the introduction of containerization in cargo management. This change brought with it a dramatic labor force downsizing across the Montreal wharf.

"And there's one last thing
I'd like to mention...
it's about the women of Griffintown
—the mothers. They were the backbone
of the family. For a lot of reasons,
they were truly the backbone of the family."

Tommy was active in many sports. If Tommy's name comes up in conversation with others from the Point, Griffintown or Goose Village, friends and acquaintances are quick to praise his abilities as a boxer. Tommy won the Quebec Golden Gloves Heavyweight Open Division in 1959. Tommy remained close to Griffintown's legendary boxing coach, Cliff Sowery, until Cliff's passing at the age of 92.

Photo: Tom with spouse Marilyn.

I was born in 1936 on Young Street in Griffintown—just across the street from St. Ann's Boys' School. We lived there for around four years then moved over to Colborne Street. That's Peel Street now. I didn't leave Griffintown until I was in my twenties.

My mother was born in Wales. She worked cleaning office buildings in Montreal. My father was born in Goose Village. His family was Irish and his father came to Canada from the south of Ireland. My parents had five children, and there is an old saying in Griffintown about the kids: "First up in the morning is the best dressed".

I went to St. Ann's Boys' School for all my education and I admired several of the Brothers that taught there. I thought Brother Edmond and Brother Stanislaus were very good. Mike McNamara, one of the lay teachers, was really excellent as well. But anybody you talk to will tell you that the Brothers at St. Ann's were never shy to use the strap or other forms of corporal punishment, and you didn't go home whining to your parents. The attitude at home in Griffintown when I was growing up was that if you were punished at school, "You probably deserved it!" When we were at St. Ann's there were no excuses for things like not doing your

C.M. SOWERY
Executive Director

"IT'S NOT THE GALE, BUT THE SET OF THE SAIL..."

WINNIFRED McCUNN
Asst. Executive Director

THE GRIFFINTOWN CLUB

homework. These Brothers lived right among us and they could see what was going on at night. They could see the Griffintown Boys' Club from their residence, and I spent a lot of time at the club. I remember one Brother used to look out his window to see who was leaving the club late at night. He'd even use binoculars. If he saw you leaving late, you could count on getting your homework checked. I always left by the back door.

When I was growing up, Cliff Sowery was the Manager and the head boxing coach at the Griffintown Boys' Club. At the club we had what we called the boxing room and that is where a lot of guys learned to fight. Griffintown produced some great boxers. Armand Savoie and Gus Mell turned pro and they were both very good. Cliff developed some top-flight amateur boxers, as well, like Jimmy Davis, Franki Fitzgerald, Emil Lamarche, Joe Caughlin and Mike Nolan. They were all *Golden Gloves* guys. My brother Timmy was a boxer from the time he was quite young and he was very good, as well. I boxed a little when I was a youngster but didn't really take it that seriously. I got back into it later, though, and remember exactly how. I was with a bunch of buddies and we were bantering around that the 1959 Golden Gloves Tournament was only six months away. They were after me to register. There was always a junior division of the *Golden Gloves* and an open division. I was 23 at the time so I was open division age. I thought about it, and decided to enter the tournament. Cliff was my coach. At the time, I was 5'-9" and 198 lbs. I trained hard and ended up winning the Quebec open heavyweight division. Then, at the nationals, or what we called the *Dominion Championship*, I made it to the championship fight but lost out.

I got to know Cliff Sowery very well over the years. The club didn't have a lot of money and Cliff was always on the move with companies and sponsors to try and ensure that we had proper equipment, boxing outfits, gloves and things like that. He worked six days a week.

With Cliff, it was always as much about character as it was anything else. For instance, if he ever saw what he thought was bullying at the club he had a process he'd use to straighten people out. First of all he'd break it up and then he'd take both boys into the boxing room. Then he would pair the bigger kid up against one of the boxers that was the same size and have them go at it.

The boxer he'd pick would usually be a pretty good fighter. After it was over he would take the three of them, sit them down and explain that bullying was unacceptable, and what his expectations were. I have even seen him do this when the smaller guy was at fault in starting the original altercation. We were brought up in the Griff not to bully, and when I was growing up I didn't ever see much of it. But if Cliff ever did, that was what he'd do.

When we were young, the Griff was heavily populated with Roman Catholics—I'd say it was around ten-to-one compared to Protestants. Cliff was a Protestant. Back in the 1940s when we were young the priests didn't like us going to the club because of Cliff's religious affiliation. We went anyway. To me, Cliff Sowery was more than the manager and the boxing coach. He knew us all and if you had a problem you could go and confide in him, and you knew he could be trusted. If any of us got into trouble, Cliff was there for us. If anyone had to go to court, Cliff was there in the courtroom with you. Usually it wasn't for anything serious, but he was there. Cliff knew all the judges in those days and I think he used to talk to them off-line and get them to scare the hell out of any of us that showed up in court.

Cliff Sowery. Date unknown.

When the Griffintown Club eventually shut down, a lot of the activities, including boxing, moved over to the Point St. Charles YMCA. Cliff coached there for a while but it wasn't the same atmosphere. By then he was already past retirement age and he wasn't getting paid at the Y. I was working on the docks by that time and we were successful in finding him a spot to work down on the wharf. We also got jobs for Armand Savoie and Gus Mell. I stayed in contact with Cliff right up until he passed away. The guys on the docks that knew Cliff always included him in our events like golf tournaments. We'd also make sure to pick him up and drive him places he needed to go. When Cliff was nearing the end of his life he gave me his scrapbooks, which included all the clippings he had collected about boxing, as well as the Griffintown Boys' Club in general. In many ways, Cliff Sowery was like a father figure to many of us. Our parents were often overloaded just trying to make ends meet for the family.

As well as boxing I always competed in the soapbox derbies when I was a kid. The big regional races were held on the road near Fletcher's Field. I always had a very good cart and remember winning the Montreal championship one year. First prize was a new bike. When I was

The Griffintown Grads fastball team. Tom is second from the right in the back row. 1962.

a kid and a younger adult, baseball, fastball and hockey was also very big in Griffintown, the Village and the Point, and I was always involved. The Village had its own league. Taverns had teams. We had community teams, house league teams, and sometimes school teams. I guess people heard the stories about how tough Griffintown was because as we got older, other teams wouldn't come and play hockey against us at the Basin Street Park in the Griff. We had to hold our home games in Lafontaine Park.

It's fairly common knowledge among Griffintowners that the Boys' Club was clipped by the bomber that crashed there during the second war. It also hit my building on the way down. I was six years old at the time. It hit our building hard enough that it knocked my father out of bed. Then it went on and crashed. A fireman by the name of Bill Gallery was the first person to get to that crash. He ran over quickly from the station and actually got there before the fire broke out. All the dead from that crash were temporarily placed at the Boys' Club. As I said, I was only six but I do remember a few of the people who were killed. I also remember that we had a barber living in our building and he was never the same after that. He got the shakes from that crash and they never left him. They were so bad that the men in Griffintown wouldn't go to him for haircuts any more. Kids would go, but not the men.

Longshoremen in Montreal unloading cargo by pallet before containerization. Date unknown.

After grade eight I went right to work. I started off working as a painter's helper, and then I got a job working on a loading dock for a while. I spent some time at General Foods, then Monsanto. After that, I went to work on the oil tankers. At twenty I got my job on the docks with the Port of Montreal and that's where I stayed until I retired. I spent 44 years on the Montreal waterfront. The docks provided work for thousands of people in those days and a lot of the guys from Griffintown, the Point and Goose Village worked there. When I started, the Montreal wharf extended from the bottom of McGill Street in the west all the way to Pie-IX Boulevard in the east. That's almost seven kilometers. Bickerdike Pier is more or less where the main part of the west end of the wharf stood. Dominion Coal used to be close to that as well. Now, the wharf extends almost to Viau Street in the east. That expansion resulted from containerization of cargo.

I started on the wharf as a cooper. They make barrels and provide for general cargo repair. After a couple of years I got a job as a checker. Back in those days we had somewhere between

The Montreal harbour at the east end of the Lachine Canal. c. 1927

7000-8000 longshoremen working on the docks and around 800 checkers. And that didn't include the guys working elsewhere around the docks like, for example, in the grain elevators or with the railway. The longshoremen worked in what we called crews or gangs. Each crew had 21 men. Back in my day a lot of these crews were composed of men who were related in one way or another—brothers, cousins, parents, marriage in-laws etc. You'd typically identify crews by the dominant family name—"he works for the so-and-so crew". Most of the crews in my day were either heavily Irish or Scottish. Now the longshoremen are mostly French. Over the years when I was there, most of the checkers were Irish, and there is still a very strong contingent of checkers with Irish heritage that carries over to today in that job. I'd say around half of the checkers are still from the old Irish stock.

Longshoremen do the heavy work—loading and unloading the ships. In the old days longshoremen used big nets, or they'd stack the cargo on pallets. Then the goods would be hoisted up by cranes and moved off into the ships' holds. Unloading would be the same process, but in reverse. Now it's all containerized.

Liberator airplane crash in Griffintown. 1944.

Checkers, on the other hand, had two main jobs—floormen and stowagemen. Floormen arranged for the placement of the cargo in sheds on the waterfront after the longshoremen unloaded it from the ships. They'd also arrange cargo there in preparation for loading onto outbound ships. These sheds were big—around 1000 feet long and about 300 feet wide. Many of them were double-deckers. At first, there were ramps built for trucks to access the second floors. Later on large booms travelled the length of both floors to move the cargo.

In 1959 there were 46 sheds on the wharf for handling cargo. When a ship was about to get loaded, stowagemen were responsible for preparing a loading plan. This is a complicated job. You had to consider ship size, cargo weight, ballast location and a variety of other things. Typically, stowagemen arranged the heaviest stuff low down in the middle of the ship and then made sure the rest was evenly balanced between port and starboard, as well as bow and stern. The captain had to approve the plan before the ship left the wharf. It took time to learn this trade and there was no course you could take. You worked and learned under the tutelage of an experienced man. Back in the day, the checkers used to come to work with ties and jackets. Both the floorman and stowageman jobs were very involved.

The Memorial Clock Tower and sheds 18 and 19. c. 1926.

In those days, the waterfront worked around the clock. It was hard work. It could be dangerous, and you worked in all weather. In the winter, the moisture from the waterfront and the snow would cling to your clothing and frostbite was a real threat. One time, after I finished work on a bad winter day the tuque I was wearing was covered in ice and snow. I didn't know it but it was stuck solidly to the top of my head and the skin had frozen. When I pulled off the tuque I ripped off some skin. I didn't even notice it when it happened. The wind in the winter could be brutal on the waterfront. Sometimes we'd walk from the wharf up to Notre Dame Street to get a bite to eat and you could feel the temperature around you rise as you began to walk the narrow streets and left the wind-chill behind.

You always had to be careful and aware of your surroundings on the docks. Booms and cranes were all over the docks and they were always on the move with cargo pallets and nets, then later on the containers. You had to be vigilant all the time and you had to take into consideration the degree and effect of wind on things. If a load swung and bumped into something because of wind, the cargo could fall, and back in my day no one had steel-toed boots or protective head-gear. When the containers were introduced that brought other issues. Containers come in various sizes. You've got 20- and 40-foot containers, and even some 56-foot refrigerated models. At first we used to organize them on what we called trays—sort of like big wine racks—the containers were slid in length-wise. One time I was working beside a tray of containers and I left for a minute to check some paperwork inside a nearby office. Seconds after I got inside, the entire tray fell over right on the area I had been standing. Some of my friends knew I was working there and ran over. They thought, for sure, I was under the pile. Then I showed up behind them. I remember one fatal accident we had once when one of the men was working inside a tray and a container was slid in alongside him. He was crushed between the ribs of two containers. It wasn't a pretty sight. Later on, things changed, and now the containers are just stacked one on top of the other by large cranes.

After some few years on the waterfront I decided to run for a position with the checkers' union. I started at the bottom and worked my way up. My first job was a Marshall. Then I moved on to one of the committees. Then, over the years, I ran successfully for the positions of Second Vice President, First Vice President, President and finally, Business Agent. In all, I spent

Containers and crane at the west end of the Port. 2014.

Top right: Entrance to Bickerdike Pier at the west end of the Port. 2011.

Right: A shed in Montreal's current-day Old Port. 2012.

27 years in one capacity or another in the union. There was always a lot of work needed to improve working conditions and regulations. I'll give you a couple of examples. Let's say a crew was loading or unloading a ship and they were working at it all day, but it turned out that overtime was required. Well, many years ago, more senior guys from other crews could bump the younger guys on this crew who didn't have a lot of seniority. The young guys would lose out on overtime even though they'd been working on the ship all day. More senior guys from other crews would finish their own shifts then run over from other parts of the wharf, sometimes miles away, and bump the younger guys. I worked to get that changed and we were successful.

But, you know, when you're in a position of authority like I was, you had to monitor the process and see that once it was fixed it was adhered to by everyone. And sometimes people would play games and you'd have to mete out discipline when it was called for. I can remember handing out a suspension of a week one time to quite a senior guy that had bumped someone's overtime well after this policy was adopted. He should have known better and I told him so. When you're in a job like that you have to be able to separate friendship from the job you're doing. Some people can do it, some can't. I always could, and I did. Sometimes that can create hard feelings, but you can't have two sets of rules when you're in that sort of position.

With containerization in the 'sixties, the downsizing and buyouts started on the waterfront. There was no longer a need for so many longshoremen loading and unloading with pallets and nets. Now, there are probably only around 800-900 longshoremen working on the entire wharf—down from over 7000. There are only about 100-120 or-so checkers left.

Today I live in Ontario, just a short distance from the Quebec border. I split my time between Florida and home. I typically go south for six months every year. My children live in the Montreal area so when I'm at home I get up to Montreal fairly regularly. I can drive to their places in about an hour. From time to time I'll take a trip into Griffintown and it still sometimes surprises me just how small the area seems. To us, growing up, it was our world and it seemed quite big. When we lived in Griffintown you never had to lock your door. No one did. The people were the best. You always had lots of friends and I'll tell you that if you bump into someone that you knew growing up in Griffintown, no matter how long it has been, it's like you saw them yesterday—and Griffintown is never out of the conversation.

And there's one last thing I'd like to mention—it's about the women of Griffintown—the mothers. They were the backbone of the family. For a lot of reasons, they were truly the backbone of the family.

Viewed from Griffintown St. Ann Park, this restored Griffintown row housing stands as an important reminder of the area's history. 2011.

" I remember that when we'd gather

at the concert hall

before the [St. Patrick's Day] parade

we always had fresh carnations

and shamrocks ready for us.

We'd adorn our top hats

with the shamrocks

and wear the carnations in our lapels.

There is a lot of tradition

that goes with those top hats.

They're handed down

from father to son

and on through the generations."

Gordon McCambridge

Gordon "Gordie" McCambridge

Gordon McCambridge was born in 1937. He attended St. Ann's Boys' School in Griffintown and then graduated from Cardinal Newman High School.

Gordie decided to attend Teachers College, then University. He went on to enjoy a distinguished 37-year career in the Catholic school system, in and around Montreal. Gordie served as a teacher for 11 years, a Vice Principal for two years, and a Principal for 24 years. For many years Gordie worked as a teacher or administrator at large inner-city Montreal high schools such as James Lyng and St. Thomas Aquinas. Both schools served students from Point St. Charles, Saint-Henri, Griffintown and some surrounding areas. St. Thomas Aquinas was a boys-only school. James Lyng was mixed. In 2007, Gordie was in the first group of inductees when James Lyng High School established a Hall of Fame.

Gordie is active in Montreal's Irish community and served two terms as President of the Erin Sports Association.

Photo: 2013.

"I sometimes take walks through Griffintown to see all the changes that are going on. The sounds of my childhood are long gone now: the tram cars, the constant clapping of horses hoofs, the steady rumbling of the big trucks coming and going along William Street as they went to and from the Canada Steamship installation just to the west of St. Ann's Church. In some ways I find these walks enjoyable. In other ways I find them sad when I think of what we had at one time down there. The sense of community that we enjoyed in those days won't ever be replicated. It can't."

CNR express truck. 1928.

My grandfather left Ballymena, Ireland for Canada around 1900. He was Catholic, and I'm told that the Ballymena area of County Antrim was about 90% Protestant when he left. Ballymena is in the part of Northern Ireland that Ian Paisley represented in Parliament. My grandfather settled in Griffintown and went to work for the Grand Trunk Railway. He retired as a foreman. My father was born in Griffintown and that's where he grew up. He went to work for the Canadian National Railway as a truck driver. On my mother's side, the family came to Canada from Scotland around 1910. My mother was about five years old at the time. Their family was Presbyterian.

My wife, Mary, grew up about a 15-minute walk from my childhood flat on Canning Street. Her parents both came from Ireland and they settled in the west end near Atwater Street. That's not too far from the old Montreal Forum. Mary's father came from County Clare, and her mum came from Galway. Mary's dad worked for Dow Brewery in Griffintown. So, our two families go back a long way in that area of Montreal.

I was the first of eight children, and the eight of us were born over a 13-year period. I have four sisters and three brothers. We lived in a three-bedroom row house on Canning, and that's where I was born. It was what you'd refer to as a cold-water flat, and we were on the main floor. As we were growing up, the boys were in bunk-beds in one room, the girls in another. I remember that during the Second World War, my grandmother moved next door to us. Five of my uncles fought in that war. Among them, I know that they saw service in Italy, Belgium, France, Holland and Germany.

Canning Street is just a few blocks west of Griffintown, but I grew up as a "Griffer". I attended St. Ann's Boys' School and St. Ann's Church. I could have gone to Belmont School, which was closer to our house, but my father sent me to St. Ann's. That's the school he attended. The Brothers and Sisters from the various religious orders that taught the Roman Catholic children of Griffintown typically lived in the community. The Sisters of Providence, for example, lived on the top floor of the building that is now the headquarters for King's Transfer Van Lines on Eleanor Street. Downstairs they offered a pre-school service for children under five years old. If both parents were working they could drop their children off and the Sisters would look after them all day. For a small fee the kids would get soup and a sandwich for lunch. The Sisters of Providence also taught grades one and two in what was known as the St. Ann's Kindergarten. It was located right beside the nun's residence and it also served the English Catholic children of Griffintown. Since it was for grade one and two, it wasn't really a kindergarten, but that's what it was called for as long as I can remember. For grade three the boys moved over to St. Ann's Boys' School across the street from the fire station. The girls went to St. Ann's Girls' School, which was beside the church. I stayed at St. Ann's until I finished

Top: Now the property of King's Transfer Van Lines, this building on Eleanor Street once served as the residence for the Sisters of Providence and as a pre-school for Griffintown children. 2011 and 2010.

Bottom: Looking south on Eleanor Street. The former nun's residence and pre-school is on the left. These two photos were taken from the same location, two years apart, and provide an example of some of the gentrification that is taking place in Griffintown and elsewhere along the east end of the Lachine Canal. 2011 and 2013.

grade eight. In my mother's time there was a Protestant elementary school in Griffintown named William Lunn. It wasn't far from the Griffintown Club. But overall, there were very few Protestants living in Griffintown, and by the time I was in St. Ann's Boys' School, William Lunn was closed. Any Protestant children living in Griffintown by that time were going to Royal Arthur on Canning Street, a little north of Notre Dame near Guy Street. I remember that when I was going one way to St. Ann's, I'd sometimes pass a few Protestant children on their way to Royal Arthur.

It was quite a long walk from our house on Canning Street to the schools in Griffintown. It took around 20 minutes. But we got an hour and 15 minutes for lunch in those days so you had time to get home and back. You could also pack a lunch, so depending on the season and weather,

Gord (left), and friends ready for the St. Patrick's Day Parade. 1960s.

that's what people would do. I remember that when we were at the Boys' School the janitor looked after us while we ate, and then he'd send us out to the yard. We used to call him "Skaboo". Don't ask my why—I have no idea how he got that nickname, but to us, he was just Skaboo! Everybody in the Griff had a nickname.

We were one of the only English families around that Canning Street area where I grew up. It was mostly a French pocket. In those days, the English and French all had their own areas around the southwest of Montreal, and if you were out of your area you'd often get challenged on the street. If you were English you'd get challenged by the French and so on. So we all learned to handle ourselves when we were young. And living where I did, I learned to speak French quickly!

Mostly any friction we had as English kids was with the French, but you could also get into tussles with other English-speaking kids from outside your own area like the west end crowd. I still get a chuckle when I think of one time in particular. After school one day, Brother Adrian was taking our class to an event in the west end. There might have been around 20 of us. I guess we were about 11 years old at the time. Anyway, we were walking along in the west end and we met up with a bunch of west-enders. They didn't know us and thought we were French so they started shooting off. We told them we were English just like them, but in the end it didn't seem to matter. We made it to our destination OK, but when we came out there was a big mob of them, likely all from Belmont School, just waiting for us. Everybody stopped for a minute and then Brother Adrian spoke up and said, "Boys, I have two pieces of advice—swing hard and run fast!"—and that's exactly what we did. To this day I'll never forget the feeling of making it down McCord Street and back into Griffintown!

We had some good teachers at St. Ann's and I'll always remember Mike McNamara as one of the very best. He was the only lay teacher at the school and he taught grade seven. In those days you had to take tests in grade seven to get into high school. If you didn't have the marks, you didn't get in. In fact, you had to take provincial exams after grades Seven, Nine and Eleven in those days. Mike's job was to get his class ready for the grade seven exams. His method was to rapidly cover the entire year's course work between September and Christmas. Then, after the holidays he'd start right at the beginning again and just drill, drill, drill! He was strict. He was a real disciplinarian, but he did a wonderful job of getting us all ready. I knew Mike later in life as well. He went on to become an elementary school Principal in Montreal's Catholic system. Mike was a guy we all admired. A lot of us attended his funeral when he passed away a few years ago.

Brother Norbert ran the choir at the St. Ann's Boys' School and he also managed the choir at St. Ann's Church. If you were young and active in the church, like I was, you'd try for a spot on the St. Ann's choir. If you didn't make the choir, and I didn't, you went into the sanctuary as an altar boy. There were usually about 30 of us in the sanctuary ranging in age from about eight to sixteen. You gradually learned all the various rituals as you went along.

Looking back now to the time when I left St. Ann's, you could really see that the population of Griffintown was dropping. There were various reasons for that. One was that things were really picking up after the war. People were getting better jobs and moving out. St. Ann's Boys' School finally closed down in 1965. There just wasn't the population there any more.

After St. Ann's a crowd of us moved on to St. Patrick's High School, but after a few days five or six of us decided we wanted to switch to Cardinal Newman up in the Plateau Mont Royal area. The same congregation taught there as at St. Ann's—the Christian Brothers. One of the guys that decided to move with us had an older sibling who was a Christian Brother. We went up to Cardinal Newman and made our case for the transfer. They didn't commit one way or the other. We were simply told to go outside the Principal's office and sit quietly in the hall. So, that's what we did—and they left us there for several days. Maybe it was a test because, let's face it, the Griffintown kids had a bit of a reputation. Well, if it was a test, I guess we passed, because they let us all in and that's where we stayed. It was a very good experience. We had some excellent teachers at Cardinal Newman. Walter Reilly was one of them. He was my homeroom teacher during my first year there, and later on I was in his French class. Brendan Fahey was another great teacher. He taught Latin and English. I remember that every now and then he'd sit a few of us down if he thought he wasn't seeing enough effort. He'd ask us, "What is it that you want to do about your education? You know you can do better". And then you'd talk things through. He was never mean. He was an outstanding man. You know, we had six or seven people from my graduating class that went on to become teachers.

Today it's just expected that you'll finish high school and then go on to some other learning. That wasn't the case in my day, and certainly not in Griffintown and places like that. Students were required to stay in school until the age of 14. After grade eight or nine a lot of students just went directly into the workforce. My own father only completed grade six or seven.

When we were children growing up in Griffintown we all spent a lot of time at the Griffintown Boys' Club. At that time Cliff Sowery was the Director and Mrs. Winnifred McCunn was his Assistant. Cliff was just an outstanding man. He did a lot for us, and it was in more ways than just recreation. For example, he had one room set aside as a dental clinic at the club. A dentist from McGill used to come down and volunteer one day a week. In my day it was Dr. Flanagan. The entire time I was growing up I had all my dental work done free of charge at that clinic at the Boys' Club. Dr. Flanagan was a man who believed strongly in providing medical and dental care for the poor. I greatly admired him.

During the summers Cliff always arranged for two special tramcars to come down and pick up a crowd of Griffintown kids every morning and take us up to Mount Royal for day camp. I know that Cliff didn't want us just running the streets in the summers. There were usually about 60 campers every morning. It only cost ten cents a day and we had an area set aside for us near Beaver Lake. We'd have all sorts of activities and we'd all get fed. It was quite an operation. The mothers of a lot of the kids were volunteers in this process. They'd prepare all the food and help with organizing and supervising games. A lot of these mothers had attended the camp in their own day. When the Boys' Club was closed down Cliff moved over to the new Point St. Charles Boys' and Girls' Club as the Assistant Director.

Before it closed down, the Griffintown Club was open every night from Monday to Friday and it was always full of kids. On Friday evenings there was always a movie for the younger children—I'd say up until about age 12. Then around 9:00 PM the young ones would leave and the older kids would come in for a weekly dance. The majority of them would have been around 16 to 18.

I remember the janitor from my day very well. His name was "Bunzy" Carroll. Don't ask me how he got that nickname or what it meant, but that's who he was to us—Bunzy! I think the club used to close down at 10:00 p.m., and then you'd see Bunzy going all over the club trying to get the kids to go home so that he could get his work finished for the day.

In Griffintown the youngsters were always up to something, and everybody tried to outdo each other. There are so many stories. I remember one day a crowd of kids—a bit older than us—was watching the ragman with his horse and cart go down the street. He was a fixture in those days. He was out all the time collecting bottles, rags and scrap metal. The ragman's horse was always old. Sometimes you'd wonder how it could still walk. Well, this particular time the ragman stopped and went off behind a house for a while. By the time he got back the horse had been removed from his harness, turned around and re-harnessed backwards facing the cart!

We always had lots of sports in Griffintown as well. Baseball and softball were very popular. As we got a little older, we liked to play the Dow Brewery guys because after the game they'd take the opposing team back to the Brewery for a beer or two in the taproom. Back in those days when the railway was a huge employer in the area, most of the porters—the *Redcaps*—working the passenger trains were black. A lot of them lived in what is now called Little Burgundy and they had their own ball team. They were very good.

I was born in the late 'thirties, and that was at the tail-end of the depression. Believe me, the depression took a real toll on places like the Point and Griffintown. These were working-class communities and the people there relied on factory jobs and other labor jobs. There wasn't much

Graduation photos from the University of Ottawa
(above) and St. Michael's College in Vermont.

money down there in the first place and the depression just piled on the challenges. Financially, it was a difficult time. But we were raised with a sense of pride in where we came from. Sure, you might find some people today that are embarrassed to say they came from Griffintown, but the vast majority of us will step right up and say "I'm a Griffer!" The same holds true of my friends from the Point.

There's no doubt that back in those days the Griffintown and Point St. Charles areas were heavily populated with working class Irish. That's not to say that there weren't other ethnic groups in Griffintown, or that there weren't Irish immigrants living elsewhere in Montreal. There were. But that area was recognized as the one where you saw the most concentrated congregation of working-class Irish. We attended various parishes like St. Ann's in the Griff, St. Gabriel's in the Point and some other churches like St. Anthony's just a little farther west. For sure, there were also other, more affluent people of Irish heritage living in Montreal. They were the doctors, lawyers, dentists, businessmen etc. Many of them attended St. Patrick's Basilica up the hill and not too far away from Griffintown.

In Griffintown we definitely had a sense of community when we were growing up, and you didn't see any stronger demonstration of that than on St. Patrick's Day. The parade was always a very important event and the St. Ann's contingent always represented their parish strongly. So did St. Gabriel's in the Point, as well as nearby St. Anthony's. By tradition, certainly in my day, the St. Ann and St. Gabriel contingent always walked near the end of the parade. In fact, I think

St. Ann's was often the very last entry in the parade. We always had a big contingent because you'd have the St. Ann's Young Men's Society, the priests, students from St. Ann's Boys' School, as well as a throng of parishioners. I remember that we often had some very colorful people walking with us on St. Patrick's Day. You'd see professional boxers, as well as politicians like Frank Hanley and others. I know that people watching the parade really enjoyed seeing the St. Ann's contingent.

Before the parade, the gathering point for everyone in the St. Ann's contingent was always at the St. Ann's concert hall. It was located across the street from the Fire Station at the corner of Young and Ottawa. The concert hall was up on the third floor, and the St. Ann's Boys' School was on the first and second. Our bowling alley was also on the first floor of that building. I'd say that the concert hall held around 300 or so people. It was used for many different functions throughout the year like plays, recitals and parties.

Now, getting back to the Young Men's Society for a minute, there is one thing you have to understand. Although it was called the Young Men's Society, there were men of all ages involved. In my time the Society wasn't as big as it was in my father's day, or the days before that, but it was still quite strong. Sometimes we'd have as many as 60 members of the St. Ann's Young Men marching in the St. Patrick's Day Parade—all dressed up in their traditional garb of top hats and long coats. I remember that when we'd gather at the concert hall before the parade, we always had fresh carnations and shamrocks ready for us. We'd adorn our top hats with the shamrocks and wear the carnations in our lapels. There is a lot of tradition that goes with those top hats. They're handed down from father to son and on through the generations. And if you look at some of those hats today that the men from the various organizations wear, you'll see that some of them are very, very well worn. You had to have one to walk in the St. Ann's Young Men's contingent. And when the parade was over and it was time to move on to the parties you made sure to give your hat to someone to look after. You'd maybe ask someone to take it home for you. You didn't ever put that hat down anywhere and walk away—these are prized possessions!

Traditionally, our signal to begin lining up outside the hall to go to the parade's staging area up the hill was when we saw the St. Gabriel contingent from the Point come through Griffintown. They always walked just before us on the parade route. First, they'd walk from the Point, through the Wellington tunnel, then along Wellington to Peel Street and up to the staging area on Dorchester. We'd wait about ten minutes or so after they went through Griffintown and then we'd head out. We'd usually have a couple of drinks at the concert hall earlier on while we were getting ready, but I'll tell you this—no one got drunk! If you had one too many, you didn't walk with the St. Ann's Young Men. They were very strict about this. Back in those days you didn't see women walking in the parade the way you saw distinct groups of men like the St. Ann's Young Men. When you did see women they were typically on floats. I do remember, though, that the nurses from St. Mary's Hospital always had their own entry in the parade—but even there, they were all in cars.

Over the years there were always parties in Griffintown after the parade. They used to hold parties at the Concert Hall, and then later on we'd have them at a nearby hotel like the Queen's. There was singing and dancing and lots of food. The older guys would take turns getting up and singing Irish songs and a lot of them could really sing. One fellow would get up and sing for a while and then someone else would jump up on the stage for his turn. One story that you'll hear circulated around by the older guys my age made it into the paper one year. It was the only time I ever remember an incident like this on St. Patrick's Day. It was at the Queen's and the Griffintown folk had a large reception room reserved for the party. But right beside them in another room was a good-sized delegation from Poland that was in Montreal doing something with the Quebec Government. I remember that they were all wearing tuxedos. Well, as the party wore on over in the Griffintown side and the singing and dancing got going, the volume quite naturally grew louder. But next door, some of them were apparently trying to give speeches. So, a few of them came over and asked if things could tone down a little.

I wasn't there at that time, because I was still over at James Lyng High School helping out. The school used to have its own entry in the parade every year. But the story goes that after the people on the Griffintown side were asked to be quiet, things somehow broke down between the two groups. I arrived in the aftermath. When I got to the hotel there were police cars everywhere. I went in right away to see my parents and there were police all over the place inside too. I found my parents sitting at one of the tables in the party room so I asked, "What's going on?", and I knew that one of my brothers was at the party so I asked, "Where's my brother?" My mother just looked at me and said "SSSHHH, he's under the table!" At that time the police were all moving around trying to find people that they thought might have been involved in any way. Sure enough, I took a quick look under the table and there was my brother—knocked out cold. I found out afterwards that someone had hit him with one of those big stand-up ashtrays you'd see between the elevators on every floor of the hotels!

When Griffintown as we knew it was really shutting down for good—I'd say around 1966 or '67, and more and more people were moving away, the parties were getting smaller and smaller. But some people hung on in Griff for a long time. One was Annie Wilson. I mention Annie because she really kept a lot of the Irish traditions alive for some time toward the end. Eventually the biggest Griffintown party after the parade was at Annie's place—singing—dancing—tubs full of beer. The family lived near the fire station. Truly, I'd say Annie was the heart of the Griffintown Irish for quite a few years near the end. My mother was very good friends with Annie.

Christmas in Griffintown was another very important day and St. Ann's Church played a big role. If I remember correctly, we'd have four masses starting at the stroke of midnight on Christmas morning. First of all you'd have the midnight Mass and the church was always full to capacity. The midnight high Mass was followed by at least three low Masses. The high Mass is much more formal than the low Masses. The Service is conducted from the middle of the church and it involves the full range of ceremonies.

Back in the 'fifties you had the option to prepare for teaching in different ways. You could complete a degree at the bachelor's level and then go to Teachers College for a year. You could also go directly to Teachers College after high school for two years and acquire a certificate to teach up to the grade nine level. That's the option I chose. Our family didn't have a lot of money, and as I said earlier, I was the first-born of eight children. So, my parents managed to help me through the two-year program and then I went on from there. The Protestants prepared at

Resurrection school where Gordon first taught in Lachine. 2014.

MacDonald College when I was starting my training, and the Catholics prepared at École Normale Jacques Cartier. So, I went to École Normale. It was predominantly a French college but the English students had a few classrooms allocated to them. École Normale was located up near Lafontaine Park. But after my first year the English sector of the school moved to Côte-Saint-Antoine and Prudhomme in NDG (Notre-Dame-de-Grâce) to form St. Joseph Teachers College. Eventually St. Joe's moved into the old Catholic High School building on Durocher.

To be honest, I really think that in that first term, when new students came in, the people running the program did their best to weed out anybody that they didn't think could make it. I still don't know to this day if I was one of the targets, but when it came time for the first student teaching assignment to a classroom, they sent me to Belmont School to teach grade seven. Yes—the same Belmont School that was near our house on Canning Street. It was considered a very tough assignment. They also told me to do it alone—and that wasn't the norm either. You usually did it in twos with someone that had some experience. At the time I was 17 and the students were anywhere from 11 to 13. You were graded for this, of course, and the person who did it was notoriously demanding. If he didn't think you were good enough you could be on your way out. Well, I was slated to teach a science class for the assessment and a friend loaned me an electrical circuit board complete with a bell. It demonstrated how conductors and resistors affected electrical current. You could use it to show the kids how some things like pennies or

St. Thomas Aquinas teachers' hockey team. Gordie is first on the left, second row.

other metal objects would complete the circuit and ring the bell, while other materials like chalk or wood, that were resistors, wouldn't. It was a wonderful teaching aid. The kids were involved and the assessor loved it. From that day on I had no trouble at all right through Teachers College.

After I graduated from St. Joe's I spent five years teaching in Lachine. First, it was at Resurrection, and then we opened Bishop Whelan High School. I taught the same group of boys for five years. We started working together at Resurrection and carried on through to Bishop Whelan. I really enjoyed that. They were a great bunch and some of the Bishop Whelan kids were excellent athletes. The big French Catholic boys' school in Lachine at that time was Piché. We used to have a winter carnival every year and the main event was a hockey game at the Lachine arena between the two schools. The stands were always packed—English on one side— French on the other. And the Lachine arena was a big venue by 1950s standards. The excitement would build up for a couple of hours before the game with warm-up events like puck-carrying contests and things like that. We always had a pretty good handle on who-was-who on Piché, but one year a player that we had never seen before skated out for the game. He was unbelievable— just a superb hockey player! We played hard, like always, but with this kid on the Piché team, it was just too much. I figured for sure they had brought in a ringer. But when the Brother from Piché came over to shake hands with us after the game he had a big smile. He told me that the player had just been brought in a few days previously by the Montreal Canadiens to attend Piché while playing for the Lachine Maroons. At that time the Maroons were an important feeder team for the Montreal Canadiens. The player's name was Yvan Cournoyer, one of the most famous players to ever lace up skates for the Canadiens.

After those five years in Lachine I took a year off in 1962 to finish my university degree. I did this at the University of Ottawa. I had already been taking summer courses toward a degree at Ottawa U. for several years. After graduation I actually thought about going into another field, but one thing led to another and I took on a short contract in teaching through a friend, then committed to the field permanently. Later on I completed a Masters at St. Michael's College in Winooski Vermont.

During my years of teaching I did a lot of work in inner-city Montreal High Schools like St. Thomas Aquinas and James Lyng. These are both in Saint-Henri and they served kids from the area where I grew up, as well as some other areas. A lot of the students were very poor. You could pretty much count on it that the kids attending these schools were not coming from affluent families. Schools like this can be tough places to teach. I know for a fact that part of the reason I was sent to work at St. Thomas Aquinas when I was young was because of my own background growing up as a Griffer. The thing about teaching in schools like this is that if you don't understand the kids, or if you can't relate to them, you can get into real trouble. They're teenagers and you can't *snow* these kids. If they think you're a phony you won't get respect and you'll lose control. And then the students don't produce or learn. I often had classes that had a good-sized contingent of challenged students. I enjoyed working with them. In fact, I requested to work with them. I grew up on some of the same streets they did and knew exactly where they were coming from. It was easy for me to talk to them, and this helped me get through to them.

Back when I was a teacher, I think I only taught what we called the "A" class once. That was the group of kids that had the highest grades and were typically the most focused. It was at James Lyng when I was there as a teacher. The Principal needed someone to teach the new math. It had just been introduced and I was the only teacher at the school at the time that had been trained in the new methods. The thing was, it was a girl's class. In those days in the Catholic system, the women, usually nuns, taught the girls, and the men taught the boys. I didn't know what to expect, but it was a great experience. They were truly excellent students. I still get a good laugh when I think about that class. It was a time when some fairly pronounced fashions for men were coming in and the girls sent me a couple of pointed messages on style. I remember they gave me a very—and I do mean very wide tie! It was beautifully made and an obviously expensive tie. They insisted I wear it at least once a month. I decided to go them one better. We had a young teacher at the school at the time and he wore very fashionable clothing—almost skintight pants etc. I asked him to lend me one of these outfits for a day since we were the same size. I wore one of his suits with the tie the girls gave me and walked into class as if everything were completely normal. The girls couldn't believe it and they had no idea that it was my colleague's suit! I still keep that tie.

Some years later when I was a Principal at James Lyng we had a very large student body— around 2000 kids. We had five Assistant Principals and 126 teachers. The staff represented a broad mix of people. We had about eight nuns on staff including some from the Sisters of the

Holy Cross in Montreal. We had teachers that had been trained and accredited elsewhere in the world in places like Hungary, Egypt, Ireland and Scotland. But we also had a sizeable group of teachers that grew up in the area, walked the same streets and experienced, first hand, the same challenges as the kids at Lyng. It was an excellent staff.

Every year at Lyng we'd welcome somewhere in the range of 400 or so new students into grade eight. And the reality was that we always received a number of kids that, for a variety of reasons, either weren't motivated to study, or had a long history of discipline problems in their elementary schools. The approach I took at Lyng was to go out in advance and talk to the teachers in the various feeder schools. I'd try to get a handle on the students we'd receive. I would ask the elementary schools to share with us the names of the kids that would likely provide us with the greatest challenges. Then we'd sit down at Lyng and pull together a plan for two classes of 20 students where we would group these kids together. Then, I'd provide them with top-notch teachers who specifically volunteered to work with challenged students and who had a track record of success in these situations. These were teachers that I knew could get through to these kids. We didn't take the approach at Lyng that these kids weren't going to make it—and we made that clear to them. We told them we had high expectations for them. They received close attention. We always checked their homework. It was never easy, but these kids ended up writing exactly the same exams as the rest of the students and we could usually get about 75% of them through the entire academic program. From experience, I came to believe firmly that the strongest educators should work with the students that were the most challenged and were experiencing the most difficulty. I also felt that it was very important for these students to know that their teachers at the front of the class had actually volunteered to work with them.

Now, one of the important things to know here is that this was a school-wide initiative. Everybody pitched in one way or another, and I'll tell you why that was the case. Our average class size was supposed to be 32. That's what we were funded to handle. So to provide for these two smaller classes of 20 on an ongoing basis for the first two years of high school, the other teachers agreed to teach slightly larger classes of around 34 or 35. After two years in classes of 20, these students moved into the mainstream, larger classes. A few of them moved into the larger classes earlier than that and did just fine, but most of them stayed in the smaller classes for the full two years. So it really was a team effort on behalf of all the teachers. Some took on more students, while others focused on smaller classes of challenged students. In today's world, there is no doubt in my mind that some of these students in the smaller classes would have been assigned to "Special Education" classes. In our day we didn't have dedicated programs like this. Our approach with these students was to work closely with them, and to really challenge them academically. I think that today we shuffle too many kids off to Special Ed. classes.

Every morning at James Lyng we used to have a prayer spoken over the loud speaker. Then, just before class started I would normally say "Good Morning", read out any general messages I might have, then I'd often say "Would the following students report immediately to my office". Then I'd read the names. Everyone knew what that meant—trouble! Long after I left James Lyng we had one of the 25-year graduating class reunions coming up and the memories of those morning read-outs served me well. These are important reunions, but I was scheduled to attend a family wedding and that came first. It was funny, though, because one of my former students who was frequently summoned to my office in the morning for one transgression or another called me a couple of times to encourage me to attend. It was great to hear from him but I had to explain why it was just impossible for me to go. But thinking about him gave me an idea for the reunion. I prepared a recording that mimicked my old morning announcements. It basically started out with a welcome and best wishes for the reunion. I followed up with an apology for not being able to attend, and then finished up by saying... *but would the following students report to my office immediately!* Then I read off a number of very well known names that I knew were in attendance and who were regularly in a line-up outside my office in the morning. And, of course, it included the name of my former student that had been phoning and encouraging me to attend. I'm told it went over well and got lots of laughs.

We did have our share of challenges at James Lyng, though. When I began my work as Principal we were experiencing a very high absentee rate, so we instituted a program whereby if a student wasn't in school we phoned home to the parents. We took attendance every day, analyzed it, and phoned—every time! In no time at all the absentee rate dropped dramatically. As administrators, you had to be flexible, as well. Today, we talk about conflict management. Well, it has always been part of the game. I remember once I got a call at the office from an old childhood friend. It was late in the afternoon. He was at a tavern on Centre Street in the Point with some of his buddies. He said to me that one of his friends at the table told him his son had just been suspended from Lyng by one of the vice principals. He told me that his friend would like to meet me to talk about it. I said, "Sure, I'll look into it and he can drop by the school". "Well", said my old friend, "he was wondering if, on your way home tonight you could maybe just drop by the tavern". So I told him, "Fine, I'll come round on the way home when I finish here". I went to see the vice principal involved and he laid things out. "C'mon, let's get our coats", I said. "We're going to the tavern".

When we arrived there was a crowd of guys around the table and we sat down. I knew most of them. One quart of beer arrived for each of us! Then another quart of beer arrived! There was no talk of the incident at school. Then the father of the student in trouble, spoke up, "So, what's the problem?" he asked. I motioned to my colleague that he had the floor and he explained the situation. The table sat in silence for a few seconds and then the father spoke up again. He just said, "Gordie, it will never happen again". And that was that. Business was over—but our visit to the tavern wasn't! They just would not let us leave—and the beer kept flowing! And, you know what? When that young man was readmitted, it never did happen again.

That James Lyng staff worked very hard to provide those kids with as much as possible. I'll give you an example. I remember one day I was watching a Notre Dame University football game on television and I was really struck by the incredible precision and skill of the marching band at half time. I thought that something like this might help our kids. I went to see our librarian on the Monday morning and asked her if she could investigate where Notre Dame got their uniforms and how much it would cost to have 40 sets made up etc. In a very short time she came back to explain to me that they were made in New York and cost $250 each. She said the company would be happy to model the same uniforms for us in our own school colors. Now, 40 years ago, $10,000 was a lot of money for a school. But the staff, the students and the parents bought in to the idea, so we went to work. We got a partial grant from the Montreal Catholic School Commission that covered half the cost. The teachers gave freely of their time to save money on a couple of fronts and we made up the rest with chocolate drives and other fundraisers. We quickly acquired some musical instruments to get going right away and we arranged for a McGill University music teacher with experience in band to come down and help us get started before the uniforms were made up.

The day finally came when we got the call that the uniforms were ready in New York. As it happened, the Sisters of the Holy Cross had a convent just across the border in the U.S., so we had the band outfits shipped directly to them. Then I ordered a school bus to take all the band members down to New York State to pick up the gear. I arranged to have five or six nuns sit in the front seats of the bus in their full habits. When the bus arrived at the border the guard asked one of the nuns where they were going, she explained that they were slated to participate in a band competition not too far from the border. Of course, all the kids were visible at the windows and playing their instruments. Off went the bus into the U.S. When the kids arrived to get their uniforms they spent some time in the local town, put their new uniforms on and got back on the bus. When it arrived at the border, the students were in full regalia and toying with their instruments. The guard asked one of the nuns where they had been and she repeated that they had been at a competition for the day. The guard immediately waved them through. Strangely enough, we didn't have to pay any duty on the uniforms!

That band was very good and very popular. One of the nuns had volunteered from the outset to understudy with the McGill Professor who was helping us. She eventually came to me and said she was comfortable with taking over, so she did. The band played at all the big school events. It was in demand elsewhere as well. The kids participated every year in the St. Patrick's Day Parade in Montreal, as well as other events like the Canada Day Parade. The other thing the kids would do is set up and play at the main entrance to James Lyng in the morning. The students were proud of that band and I can tell you that it had a very calming effect on the student body when they were playing in the morning. It was a wonderful program for the seven years it lasted. As fate would have it, though, the instruments were all stolen. Then the uniforms were destroyed when the St. Pierre River, which runs underground near James Lyng, completely flooded the three underground floors of the school. That was where we stored the uniforms.

When I was a principal I always did my best to help young teachers coming into the schools, as well. From time to time over the years when I was in administration I'd see a young teacher, with the very best of intentions, taking an approach in one environment or another, whether in the inner city or elsewhere, that I had seen lead to real problems in the past. What works in one area of a big city like Montreal doesn't necessarily translate into teaching success in another. When I saw a situation like this I'd sit down with the teacher, share some experiences and try to help with some advice on how to connect and get through to the students. I remember one instance at James Lyng where a student teacher introduced himself to the students using his first name. I know that he just wanted to connect with the kids and build a relationship, but it was the wrong approach in the wrong place. The response from that group of students was predictable. You could see it coming. In no time they were joking around, making rhymes with his first name and things like that. I sat down with him and gave him a friendly piece of advice that in the future he should introduce himself as "Mister so and so". I remember another situation where a teacher came to me in despair. When he had entered the cafeteria at lunch that day, everyone in the room had met him with a table-thumping chant. And, as I said, James Lyng was a big school. Perhaps he thought it disrespectful—but it wasn't a mean chant or anything. After we talked for a while I simply told him that in some situations, and in this environment, the best thing you can do is just laugh some things off. Everything worked out fine.

Looking back on my years of involvement with thousands of young people all over Montreal, I was very fortunate. I loved working with the students and was very grateful when I was inducted into the James Lyng Hall of Fame. You know, when you work with kids for four years—you see them in the halls every day—and you remember them later in life at special events like reunions after they mention their names. Some kids, though, you just never forget! As often as not, they're the ones that were frequently in your office for one reason or another. It is fascinating to see where some of my students ended up: doctors, lawyers, dentists, police officers. One holds a key position in a National Football League organization in the U.S., and several have gone into the field of education. My former students from Lyng are all over the world and some of them travel a very long way for these 25-year reunions that I mentioned earlier.

When I was still working, former students would sometimes come back to visit. I remember my secretary came to me one day and told me that someone was in the lobby and had asked if he could see me. I said, "Sure". He came in and told me his name. It took me a second or two but then I recognized him. I had taught him about 13 years earlier. He was a very quiet boy who had just arrived from Italy and was assigned to my class in grade ten. He didn't speak a word of English at the time. He just sat at the back, listened, and took it all in. After only one year, I remember he was writing very well and he was a whiz at math! He said that he had dropped by to see me to say thank you and to tell me that he had just finished his internship in neurosurgery at the Montreal General Hospital.

I have been retired now since 1994. My wife, Mary, who was also a teacher in some inner-city Montreal schools, is retired as well. Today, we still live in the same house we bought here in Pierrefonds in 1975. We brought up four boys here and they are all doing well. One is in Montreal. Two are in Toronto and one is in Vancouver. One even decided to go into teaching. We enjoy travelling and move around quite a bit, so we see them all frequently.

So, yes, we keep busy. I stay active with the Irish community here in Montreal, and I really enjoy my involvement with the Erin Sports Association. I'm very proud of the work that organization does in support of underprivileged children. I still have a lot of extended family in Montreal and we even have our own contingent that marches under the "McCambidge Family" banner in the St. Patrick's Day Parade every year. I don't always walk in the parade now. Mary and I often just park near St. Patrick's Basilica, walk up to St. Catherine Street with our grand-children and watch the parade as it passes the reviewing stand near Phillips Square.

I left Canning Street in 1959 when I was 22 years old. When I have the opportunity I some-times take walks through Griffintown to see all the changes that are going on. The sounds of my childhood are long gone now: the tram cars, the constant clapping of horses hoofs, the steady rumbling of the big trucks coming and going along William Street as they went to and from the Canada Steamship installation just to the west of St. Ann's Church. In some ways I find these walks enjoyable. In other ways I find them sad when I think of what we had at one time down there. The sense of community that we enjoyed in those days won't ever be replicated. It can't.

I meet with my childhood friends from the area regularly, though, and one of the places where we like to have lunch is at the Capri tavern down by the canal in the Point. And when I do, there is rarely a day that a waiter won't come over, drop down a beer and point to someone at another table. I can almost guarantee what that means. Nine times out of ten, when I look over I see one of my former students waving to me and smiling. And when they come over …they still call me "Mr. McCambridge!"

Gordon and Mary McCambridge at home, 2013.

"I can still hear the sound of the guys

under the street lamps

in the evening,

singing in harmony.

Usually it would be four of them

—no musical instruments—

just singing.

It was just marvelous."

Betty Dwyer

Betty Dwyer
nee Daigle

Betty was born in 1929 and lived in Goose Village until just before the demolition in 1964. Betty raised seven children and she is a graduate of the Thomas More Institute's Early Childhood Education Program. Betty enjoys music and has always been interested in creative writing. She now resides in a senior's residence in Montreal.

Photo: Betty at home. 2013.

"When I was young my dad had a band of his own. He was very musically inclined. Maybe part of it was his Acadian background… My dad taught me the spoons and I'd always play at get-togethers."

My mum came to Canada in 1928 from Lanarkshire, Scotland. Her sister had come to Canada a year before and, as it happened, the two of them ended up marrying two brothers here in Montreal—the Daigles. They were from Griffintown. They lived on William Street over near Duke. That's not too far from Haymarket Square. My dad, Frederic, was born in Montreal but he had an Acadian background. He was fluently bilingual but his first language was English, so I was brought up speaking English.

I was born at home in 1929—the year of the great stock market crash. I was very much a premature baby and weighed only four lbs. My parents were living just north of Wellington on Bridge Street at the time. Not long after I was born we moved a few blocks south into Goose Village. Over the years I lived on various Village streets: Conway, Forfar, Riverside and Britannia. I got married in 1950. I had three sons and one daughter of my own, but I also adopted three foster children. We stayed in Goose Village until just before it was demolished in 1964. Then we moved over to Magdalen Street in the Point. We had a very nice place there but eventually went just across the river to St. Lambert in 1967. There were more parks and things like that for the children in St. Lambert.

I was the eldest of ten children. I had seven brothers. All the children were born very close to a year apart. We were born into tough times during the depression but my parents always found a way to look after us. We always had food on the table. My dad had several different jobs over the years. When he met my mother he was in the Merchant Navy. After that he worked at places like Wilsil's and Canada Packers. They were right across the street from each other. I know

Betty (second from the left) with father (seated) and all of her siblings.

that one of the jobs he had was counting the animals as they came in for processing. For a while, he also spent some time working in shipbuilding and repair. He was always on the go. He did a lot of different things on the side to make sure we all had what we needed. He used to keep a small boat right under the Victoria Bridge and he'd go fishing all the time in the St. Lawrence River. We always had lots of fish to eat. I remember he also used to hunt and trap muskrats up and down the riverbanks along Riverside Street as well. He'd clean and fix up the hides and then take them down to the Main and sell them to merchants that used them in their clothing lines.

My dad also drove *calèches* with Leo Leonard over in Griffintown. My father was really quite close to Leo. The St. Patrick's Day Parade was always a big event in Montreal and I remember my dad driving the "Irishman of the Year" a few times. When he was on the *calèches* he'd meet celebrities too. I remember him talking about meeting Liberace and Harry Belafonte. He told me that Harry Belafonte was very generous. My dad spent a lot of time at Leo's Horse Palace. The deal with Leo was always 50/50. Whatever my dad made driving *calèches* in Old Montreal or elsewhere, he'd just go back to the Horse Palace and split it up right down the middle with Leo. My dad was over at the Horse Palace well after he retired from full time work.

When we were children my dad used to take us over to the boat after church in the summer and row us out to Nun's Island. There were lots of green spaces there and we could play in the woods and along the shores of the St. Lawrence River. We always started the trip by rowing

Looking across the span of the Victoria Bridge toward the south shore. In the foreground is where Betty's father negotiated his way under the bridge to Nun's Island. 2013.

between two of the Victoria Bridge's huge stone supports. That part scared me, but we always had a good time when we got there. My dad was a very kind and caring man, but once on the way to Nun's Island this almost cost us dearly. As we were about to leave for the island one Sunday, a neighbor asked if my dad could take her children over to the island with us. He agreed, but I guess maybe my dad overloaded the boat. It capsized. I couldn't swim at the time, but I can still remember someone just grabbing my arm and pulling me up. In the end everyone was OK. Unfortunately, someone who was watching from the bank ran back to my mother in the Village and told her that two of us had been lost.

When I was young my dad had a band of his own. He was very musically inclined. Maybe part of it was his Acadian background. He was an excellent mouth-organ player and he'd play the spoons at the same time. There were five people in his band and they'd practice at our place. I can still remember so clearly lying in bed listening to them get ready for an event. They loved to play "Oh, The Lady in Red". They'd play regularly and they got paid for it. Music was important to us. Whether it was learning an instrument or singing, everybody in the family did something. One of my brothers picked up the guitar and piano. He was self-taught on the guitar but had some help from the Clahanes on the piano. Another sang. My dad taught me the spoons and I'd always play at get-togethers. I still do. I always keep my spoons handy! Just last weekend I went to a big Daigle/Dwyer reunion. There were 125 people there. Things were going a bit slowly at

Looking north on Bridge Street, a very short distance from where Goose Village stood. The catwalk inscribed with the words Domestic Shortening served the stockyards. Betty worked at Wilsil, one of the meat packing plants in the area. 1935.

one point so I pulled out the spoons and sat down beside the DJ and started playing. People loved it! We played some polkas and that got things going. After I finished playing I got a standing ovation and that boosted my morale for a few days. The thing about playing the spoons is that you can beat yourself up pretty badly playing those things!

When I was a child I used to always look forward to going over to my grandfather Daigle's place in Griffintown. He was such a charming man and he was always so happy to see us. When we'd arrive he would prepare us his special home-made potato chips. He'd start off with fresh potatoes and slice them very, very thinly. Then he'd lay them out across the top of the wood stove and keep turning them over until they were brown on both sides and nice and crispy. Then he'd put some salt on them and we'd have hot potato chips. We had no television or video games or things like that in the 1930s, but we did have radio. I just loved listening to the serials like "The Shadow". We would often listen to serials at my grandfather's place. When we'd get there he would already have an area near the kitchen all set out with things like pots and pans hanging from the ceiling, as well as other gadgets he could use to make sound effects. Then, when the Shadow or some other serial was on we'd all gather around the radio while my

The same view today. Only the derelict building that once served as an administrative office remains.
Betty was born just a short walk up Bridge Street from where these photos were taken. 2014.

grandfather was off to one side matching the dialogue with sounds from all the things he had set up. That's what we looked forward to as children. It was always so much fun.

When I was playing with my girlfriends we were usually on the streets or in each other's houses. Sometimes we'd go to this little restaurant on the corner of Menai and Forfar owned by Mr. and Mrs. Revenda. They were very kind and they'd let three or four of us sit in one of the booths and do things like play some cards. We'd also do some of the same things the boys did in the Village, like if we could manage to grab a soft drink off one of the trucks and things like that. I even went over with my brothers once and rode a cow in the stockyards. If I wasn't with my girlfriends I was playing all kinds of sports with my brothers. All seven of my brothers were boxers. My dad started them off. He built up a small ring at home. Fred ended up staying with it the longest and he was a very good boxer. He went to the Olympics with the 1948 Canadian boxing team. Fred trained at the Griffintown Boys' Club so he benefited from Cliff Sowery's coaching. I used to box with my brothers until I was around 13. I really enjoyed sports and played softball until I was an adult. It all came very easily to me growing up with seven brothers.

I started off at St. Alphonsus School in the Village, just like everyone else, but I was sent to St. Gabriel's in the Point after grade two. It was quite a bit farther away and, believe me, it was a cold walk in the winter. The three cents for the bus was simply out of reach for us most of the time.

And you had to be careful walking to school back then. It was a very busy area. Once, one of my brothers was hit by a car on Bridge Street, but it turned out OK. We used to have to cross some train tracks along the way to school as well, and quite often the freight trains would stop and block our crossing. It was quite common for some of the Village kids to arrive at school late because of the trains. You'd be standing in the cold waiting for the train to move on before you could get back on the road to school. Every now and then someone would take a chance and sneak through between the boxcars while the train was stopped. Well, you're never supposed to do that because you have no idea when the train will lurch forward and then you're in real trouble. One of the children I knew did that once and got caught. He lost both legs.

I stayed at St. Gabriel's right through until grade nine and then I went straight to work. And when you started working in those days in the Village, the Point or Griffintown, it was like going back to school. Right away you'd see lots of your old friends. It didn't matter where you worked, you'd see people you had known for years. People got jobs in the area and walked to work. And the linkages between Griffintown and the village were always strong anyway. Not too far away and nearer downtown you also had places like Sun Life Insurance. That was always a popular place to work. When you worked for organizations like that it meant you started receiving benefits. A lot of the women from the Point, the Village and around the area used to work as after-hour cleaners in some of those places as well. My own grandmother used to work as a cleaner.

My first job was at Wilsil's meatpacking. Like I said, they did the same things as Canada Packers. They had their own slaughterhouse and everything. I worked there for two years and I did various jobs. First off, I worked slicing and packing bacon. We had to slice it very thinly so that it would go a long way. I also worked preparing sausages. For a while I was involved in getting lard ready for sale. I didn't ever work in the slaughterhouse. In fact, I only ever walked through it once. I remember that day well. I had a terrible headache, and to get to the nurse's office from my workstation I had to go through the slaughterhouse. It was in full operation at the time. I still remember vividly looking over and seeing a cow getting its throat slit and the blood surging out. That was the one and only time I went through that area. Wilsil's was very good to its employees. Every week you could put in your order for the different kinds of meat that you wanted and they'd package it up and give it to you at a greatly reduced price. So, as a family, when I was there and when my dad worked there, we always had plenty of meat. At a time when there wasn't much money around, something like this was very important. We considered ourselves a very fortunate family.

My whole life I have always been very industrious and I really enjoy learning. I never really stopped learning. When I was at Wilsil's for those two years I was taking courses in typing and shorthand and things like that. It served me very well because I got a job at Northern. I stayed at Northern for five years, mostly in the blueprint department. While I was there I enrolled in the Early Childhood Education at the Thomas More Institute and completed the diploma program. After that I stayed home with the children.

What are some of the sights and sounds of the Village that I remember the most? Well, there were lots, but the one that keeps coming back has to do with music. I can still hear the sound of the guys under the street lamps in the evening singing in harmony. Usually it would be four of them

—no musical instruments—just singing. It was just marvelous. The Clahane family is well known for their music and often you'd see one of them in the group.

I'm 83 now, but like I said, I really enjoy learning and I like to keep busy. Some years ago I took some courses in creative writing. I'm thinking about getting a computer and getting back into it again. I'd like to write something about the Griffintown Horse Palace, and I have always enjoyed writing poetry. Here is one of the poems I wrote about Camp Chapleau—a summer camp. The Brewery Mission was a big supporter of Camp Chapleau. A lot of the kids from the point and surrounding area went there. I went as a camper and so did my children. I worked at Camp Chapleau in the summers until I was 65.

The Lake

The lake that rests so calm and still now
At the end of a beautiful day
Has fulfilled its duty to us.
We've looked, we've dreamed, we've played.
But now it's time to say good-night
And thank God for this wonderful sight.
Tomorrow when the sun comes up
And all the world is new,
Our lake takes on a new look
Of bright and shining dew.
It sparkles and it shimmers
It beckons to us all
To come and have a good time,
While always being aware
To thank God for this treasure
Of beauty that we share.

—Betty Dwyer

"…employment was available

for anyone in Montreal

that wanted to get busy.

Griffintown, the Point and the Village

were alive with opportunities.

Just to mention a few of the places

you could work

in Griffintown alone,

we had two big breweries,

the Lowney's chocolate factory,

a big bus terminal, and Canada Steamships

had a large facility down by the canal.

We had a company that built and sold large trucks.

We had foundries, spring manufacturing, two dairies,

stables, box manufacturing, a huge Simpson's warehouse,

oil drum cleaning facilities, Donnelley's trucking,

food preparation outlets and much more."

Maurice Harkin

Maurice "Moe" Harkin

Maurice graduated from Cardinal Newman High School in Montreal and began working full time at 16. He spent almost 55 years working in the oil and gas industry. Moe now lives in Ottawa but still looks forward to getting together regularly with his old friends from Griffintown.

Photo: 2013.

"I'd say anywhere from 80-90% of people in Griffintown, the Point and the Village lived, worked and played right in the area at the east end of the Lachine Canal.
A lot of these business enterprises were side-by-side with the housing.
Everything was right there."

I was born in 1937 on Ottawa Street in Griffintown. Altogether, I lived at 1202 and 1200 Ottawa for 20 years. Our building was right next door to the old Griffintown Horse Palace.

My father came from Ireland with my grandfather in the early 1900s. I'm told they came from the Churchill area, which is in County Donegal in the Republic of Ireland. My mother's name was Juliette Côté. She was from Montreal and didn't speak any English at all. So, I grew up speaking English and French.

There were eight children in the family. I had five brothers and two sisters. In the first seven years of my parents' marriage they had three boys and one girl. Then, for seven years they didn't have any more children. Then, in the next seven years they had three more boys and one more girl. I was the 7th born. At first we lived upstairs at 1202 Ottawa Street. We were lucky when we lived in the first place because we had a bath. Lots of places didn't. Later on we moved downstairs to 1200 and there was no bath there. We had lots of room, though. By that time there was only me and my younger sister left at home with my mother.

My father died when I was about one. He was only 38 years old. He was a caretaker with the City of Montreal at the time. At first my mother was on welfare but she found a job cleaning offices and did that for about 15 years. When my father died the older kids in the family were in their teens so they all went to work. In those days in Griffintown that was very common. Most people went to work in their teens.

By the time I was six or seven I had lots of freedom to move around Griffintown by myself. I lived two blocks from the school, three blocks from the Griffintown Boys' Club and two blocks from the church. Basin Street Park was right behind the church and corner stores were all over. So, everything was right there for me. I had lots of older brothers and sisters to look after me as well, if I needed any help. Everyone knew everyone else in the area anyway. We all had groups of friends in our own little areas of Griffintown.

The building where Moe grew up. with a *For Sale* sign in the window. New condos were recently built to either side. 2013.

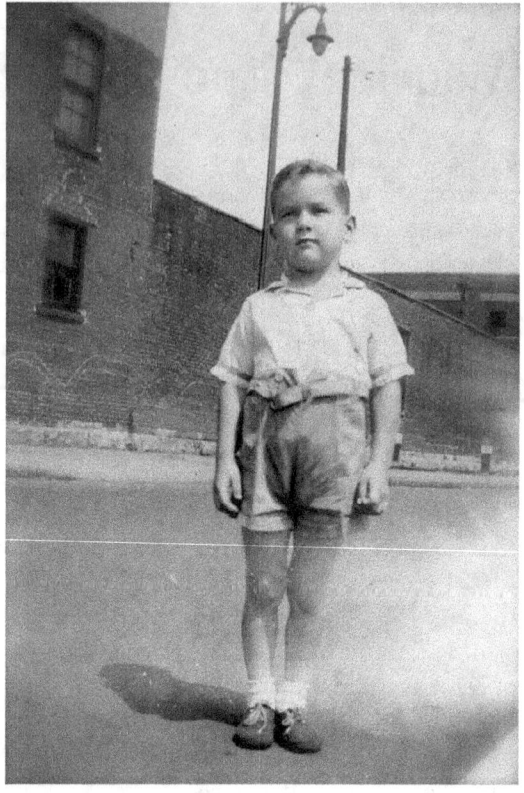

Young Moe. c.1941.

When I was a kid growing up in Griffintown I had French and English friends, and later on I could work in either language. I don't remember any real ongoing friction in Griffintown between the French and English. The French and English were sprinkled all through the Griff. We played on the streets together and we all played on the same sports teams. Sometimes we'd have kids' craps games and play for pennies.

Griffintown was a small but very close community, and any stranger in Griffintown really stood out. In fact, if a guy was walking down the street in Griffintown and nobody recognized him, you'd often see the person challenged by a group of Griffintowners—"Who are you and where are you going?" If it was to go to work or to go to another guy's house that we knew—fine. If the response was to go and see one of the girls from Griffintown, then that was the wrong answer and they'd get sent packing. I've seen it happen. If someone from outside Griffintown was seeing a girl from the area and was walking her home, they'd often stop at Notre Dame Street, the northern border, and then let the girl carry on alone into Griffintown. Sometimes they'd drop her off by taxi at her house and leave by the same taxi. When I was growing up in the '40s and '50s, I can tell you that 50-60% of the people that I knew married from within or across the three different communities of Goose Village, Griffintown and the Point.

I attended St. Ann's Boys' School and I thoroughly enjoyed my time there. Brother Edmond probably had the greatest influence on me of all the Brothers. We played a lot of sports at St. Ann's but most of it at school was informal. There were lots of other opportunities for community sport, though, and baseball was very popular in Griffintown, the Point and the Village. There

Moe (first row, first on the left) with his mother and his seven siblings. c. 1941.

were some very good teams. I took advantage of this and played a lot of baseball and hockey when I was young. I continued to play well into my adulthood.

I was also very active in the church from the age of eight until about 16. I was an altar boy, or as we say, I was in the Sanctuary. I would help the priests with Mass. I'd serve at weddings, funerals, and all the big religious events like Easter, Christmas, and Corpus Christi. Altar boys always helped at the Tuesday devotions at St. Ann's as well. People were truly committed to attending devotions. Corpus Christi was always a big event in Griffintown when I was young. I have a number of photos of this event. It is celebrated two months after Easter and it honours the body and blood of Christ. An important aspect of the Corpus Christi celebration was a procession through Griffintown starting and ending at St. Ann's Church. The procession included the Knights of Columbus, the Ancient Order of Hibernians, the local priests, nuns, all the Brothers from St. Ann's School, the altar boys, choir members, as well as local dignitaries and others. You'd almost always see a Bishop or a Cardinal. Right after Mass, the procession would wend its way through Griffintown to the fire station where an altar was always set up. We'd have a small service there, then the procession would go back to the church. In preparation for this event, the people of Griffintown washed down the exteriors of their houses and hung religious flags and artifacts from the windows. They lined the streets and looked out all the windows. You don't see this today, but it was quite an event back in those days.

Moe (back row, fifth from the left) and the rest of the Griffintown "Grads". c. 1956.

Yes, the church had a big influence in Griffintown. One of my brothers joined the *De la Salle* Christian Brothers. That's the same order that taught at St. Ann's Boys' School. One of my sisters joined the Grey Nuns. Their mission was teaching and nursing. Both remained in their orders for about 15 years. My brother left and married someone who had previously been a nun. While my sister was serving in Toronto she met a fellow that she had known in Griffintown. She left the order and they got married. Growing up, I faithfully attended Mass, but after I got married and started a family, things trailed off. Now, I mostly attend on special occasions such as weddings or funerals.

After I finished grade nine at St. Ann's I moved to St. Patrick's High School. That only lasted for a short time, though, because the School Board shifted us all to Cardinal Newman High School up on Christophe Coulombe and St. Joseph. I graduated from grade eleven and went right to work. At that time, employment was available for anyone in Montreal that wanted to get busy. Griffintown, the Point and the Village were alive with opportunities. Just to mention a few of the places you could work in Griffintown alone, we had two big breweries, the Lowney's chocolate factory, a big bus terminal, and Canada Steamships had a large facility down by the canal. We had a company that built and sold large trucks. We had foundries, spring manufacturing, two dairies, stables, box manufacturing, a huge Simpson's warehouse, oil drum cleaning facilities, Donnelley's trucking, food preparation outlets and much more. We didn't have

Moe's class photo for his first year at St. Ann's
Boys' School. 1945.
Right: Altar Boy Moe Harkin. 1947.

cars, but all of these places were within walking distance for us and the jobs were plentiful. If you wanted to work, it was there. I'd say anywhere from 80-90% of people in Griffintown, the Point and the Village lived, worked and played right in the area at the east end of the Lachine Canal. A lot of these business enterprises were side-by-side with the housing.

Everything was right there. I can remember that when I was a kid at school in Griffintown, we'd see foam floating by overhead after it was released from the Black Horse and Dow breweries.

When I went to work in 1954, I joined Canadian Oil as an office-boy. I was at the head office located just north of Goose Village and south of Griffintown. It was across the street from Canada Packers and the Stockyards. Canadian Oil controlled the White Rose gas station chain across Canada and they were big players in various other oil-related initiatives like lubricating and heating oil. The company was eventually bought out by Shell Oil in 1966 and I shifted over to Shell. I was there for 38 years. Over the years at Canadian Oil and Shell I moved through a lot of different positions. I was put in charge of fuel oil for homes. I worked in wholesale sales, heating and equipment sales, and I ended my career at Shell as a plant foreman in 1991. But I didn't stop working. When I retired from Shell I was located in Ottawa and I went directly to work for Mr. Gas for over 15 years. Overall, I worked for almost 55 years. I did my share! I was 70 when I finally stopped working.

Forty or fifty years from now, what should people reading about our area understand? First off —that area of Montreal around the harbour is where everything started. That's where the first ships came in. Later on, Griffintown was the heart of Montreal's industrialization. Back before there was a Westmount, Outremont, Mount Royal or Montreal West, people were living and working down beside the water. I expect that a lot of people would be very surprised to find that if they conducted a study of their family tree, they'd trace it somehow back to our area of Goose Village, Griffintown or the Point. A lot of what was down there is gone now. Is that progress? I can't really say, but you can't stop change.

Flanked on either side, Moe carries the cross during a Corpus Christi procession in Griffintown. c. 1951.

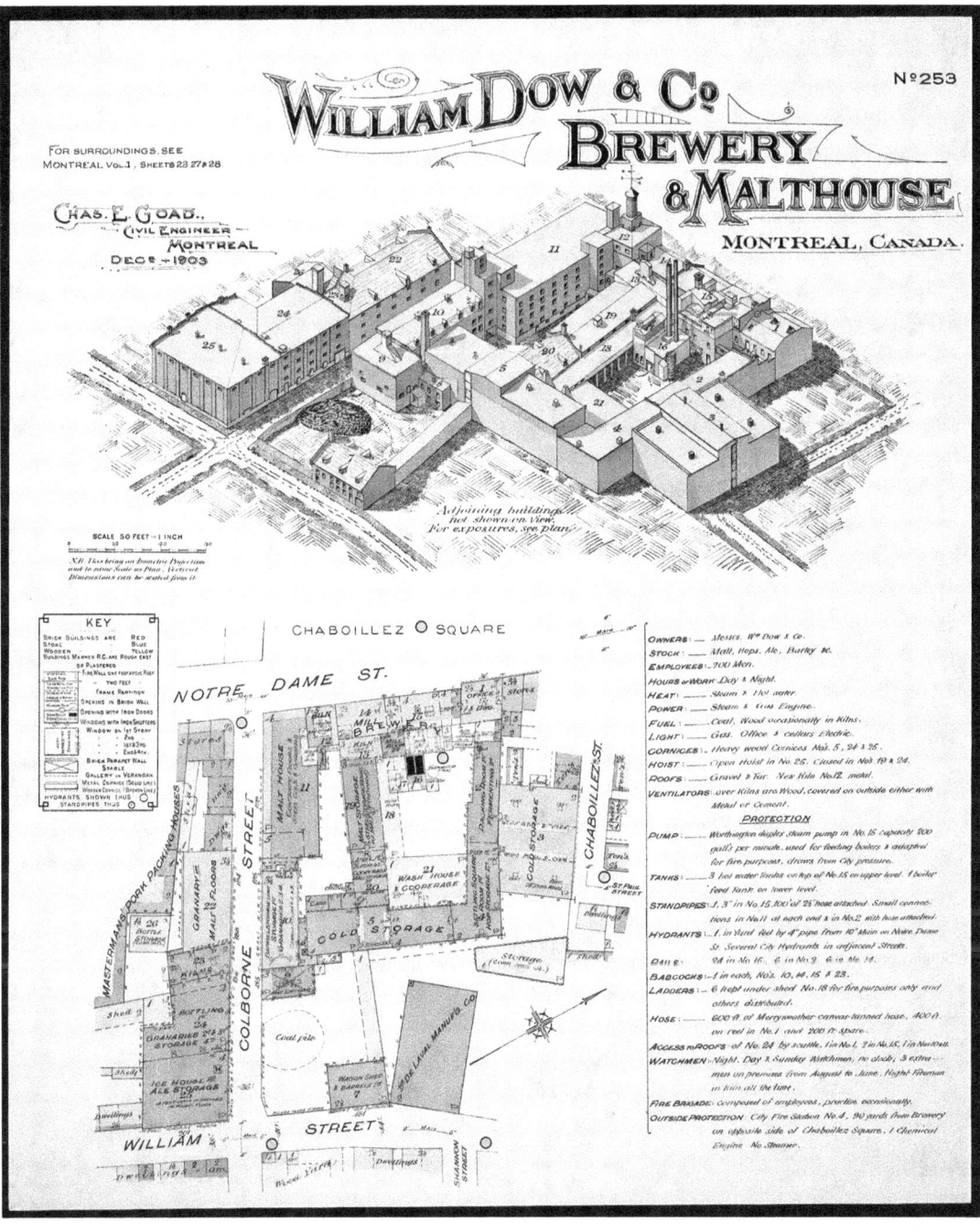

Dow Brewery served as one of the area's main employers.

"Pointe-Saint-Charles

has a great history.

I have very fond memories

of my childhood living there.

We lived across the street

from Marguerite Bourgeoys Park.

We were entertained every night

with movies in the park,

on Wednesday night

with Band Concerts

and on Saturday

everyone gathered

for street dances."

Margaret Healy

Margaret Healy

Margaret has been a volunteer and community organizer in *the Pointe* for decades. Margaret is a Past President of the United Irish Societies of Montreal and was the first, and only, female Grand Marshal of Montreal's St. Patrick's Day Parade.

For all of her efforts and accomplishments in support of the people of the area, Margaret was inducted into the Pointe-Saint-Charles Hall of Recognition in 2009, and in 2011, Margaret was awarded the St. Patrick's Society Community Award. At the

"The Pointe—a gem in the crown of Ville de Montréal."

2012 Untied Irish Societies' post-St. Patrick's Day Award Banquet, the Irish Ambassador to Canada, Dr. Ray Bassett presented Margaret with the prestigious certificate of Irish Heritage for her long-standing commitment to the Irish community. In his speech, Ambassador Barrett described Margaret as the "soul of the Irish community in Montreal".

Margaret remains active as President of the Centre Communautaire St.-Antoine (a senior's centre). Margaret's basement still serves as the hub for the United Irish Societies' annual Christmas food drive.

Photo: Margaret Healy as Grand Marshal during the St. Patrick's Day Parade in Montreal. Her grandchildren Jonathan and Matthew Showers accompany her. 2005.

In 1931 I was born Margaret Maude Healy. My parents were Thomas Patrick Healy and Lucy Irene McCarthy. I am the eldest of three children. I have a daughter, Sheila, a son Michael, from my first husband who came from Griffintown, and two grandchildren Jonathan and Matthew.

My dad and his siblings were brought up by their widowed mother, Bridget Healy, following the passing of her Irish immigrant husband, Michael Healy who came to Canada in the 1800's from County Clare, Ireland. He lived on Duke Street in Griffintown and attended St. Ann's School. He married my mother Lucy Irene McCarthy in 1929 and they made their home in Pointe-Saint-Charles.

My sisters and I were brought up in Pointe-Saint-Charles where we were baptized, made our First Communion, were confirmed and finally married in St. Gabriel's Parish. We all attended St. Gabriel's Elementary School. After elementary school, I had the option of choosing where I would like to attend high school. I chose to attend a boarding school in St. Laurent, run by the Sisters of the Holy Cross. It was a very unique and wonderful experience for me. My classes were small and the academics excellent. We received a broad and practical education. This boarding school is now Vanier College. After graduation, I attended the Congrégation de Notre-Dame Mother House, presently Dawson College, on Atwater Ave. where I followed business courses.

Margaret (centre) together with her parents and sisters (Sheila (left) and Irene (right).

Thomas Healy. Date unknown.

Pointe-Saint-Charles has a great history. I have very fond memories of my childhood living there. We lived across the street from Marguerite Bourgeoys Park. We were entertained every night with movies in the park, on Wednesday night with Band Concerts and on Saturday everyone gathered for street dances. Unfortunately, this has long since disappeared.

The church played an important role in our lives. The community gathered for both Mass and for social events, one of which was St. Patrick's celebrations. As a young girl I danced in the many Irish concerts.

Just two blocks away on Dublin Street, you will find La Ferme St. Gabriel. On this site is the original home of Marguerite Bourgeoys where, on her arrival from France, she instructed the *Filles du Roi* as well as many Quebec and First Nation children. When we were young, our family purchased fresh vegetables and fruit from the Sisters. Now, the farm is a museum with many antique articles and, today, there are many cultural events held on these premises.

My mother stayed at home with the children and my dad worked at various jobs, eventually operating his own business, Healy Brothers, which was a distributor for Pepsi Cola.

My dad's political career began in 1938 when he was elected as a City Councilor in Montreal for St. Ann's Ward. In 1940 he was elected to the House of Commons as a Liberal MP for the same district. This opened a whole new world for our family. We were then introduced to a political life in Ottawa where we made many friends, met many dignitaries and attended government events. Dad was a very humble man and was kind and caring to his constituents. He

Memorabilia from the St. Patrick's Day Parade, 1943, when Margaret's father, Mr. Thomas Healy served as Grand Marshal.

Thomas Healy garage. Date unknown.

served his two political offices until his death in 1957. My sisters and I felt very loved by both of our parents. We were taught through example that our duty was to love God, respect others, care for our neighbors and help those in need.

In 1942 dad had a triplex built opposite Marguerite Bourgeoys Park and later, a larger home built alongside where I now live with my husband Kenneth O'Donnell. As was the custom at the time, our widowed Grandmother, Brigit and our Uncle Eddie lived with us.

After my children were grown I decided to enter the business world and worked for an Advertising Agency. I also volunteered in various organizations, one of which was the Cedar's Cancer Fund at the Royal Victoria Hospital. I became a member of the United Irish Societies of Montreal where I served as Secretary and as President for two years. I also was honoured to be named the only female Grand Marshal of the St. Patrick's Parade. It pleased me because my dad was also the parade's Grand Marshal in 1943.

I have served on several other Boards of Directors and Executives over the years, namely: English Catholic School Council, Catholic Community Centre, and as Warden of St. Gabriel's Parish.

One of the special events that I remember most was my involvement in raising funds for the establishment of an Irish Studies Program at Concordia University. The United Irish Societies was asked to contribute to this fund. At this time, the Notre Dame Concert Band was touring the Eastern United States. As Chair of Fundraising for the United Irish Societies, and with the help of others, we arranged for the Band to come to Montreal to perform at St. Patrick's Basilica. We

Thomas Healy (third from the left) and friends beside St. Ann's Church on St. Patrick's Day. Date unknown.

raised $22,000 which was donated to Concordia Irish Studies Program in the name of United Irish Societies. Consequently, these monies continue to assist students to this day.

I was also part of the organizing committee for the visit of the Irish Immigrant Ship, "Jeannie Johnston". We organized entertainment at the Old Port in Montreal during its stay and this was enjoyed by many visitors and tourists.

All in all, I have had a very interesting and fulfilling life. I am now 81 years of age. I move a little more slowly now than in the past, but I remain ready to do what I can for others in life. I was recently awarded a certificate of Irish Heritage from the Irish Government of which I am very proud and a Community Medal Award from the National Assembly. How more fortunate could I be?

The Pointe will always be an important part of my life. It is a wonderful community and I am happy that I have experienced such great times here. Every morning I look out my window and see beautiful Marguerite Bourgeoys Park, with its majestic trees and well-trimmed lawn and thank God for all the blessings he has bestowed on me.

Margaret Healy as Grand Marshal and the other Marshals during the St. Patrick's Day Parade in Montreal. Margaret is third from right, first row. 2005.

Margaret, with husband Ken O'Donnell (left) and Raymond Bassett, Ireland's Ambassador to Canada. 2013.

"We did not have a lot

when we were growing up,

but we made our own fun.

We had a wonderful social life.

Sometimes we would go

to three or four dances a week

at places like the

79th Battery or the Polish Hall.

We still remain very close."

Patrick Duffy

Patrick "Paddy" Duffy

Growing up in the Point, Paddy was an outstanding athlete. He played guard and inside linebacker on two Canadian champion senior football teams: the Lakeshore Alouette Flyers in 1959, and the Verdun Shamcats in 1961. Paddy also won two Dominion (Canadian) championships paddling for the Grand Trunk Boating Club in Verdun.

In 1962 Paddy faced the difficult decision of accepting an offer from the Edmonton Eskimos football team or staying in the Point where he was already established in a career at Northern Electric. Paddy and his wife, Mary, decided to stay in Montreal and Paddy began turning his football interests to coaching in the Point. Says Paddy, "The kids in the Point needed the support, as well". Paddy coached at several different levels in the Point, and in the mid-1960s steered two teams to national championship victories at the juvenile level (age 17-19). Paddy still hears from some of his players.

In honour of his accomplishments over the years as an athlete, coach and mentor Paddy was inducted into the Point St. Charles Hall of Recognition in 2009.

Photo: Paddy Duffy at the 2013 "Walk to the Stone".2013.

"Today, I remain very much connected to the Point and to the people I grew up with…
What is most memorable for me about the Point?…the friendships I made, the lifelong friendships."

I was born at the Reddy Memorial Hospital near the old Montreal Forum on August 20th, 1935. My parents were living in the Point at the time. I grew up in the Point and stayed there until 1967. I was 32 when my wife, Mary, and I moved to 90th Avenue in LaSalle. After a while we moved to 37th Avenue in LaSalle where we bought the triplex we still live in today.

My parents were both born in Ireland. My father was born in 1908 in County Tyrone. My mother was born in 1910 in County Down. They didn't know each other in Ireland. They met here in Montreal. My father moved to Canada first and my mother came later. She was 18. I don't remember them talking very much about Ireland. Even when we had family over to the house in the Point they would talk only quietly about the old country. Sometimes they'd say a few words in Gaelic here or there if they didn't want us to understand what they were talking about. No, they didn't talk about it much, but I do remember my mother telling us that when she

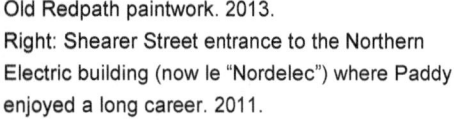

Old Redpath paintwork. 2013.
Right: Shearer Street entrance to the Northern
Electric building (now le "Nordelec") where Paddy
enjoyed a long career. 2011.

was in County Down, which is in Northern Ireland, she would have to walk up into the mountains to attend Mass.

There were five children in the family. I was the third born. My older sister lives in Oakville, Ontario. I had a younger sister too, but she died of cancer when she was 41. Through all her difficulties, she was very serene and she took things really well. Both of my brothers, Cathal and Kevin have passed away. I never knew my grandparents and my parents never mentioned them. I used to have a lot of relatives in and around the Point, but not any more. A lot of them left for Ontario and western Canada.

When I was born the family was at 801 Charon but we moved to 2722 Rozel. That is the place I lived in until I got married. Our flat on Rozel wasn't very big. We had a living room and kitchen on the main floor and two bedrooms at the top of the stairs. All of the children slept in one room. The three boys slept in one three-quarter-sized bed and the two girls had their own bed. We had one bathroom at the top of the stairs and it was very small. I remember that when I broke my leg one year and had a cast on it, I couldn't sit down and close the door at the same time. Mary's situation was similar. There were five children in Mary's family, four boys and Mary. They all slept in one bedroom too.

During the depression my father hauled stone by horse-drawn wagon to build roads. After things got a little better he got a job at Northern Electric, and that is where he stayed until he retired. I'd say he was there for around 40 years. He rose over the years to be a production

Paddy's Charon Street building. 2014.

Paddy's Rozel Street home. 2104.

manager. A big part of Northern's business was manufacturing various kinds of wire for communications. Many of the products had to be covered by rubber. My father would oversee this process. He'd make sure things were running smoothly and ensure the quality of the wrapping processes.

My father always worked the night shift at the Northern. My mother worked nights too and I hated that. She used to clean offices. My father typically worked from 11:00 at night until around 8:00 in the morning. Then he would go across the street to Sauvé's Tavern, have a few beers, come home and go to bed. Everybody in the Point knew Sauvé's. It wasn't open to the public in the morning, but they'd open the doors for their good customers.

When we were growing up my parents had a hard time making ends meet. They pulled enough together to be able to send my older brother to Catholic High School. It was a private institution that cost $10 a month. I remember my father telling me he was sorry he couldn't afford to send me as well. I told him not to worry about it and I just did what I could in the way of jobs when I was young to try and help out. I had many jobs over the years when I was going to school and some of them were very physically demanding.

One summer when I was in my teens I worked at the Redpath Sugar Refinery alongside the Lachine Canal. My job was to pick up 60 lb. bags of sugar from inside the refinery, load them on my shoulder, then carry them about 50 feet or so and stack them inside railway freight cars for shipment. I did this all day. That was a very hard job. I used to come home at night, eat and fall

Paddy Duffy (fifth from the right, back row) and the rest of the Canon O'Meara hockey team. HNS on the game jerseys represents the St. Gabriel Holy Name Society. 1951.

into bed by around 7:00 p.m. My mother would say, "What's wrong?" I was just exhausted. Then I'd be up the next morning to do it all over again.

I had a similar job with an ice delivery company for a while. This was in the days when most people in the Point didn't have refrigerators. We used to deliver big blocks of ice to people for their iceboxes. I would say they weighed between 30-40 lbs. You'd have a piece of rubber on one shoulder and one rubber glove that the company would give you. You'd hike the ice-block on the one shoulder and go. In the Point there are a lot of three-storey walk-ups. They're all over the place. The guy I was working with at the start says to me, "OK, you're responsible for taking the blocks up any stairs". I told him we'd share that role or I was gone. We shared the stairs.

Another job I had for a while was helping demolish old buildings. That was very difficult too. I remember helping to demolish the building that stood right where the current RCMP building is up near Atwater.

I also worked stocking shelves at Thrift's, the grocery shop on Wellington Street, and I spent some time at Sterling Teas and Coffee. I used to mix different brands of teas for places like Steinberg's. We were never short of tea or coffee at our place when I worked there.

I went to Canon O'Meara School in the Point for all of my education. I didn't really like school very much. I enjoyed playing hockey and other sports a lot more than studying. I just wasn't interested in academics. After I finished grade seven and would normally have moved on to another school, Canon O'Meara extended their program by another two years. I decided to just stay there. After that, I went to work full time.

We had some good times at Canon O'Meara. The Presentation Brothers also ran two other schools that weren't too far away, so we used to play sports against them. The kids in the school pushed the Brothers hard to integrate as much sports as possible into the life of the school. The Brothers used to organize skating parties for us as well, and we would bring our girlfriends over on Friday nights. They would have hot chocolate and doughnuts ready for us. It was a lot of fun.

Frank Hanley's son went to Canon O'Meara at the same time and that was when Frank was a pretty important guy in the Montreal scene, especially in our area. Frank's son would get us free movie tickets and things like that. Frank owned a big garage at that time too, and Frank's son would arrange for a vehicle to come and pick us all up and take us swimming.

From time to time there would be fistfights in the schoolyard between O'Meara boys. If the two were caught by any of the Brothers they would immediately be taken downstairs to the basement of the school and each given a pair of boxing gloves. Brother Iraenus was the Principal and he was a very straightforward guy. He would oversee the continuation of the fight. When it was over he'd have the two shake hands. I found myself in the basement a couple of times. Brother Iraenus was one of the people I looked up to at the school. So was Brother Borromeo. He looked after the choir and was in charge of our entertainment, like skating parties.

When I was growing up in the Point each street had its own group of kids that hung around together. When you would have a street hockey game or something like that it would usually pit one street against another. We'd use frozen horse manure for pucks. In those days there weren't very many cars on the street. Our area was on Charon, from Wellington to Coleraine. We used to play baseball on the streets as well. We often played on the corner of Coleraine and Liverpool and that led to broken windows on a number of occasions.

We'd swim in the Lachine Canal all the time too. Obviously we weren't supposed to, but we didn't care. The police would come and try to get us out but we had a system worked out. We'd hide our clothing in the lumberyards beside the canal and then jump in wearing our underwear. If we saw the police approaching from one side of the canal we'd just ignore them and swim over to the other side. Then if we'd see them coming over to the other side, we'd cross back over and so on.

The relationship between the people of the Point, Griffintown and Goose Village was good. There were never any real issues between the three areas. Many of the kids ended up in the same schools. My wife, Mary, for example, went to St. Ann's Girls' School in Griffintown, and there was always lots of intermarriage between the communities. Two of my own siblings married Villagers.

What could lead to trouble in the Point when we were younger, though, was if groups like what we used to call the West End crowd would come into the Point and start stirring things up. This was a very hard group of guys that lived across the canal just north of Little Burgundy around the Saint Antoine area and points farther west out toward the lower Westmount/Greene

One of the buildings that housed Paddy's past employer (Northern Electric) looms over today's Fine Pointe Restaurant on Centre Street. 2011.

Avenue areas. Incidents with them didn't happen all the time but one that people still remember was at one of the dances in the Point on a Friday night. One thing led to another and there was a very big fight outside. There were probably about 40 people involved in that.

In those days in the Point there were no guns involved, and only in the very rarest of circumstances would you hear of a situation involving a knife. Back then in the Point it was fists and boots, and every now and then you'd have to defend yourself in the streets. I remember one day I came home and I had a big black eye and cut nose. My father just took one look at me and said—"Well, you must have deserved it". Another time, a guy I knew jumped me from behind on the way home at night. I didn't see him coming and I don't know why he did it. I don't know if he even knew it was me that he hit when he started it, but he certainly knew after it was over.

Anybody that you talk to from our generation will always talk about the Victoria Day fires in the Point. My mother would say, "Well, we are going to need some coal soon". And I'd say, "Don't worry". My friends and I would decide on a time and go over to the coal yard. It wasn't too far from our house, but they always had a big guard dog there. We'd pick the fastest guy in our bunch at the time and send him over the fence to start yelling to distract the dog. While he was engaging the dog, we'd hop the fence and throw coal over for the Victoria Day fires.

People got very creative at those fires. One of the things that people did was to grease the wooden hydro poles at the side of the roads with the same stuff used to grease car wheels. When these poles were set on fire, the whole thing would go up. I can even remember a situation involving the Fire Department one year when someone grabbed an axe off the fire engine and axed the fire hoses.

For a lot of the boys of my generation, what was really important to us was a place called the 79th Battery. It was a federal armory on the corner of Congregation and Wellington. It is no longer there now. It doubled as our Boys' Club for the Point. It really had a lot to offer the boys of the Point up until about the age of 17, and even after that they had a teens-and-twenties room upstairs. When I was 15 or so I served as a leader at the Battery and helped out with the younger kids. We would take them on picnics or on different outings like to the chocolate factory in Griffintown. We'd also take them to the beach.

Paddy Geary was the general manager at the 79th Battery. He was Bob Geary's father. The Gearys were very active and very well known in the Point. Bob was my age and a star football player who eventually made the *Alouettes*. He went on to be an executive with the club after he finished playing. I played with Bob on some football teams over the years. He was very, very tough. When we had dances at the 79th Battery, Bob and I were usually the monitors. There was no drinking inside at those dances so we'd monitor that. We also knew who the troublemakers were. So we had to keep an eye out for them.

Bob was as tough off the field as on it. I remember, in particular, one situation when Bob was a little older. He was in a bar at closing time and there were three Italian guys there. The four of them were the only ones left in the bar. For some reason, they locked the door from the inside so that Bob couldn't get out and they beat the hell out of him. When we all found out about this we were angry as hell, but Bob just said, "…nobody does anything. Just leave this to me". We did. Bob waited his time and, one by one, he found those guys and settled the score.

Hymie Rothstein was deeply involved as an organizer with the 79th Battery. He was about ten years older than us. His family was from the Point and they were quite well off. They owned

Bob Geary. Date unknown.

some businesses in the Point. Hymie had served in the Navy and he played on the Navy football team. He was instrumental in starting a juvenile football team in the Point. Hymie acquired the equipment and he was the head coach for the team. Lorne Dixon was the assistant coach.

I played on his team. So did Bob Geary and many more of my friends. It was my first real exposure to the game of football and it became very important to me. It was a good team and we did very well. Almost all of the players on the team were from the Point. I still see some of them from time to time.

After playing for Hymie, I went on to play for the Verdun Shamcats Juniors for a couple of years, then to the Lakeshore Alouette Flyers out in the West Island. It was a senior team. Moving to senior was a difficult transition because I was still quite young by the standards of that team. But I stuck with it and did fine. The Flyers played in what was called the "Little Big Four". The Canadian (professional) Football League had two divisions at the time; the Western division and the Eastern division. The Eastern division was called the Big Four (Montreal, Hamilton, Ottawa and Toronto). Each one sponsored a team in the "Little Big Four". We represented the *Alouettes*. The idea was to develop players that had the potential for the pros. It only lasted a short time. Hamilton couldn't afford a team.

We won the Dominion Senior Championship with the Lakeshore Alouette Flyers in 1959. Herb Trawick was the coach. He was a wonderful person and I learned a great deal from him. In 2009 we decided to have a reunion in Montreal of former Flyer players and coaches. It was very successful. And for those that live in the Montreal area, we still meet every three months for lunch at the Capri Tavern on St. Patrick Street in the Point.

Herb Trawick Park is in Little Burgundy, a five-minute walk from Point St. Charles. 2012.

In 1961 when I was playing for the Verdun Shamcats senior team we also won the senior Canadian championship. In the championship game we were down with just a few minutes left in the game. I have never been shy to speak my mind and I remember suggesting that we try and change things up by switching quarterbacks. The switch was made. We rallied and won the game.

I was invited to try out for the pros with the Montreal *Alouettes* one year and it was a good experience. Perry Moss was the coach of the *Alouettes* at the time. I played for them in the exhibition season and made the trip out to Calgary and Vancouver. I was released from the *Alouettes* when I got back to Montreal, but I guess the Edmonton Eskimos must have seen or heard something they liked. They called and made me an offer. I asked them how much they would pay me and they said $2,500. Mary and I were married by then. We thought it over, but by that time I was established at Northern Electric. We came to the decision that, overall, it wouldn't be worth it, so I passed and decided to stick with Northern and go into coaching football. The kids in the Point needed the support, as well, so that is what I did.

I played football until I was 26. My mother never missed a game. She was always there, but my father didn't come to watch. He played a little lacrosse, himself but was never really interested in sports that much. He always worked night shifts at the Northern.

I usually worked the night shift at the Northern too, so that worked out fine as far as my interests in coaching. I coached for many years, starting out at mosquito and moving up to juvenile, which I really enjoyed. Most of the time I coached Leo's Boys teams in the Point and the majority of boys I coached were from the Point. I always made sure to play each and every one of my players. Once in a while parents would come to me complaining that their son should be doing this or that. I just used to politely tell them that everybody played equally on my teams, and if they weren't satisfied they should look elsewhere.

I always found it very rewarding to watch these young players grow as they learned the game. I coached two juvenile teams to national championships—one in 1964 and the other in 1966. Ken Dixon was the head coach of the 1964 team and I was the head coach of the 1966 team. When the 1966 team returned to Montreal after the game, we were given a parade down Wellington Street in the Point. Keating Ford supplied the team with convertibles. I still receive

Canadian National Railway shed. 1929.

letters or messages from some of the players I coached. When I was inducted into the Point St. Charles Hall of Recognition for my coaching efforts I felt very honoured.

For a while I also helped out coaching at Loyola College. That's Concordia University now. One year they asked me to be the head coach of their junior varsity team and I enjoyed that.

In those days the Point's Amateur Athletic Association took over most of the administration and management of amateur sports for people over the age of 19. This was a very active association too. There was a senior football team from the Point, as well, and it had some very good players on it like "Bucky" Buchanan, Jim Montgomery and Billy Killen. There was no age limit for that team. Billy Killen became a coach too, and he was very popular.

As I said before, the 79th Battery was a big part of our life during my time in the Point. It offered us a lot. But another important facility for the young people of my generation was the Grand Trunk Boating Club. It was just across the border from the Point in Verdun on the other side of the underpass at Butler Street. You turned left for a very short distance after the underpass

Paddy Duffy (left) with many of the players he coached for the 1964 National Juvenile Football Championship. (Point St. Charles Hall of Recognition induction) 2013.

and you were at the water. They had a very successful competitive racing program there in paddling. I was a member and used to pay my annual dues by putting the wharves in the water in the spring and removing them in the fall. My specialty was war canoe racing and my position in the boat was in what's called the "motor". That means the middle of the boat. I was also on the juvenile and senior *Dominion Championship* teams with Grand Trunk in the 'fifties. It was a good place. We had a large hall on the second floor for dances and get-togethers and we had a snack bar in a separate building.

The Boating Club was close to what was referred to at the time as "Shit Creek". It was a stream that carried some of the effluent from Verdun to the St. Lawrence River. We had some outdoor toilets at the time at the Boating Club and they were right beside the creek. I remember a gang of us was there one day and one of my friends was busy in the toilet. Let's just say for the record that the toilet slipped into Shit Creek while he was inside. After the yelling died down and he climbed out we used a hose to spray him down.

When I was a young adult in the Point jobs were plentiful. You could work at the Northern, the Canadian National Railway, or Belding Corticelli, as my wife Mary did. And there were lots of other places. It wasn't difficult to find work.

Manufacturing - Electric

2187

Unidentified employee making cable at the Northern Electric plant in Montreal. Date unknown.

My father offered to get me a job at the CN as an electrician trainee when I left school. I thought that was a good idea so I said OK. Well, what actually happened was that I was cleaning the grease pits under where the locomotives were serviced in the railyards so I said no way for that and quit. My dad wasn't happy, but that was it! Then he got me fixed up at Northern and things went really well. I stayed there for 39 years and I did many different jobs. For most of my career I was a production manager. The Northern typically moved people around every two years or so. We learned our trades inside out at the Northern. I worked at the Shearer Street plant in the Point, as well as the Lachine installation and the Connor Building, which was also in the Point. It wasn't far from where the old Arrawana Social Club was located. And, by the way, the Arrawana was a very tough place!

We worked hard growing up in the Point. But I can remember wondering when I got married if I would be able to provide the level of support that I wanted to.

79th Battery (Point St. Charles) juvenile champion football team. Paddy is the third player seated from the right in the first row. 1952.

Mary and I saved as much as we could. Before we even got married we had saved enough to buy all our furniture. Other than the mortgage on our triplex here in LaSalle we have never had a debt. And we paid off the mortgage in ten years.

Today, I remain very much connected to the Point and to the people I grew up with. Mary and I attend church services at St. Gabriel's and there is a group of about 20 of us from the Point that remain very close. We all go out for lunch in Verdun after Sunday Mass. We have a table reserved every week. We attend dances and other social events with our old friends from the Point as well.

`I have five old colleagues from the Northern that I get together with for lunch every second Friday at the Greenstop in Châteauguay. I also enjoy our Dominion Championship football get-togethers every three months at the Capri.

These are the people we grew up with. We did not have a lot when we were growing up, but we made our own fun. We had a wonderful social life. Sometimes we would go to three or four dances a week at places like the 79th Battery or the Polish Hall. We still remain very close.

What is most memorable for me about the Point?…the friendships I made—the lifelong friendships.

Looking out from "the Northern" over St. Patrick Street, the Redpath complex, the Lachine Canal and on to downtown Montreal. One wing of "the Northern" is visible on the right. 2013.

This photo was taken from the old Northern Electric Company building where Paddy worked. It looks west across Point St. Charles. The steeples of St. Charles Church stand out at the centre of the photo. St. Gabriel Church is located just to the other side of St. Charles. 2012.

"Belding Corticelli

was a very well-known company.

The symbol for the company was a kitten

playing with a bobbin of thread

and it was well known too.

When Belding Corticelli

went under

it was a difficult time

for the people that worked there."

Mary Duffy

Mary Duffy
nee Burton

Mary Duffy grew up in Point St. Charles and worked at Belding Corticelli Ltd in the Accounting and Payroll departments from 1966 until 1983 when the company went out of business. For decades, the company had been an important employer in Montreal's southwest. In a short publication entitled The Belding Corticelli Story, which covers the history of the company until the year 1951, George Stevens summarizes 74 years of the company's activities. He describes how the Belding Paul & Company, as it was established in Montreal in 1877, was an offshoot of the efforts of three Belding Brothers from the United States. The focus of the enterprise was the silk trade and a broad range of related goods such as ribbons. And as Mary explained to me, the company became very well known for women's full-fashioned stockings/ hosiery.

"I was one of the last people to leave the factory when it finally shut down. My last job was to make sure all of the final payroll actions were completed."

The property has since been converted into condos (Les Lofts Corticelli). It stands as a Point St. Charles landmark and is located on the south bank of the Lachine Canal beside the historic St. Gabriel Locks. The buildings' north-side windows overlook the canal as well as the City and it sits next to two other historic locations: the old Redpath Sugar site and the iconic Northern Electric Company Ltd. building (the "Northern").

Photo: 2012.

I was born in 1934 and I grew up in the Point. I lived on Sebastopol Street until I was 21 and got married. Our house was just a two-minute walk from the entrance to the CN Railway yards. Every day, when the workers from CN finished their shifts, they would come streaming up our street and joke with us as we all played and watched them go past.

My parents and grandparents were both from Montreal but our family history goes back to England and Ireland. My grandmother on my mother's side was a Geary and that's a pretty well known Irish name in the Point. I had two older brothers and two younger brothers and all of them were boxers.

Row housing on Sebastopol Street not far from where Mary grew up in the Point. Several of these renovated row houses show murals depicting the history of the adjacent railyards. 2013, 2011.

I went to Jean Leber School for grades one-four. We received our instruction from nuns from the Congregation of Notre Dame, and also from some lay teachers. At that time the school had English and French students. The English girls studied in English and the French girls in French. Things changed after I finished grade four, though. The school was designated French only. The English children had a choice: study in French at Jean Leber, or switch to either St. Gabriel's in the Point, or St. Ann's in Griffintown. I chose St. Ann's because the teachers there were also nuns from the Congregation of Notre Dame. It was almost a 30-minute walk to school in Griffintown, and I did it four times a day, because I'd hurry home for lunch. We had no cafeteria at St. Ann's.

I went to St. Ann's until I finished grade nine and then moved on to Business College. My first job was with a printing company over in Saint-Henri. Then, when we had our only child, I took six years off to stay home and care for her. When my daughter started going to school I decided to go back to work and I was offered a job at Belding Corticelli. Most of the people that worked at Belding were from the Point, Griffintown and Goose Village. There were also a few people from Verdun.

I started work on January 31, 1966. My pay at the time was $240 per month. I was well trained in Business College and I worked in Accounting and Payroll. Compared to some of the factories along the canal, Belding Corticelli was a very clean and safe place to work. At that time our installation was still focusing on various kinds of ribbon, thread, hemming material and things of that nature.

In 1966 Belding was one of the smaller factories in the Point. When I went to work there the company had already been in operation for a very long time and I was one of only a very few young people there. It was definitely an older workforce by that time. But I do remember that some young people would come to Belding to acquire some initial experience and then use it as a stepping-stone to move on to one of the much larger operations like the Northern. I decided to stay at Belding.

Top left: A variety of products showing the two names Belding, and Corticelli. 2012.

Top right: Northwest across the Lachine Canal from the old Northern Electric building. Centre is the old Belding Corticelli factory. The foreground shows the ongoing development of the Northern site ("Le Nordelec"). 2013.

Bottom left: Looking south across the Lachine Canal toward Point St. Charles and the condo that once housed Mary's employer, Belding Corticelli. 2012.

Bottom right: Looking south across the canal and the St. Gabriel Lock to "Lofts Corticelli". The tall brick structure to the left is one of the wings of the old Northern Electric building. 2012.

I would say that for most of the time I was at Belding Corticelli there would have been between 300-400 people working there, but the variety and amount of items produced wasn't what it was in the company's heyday. By the time I had started at the company, the east end of the Lachine Canal was already closed and marine traffic was considerably less than what it had been in the past. I remember that we used to sit on the banks of the canal in front of Belding on nice summer days and eat our lunch. It was very pleasant, but we didn't see the number or variety of ships that we used to see when we were children.

I spent 17 years at Belding until it finally went bankrupt in 1983. In fact, I was one of the last people to leave the factory when it finally shut down. My last job was to make sure all of the final payroll actions were completed. Belding Corticelli was a very well-known company. The symbol for the company was a kitten playing with a bobbin of thread and it was well known too.

This once-busy railway property sits adjacent to Sebastopol Street. 2011.

Looking south down Sebastopol Street toward the once-bustling Canadian National Railway shops of Point St. Charles. 2013.

When Belding Corticelli went under it was a difficult time for the people that worked there. When I started at Belding, the company had just initiated a pension plan. We had the choice as to whether or not we wished to participate. My husband and I thought it over but decided to opt out as he already had a plan in place at the Northern. Other people working at Belding signed up when the program started, but unfortunately they lost their pension when the company went bankrupt. At that time, some of the people at the company had been there for 50 years.

Mary and Paddy Duffy at St. Gabriel's Church Hall. 2013.

"I can't put an exact number on it,

but many of the Italians from the Village,

I'd say around 40% or so

worked at the Point St. Charles railyards.

All my uncles worked there

and so did my grandfather.

And then of course,

a lot worked in construction.

There were different kinds of trades people

like plasterers and electricians.

We also had some experienced coal miners.

They would get jobs at Dominion Coal

near the Village."

Linda Frainetti

Linda Frainetti

Linda lived in Goose Village from 1949, when she was two, until the Village was destroyed. Linda has spearheaded three separate reunions of Goose Village residents. Forty-seven years ago, when Goose Village was about to be demolished there were about 400 families in the community, yet 258 people attended the last reunion in 2001. They came from places as far away as Vancouver.

Linda and her husband, Ron, currently reside on a quiet, tree-lined street in St. Hubert, Quebec, just a short distance from Montreal.

Photo: Linda at home. 2011.

"The people in Goose Village cared about each other, and they helped each other. If I ever needed help in the Village there was always someone there. The closeness was really indescribable. I have never seen anything that compares with this in other communities."

I was born in Montreal at the Reddy Memorial in 1947. I lived on 2nd Avenue in Verdun for two years, then we moved to 179 Menai Street in Goose Village. I have five sisters and two brothers. I am the second oldest. I have one son and three grand-children. They live in Ville Émard.

My grandparents came to Canada from Presidio Italy, where apparently there is a monument for a Frainetti, but I haven't seen it. My grandfather married Octavia Todi. She died in 1949 and that was when we moved to the Village on Menai Street with my Grandfather. My grandparents lived on Grand Trunk in the Point before they moved to the Village.

He raised goats right in the Village. He kept them in the small backyard. Since there was no grass to speak of in the Village, he used to walk them up to the Dyke on Riverside to feed them. There was also some grass up near Bridge and Wellington where they could eat as well. So you'd see him walking through the Village with his goats.

My father's name was Joseph Frainetti. He was known as Pepe. He was born in 1917. He worked seasonally in construction early on. He was a plasterer. He used to commute to Ottawa for work. He'd leave on Sunday night and come back on Friday. Eventually he got a maintenance job at the Royal Bank up at the Place Ville Marie and he stayed there until he retired. My mother didn't work outside the house. She volunteered at the Victoriatown Boys' and Girls' Club.

On Menai Street we had a two-storey house. On the main floor we had the parlor, the dining room and the kitchen. Upstairs, we had the bathroom and three bedrooms—the big one for the girls, the medium-sized one for my parents, and the small one for my brother Eric.

Baby Linda. 1948.

Left: Linda's grandfather, Gaetano. 1929.
Right: Grandmother Octavia (Todi) holding Linda's sister, Sandra. 1948.

My first husband was killed in the Bluebird Café Fire in Montreal in 1972. After the fire, my mother looked after my son when I was working. Thirty-seven people were killed in that fire and 54 people were injured. It just seems like that fire has been forgotten. The site is a parking lot now. We held our own memorial on September 1, 2011. Some work is being done now with the City of Montreal to try and get a monument of some sort on the site. One hundred and forty-five people have signed a petition already. The response from the City has been quite positive.

Until grade three I went to St. Alphonsus School in the Village. Then I went on to St. Ann's Girls' School in Griffintown. After that I went to high school at St. Patrick's up near the Cathedral. I went to Verdun Catholic High School for a while too after the Village was torn down. I wanted to take the secretarial course at Verdun but they told me I couldn't. They wanted me to study biology so I just left school after grade ten.

I started working part time at Lovell's Directory in Old Montreal in 1962. It was a summer job. In 1964 when I was at Verdun Catholic for a while I worked at the Royal Victoria Hospital from 4:00 p.m. until 8:00 p.m. every day. I was a dietician's aid. I always tried to look after the patients really well and make sure they all had their helpings of the various types of food they were supposed to get, and I always would ask if they'd like a tea or something like that. Sometimes the nurses would get upset with me, telling me that everything was so hectic I didn't have time to be getting people tea, but I kept doing it anyway.

When I lived in the Village we had one gas station. It was on the corner of Bridge and Britannia. It changed into a restaurant called Norman's and it became our "Fonzie"-type place. In the Village, it seemed like there were small establishments of some sort on every street corner. I remember once I counted 15. We had a hardware store, and lots of corner groceries, beer stores, candy stores and the like. Some of the ones I remember are: Piché's Grocery, John's Beer store and Dépanneur, Pace's candy store (where they played bocce in the back yard area), Rotella's Pizza which was owned by the Gagliardi brothers, Salvatore's, which sold things like ice cream and candy. He made it into a small restaurant too. I remember it had two booths and six stools; Arciero's Grocery, and the Bridge Restaurant.

Why were there so many corner stores in the Village? I'll tell you why. There were 385 families living in Goose Village and there wasn't much money. People in the Village lived from paycheck to paycheck during the week and the small corner stores gave credit.

My Dad, like others, worked seasonally and it was very difficult financially. Our rent was $44 a month. Sometimes we couldn't make our payments at the grocery store or the rent. In those situations my Dad would tell me to "Go tell Toncia at the store", or "Go over to the landlord's and tell him that I can't put anything down this week". It was always me that he sent. My father had to kind of balance things between the two stores we went to for our groceries, and the landlord. In those days, you ate everything that was put down before you. To this day I cannot stand shepherd's pie.

In those days the flats had coal heating: a big pot bellied stove stood in the hallway of our flat. It had large round ducts that ran across the ceiling sending the heat to the different rooms.

School days. 1954.

My father and I would take apart all these ducts regularly and knock out all the soot to clean them out. It was a big job. Sometimes we would even paint the ducts, and we used to paint the flat regularly as well. Before we had parties my mother would have us wash all the walls. We did "spring" cleaning twice a year. Nobody would come in unless the house was to my mother's delight. We cleaned all the time. For cooking we had a wood-fired stove. I remember I was told one day to start the fire, but I had never really been taught how. I burned myself in the stomach with a hot ember that day.

At school the girls all wore tunics and blouses. A day for us would involve going to school, always coming home for lunch, then going back to school. If we finished our homework right after school we were allowed to go to the Victoriatown Boys' and Girls' Club where we had a lot of activities we could take part in. The Club had a gym and we played shuffleboard, floor hockey, soccer and dodgeball. We had an arts and crafts room and a woodworking shop as well. After supper, we were allowed out for one hour.

In the Village the kids were always occupied and busy. There were always lots of activities in the Village. We used to have dances at the Boys' and Girls' Club, and in the summer we would have things like street dances. My cousin had a band and they would play '50s and '60s music. We also used to have soapbox derbies. You had to completely build the derbies from scratch with old carriage wheels etc. One person steered and another person pushed the derby. The

Norman Snack Bar at the corner of Bridge and Britannia. 1964.

Boys' and Girls' Cub also had bus trips for us. They would take us to the Lowney's Chocolate Factory or to St. Helen's Island and things like that. I remember getting lost on the St. Helen's Island trip once and I got a good smack on the head for that one.

Halloween in the Village was something else too. Mrs. Hart used to make the best taffy apples and give them away. I can remember the girls dressing up as hobos and the boys dressing up as girls. They used potatoes in bras. Some of the guys made pretty good-looking women!

At Christmas-time everybody went out to visit around the Village. And, regardless of age, you couldn't leave an Italian's house without a glass of wine—just a small one for the kids. Easter, Christmas, it was always the same. We'd visit. We took the time.

Village kids used to go to dances and things like that in Griffintown and the Point. Things were fine between the three neighborhoods. We used to go to the dances at the Griffintown Boys' and Girls' Club on Ottawa Street. We got along fine. But the Goose Village girls were not allowed to date boys from outside the village. And if an outsider came into the village, say from Verdun, to take out a girl he could get the dickens beat out of him. And in some cases there would be other trouble with groups from farther out again, like Verdun. In those cases the guys from the Point and the Village would join forces against Verdun.

We also had some fights within the Village itself between boys that lived there. The best fight I ever saw was just outside my window. Girls weren't supposed to see fights in those days but I went upstairs and looked out the window. This was something else. It was between two people I knew. Those two stood toe-to-toe and exchanged blows one after the other. It was a real knock down, drag out affair. There was no phony-baloney stuff here like you see on TV today; just blow after blow. But, you know, when it was all over, they just shook hands. We had a lot of razing and fighting in the village, but we always shook hands.

Top left: John's Licensed Groceteria. Right: Pizza Rotella. Bottom left: Dominico Pace Restaurant. c. 1963.

I couldn't put an exact number on it but I know that in the end, a lot of Goose Village, Griffintown and Point kids ended up marrying into each other's neighborhoods. A lot!

We had some real characters in the Village. I remember Philip Tamburino; he was always absolutely dressed to the nines and he always had the most beautiful car. I remember one of the guys our age got so drunk once he passed out on the sidewalk, and when he woke up his friends had shaved his head completely bald and covered his face with black shoe polish. Another was always in some sort of trouble somewhere or another. I also remember a girl about three years older than me; she was a real scrapper—came from another big family. She was always fighting, literally! What the guys could do, she could do. Another friend of mine once went to the stock-yards beside the Village and somehow managed to get a cow out; he took it over to someone's house, sneaked it into their backyard and left it.

I remember Muriel Pierson Clahane too; she was a very beautiful woman with a very beautiful voice to match. She would start sing-alongs either outside the front of their house or in their back yard. Others would just join in. It was a lot of fun. Actually, anybody could start one. It could just take someone bringing out an accordion or another musical instrument.

There were a number of people I looked up to when I was growing up in the Village and then later on going to school in Griffintown. Sister St. Columbus was one. She was the Principal

Left: Piche's grocer and butcher on the corner of Bridge and Forfar. Right: Salvatore Snack Bar. c. 1963.

at St. Alphonsus and then at St. Ann's Girls' School. She was stern but she was also very fair. You could talk to her. Sister St. John taught grade six at St. Ann's Girls' School in Griffintown. Never have I seen a nun like that. She loved to drink Coke; only one I ever saw that drank Coke. We'd argue over who could bring her a Coke. We would take turns. We'd arrive with a Coke and it would make her so very happy. We just loved to see the gleam in her eye when we'd bring her a Coke. Sister Irma was another person I really looked up to. She was at St. Pat's. She grabbed my attention and really made me want to learn. She was another person that you could sit down and talk to.

At the Victoriatown Boys' and Girls' Club I really respected Joe Berlettano. He was similar to what you would call a social worker today. He was a volunteer in the Village working for the Catholic Services. He was a very deeply-rooted person in the Village. He was our landlord's son. Leo Roberts was another person I really liked. He worked at the Boys' and Girls' Club too. He was the boxing and hockey coach.

When I lived in the Village I don't remember any Protestants at all. I think everyone was Catholic—the Italians the Irish, the French. There must have been French people in the Village because quite a few came to the reunions, but to be honest I don't remember meeting any in my time there. And when I met my second husband, Ron, from Verdun, he told me he was a Protestant. I remember telling him he'd have to teach me all about it because I didn't really know anything about the faith.

For me, the Lachine Canal was just a great big dump. I bike along it now that it has been fixed up, but back then it was just a dump! We had several drownings but many of the people from Goose Village learned to swim in that Canal, my brother included. He was a real daredevil and he almost drowned. I saw him jump in the canal and he didn't know how to swim at the time. He went up and down several times and eventually grabbed a log. That is the way some of the kids learned to swim.

Benedict Labre House. "...a home for the homeless, a refuge for those in need". 2012, 2011.

My brother was also mad about pigeons and he used to feed the pigeons in the Ogilvie Flour Mill. He'd sneak inside and climb up the wall ladders to where the pigeons were and that's where he would feed them. I used to fight with my brother all the time. I remember one Christmas he got boxing gloves. I looked at my Dad and asked him where mine were. He bought me some and my brother and I would go at it. We'd mark off a ring in the back yard. I think one of my biggest challenges growing up in the Village was learning to be a girl! I didn't like sports in general but I loved boxing.

I can't put an exact number on it, but many of the Italians from the Village, I'd say around 40% or so worked at the Point St. Charles railyards. All my uncles worked there and so did my grandfather. And then of course, a lot worked in construction. There were different kinds of trades people like plasterers and electricians. We also had some experienced coal miners in the Village. They would get jobs at Dominion Coal near the Village.

The other thing that Italian families would do in the Village to make ends meet was to rent out rooms. My grandfather did this before we moved in with him. They would sponsor a person from Italy. It would work like this. First of all, a person coming from Italy would pay dues to be sponsored and then they'd pay rent to the sponsor. The sponsored person would then work and save enough money to bring his family over from Italy. Personally, I think that that is how the Village transformed into such a heavily Italian community, because part of the deal and understanding was that the person being sponsored would do the same thing for someone else once they got established. Pass it on! These people were smart enough to live together, work together, pay their dues, buy property and then pass it on.

Inside a Goose Village corner store. c. 1963.

When the Village was torn down it was difficult to find places to live. We left in 1963 and went to Verdun. Our landlord didn't like having such a big family, though, so he asked us to leave after four months. He shouldn't have done that. We found another and bigger place over a horsemeat store. It had four bedrooms.

After I started working, I lived in different places for periods of time. I lived in LaSalle, Verdun and NDG (Notre-Dame-de-Grâce), then settled here in St. Hubert. I worked as a waitress for a number of years then moved to the Royal Bank at Place Ville Marie until I retired.

I took two years off after retirement, then I went to the TD Bank just for a year to help out a friend. Now, I'm a full-time Grandma.

When the Village was destroyed, people were displaced all over, but a lot went to Verdun, LaSalle, the South Shore and St. Michel. There are a lot of Italians in St. Michel. Once everyone vacated the Village, if you were looking for them it was almost like trying to find a needle in a haystack.

I have organized three reunions now of ex-Goose Village residents. The last one was in 2001. It attracted 285 people from as far way as Vancouver and there were less than 400 families in total in the Village. It is a lot of work but we did get a lot of support from Freddy Pine at the St. Ann Society. Without them it would have been a bust and we would have been in the hole about $4500. But as it turned out, we made a profit of $1500, which we donated to the St. Ann Society. It is a benevolent association located in LaSalle and it supports causes like Labre House for the homeless, which is in Griffintown, as well as St. Columba House in the Point, and it is also active with seniors. My husband, Ron, really helped me a lot getting things set up, but I won't be organizing another.

When you look at some of the pictures that were taken of the Village prior to the demolition it looks like a dump, but it wasn't. Look at the pictures of some of these interiors I have of the Village. Everything is neat. Some of the exterior pictures are of back yards where people have their own gardens and clotheslines are full, but we needed a place to dry our clothes.

Looking back, I can tell you that when the Village was destroyed the people that lived there were not *happy campers*. We were all in shock at the beginning. Mostly, I was angry. I did not want to move. We were never consulted. Personally, I miss the closeness and the sense of community. I would have been very happy to stay in Victoriatown and so would many others. It was not a slum. This was a place where you left your door unlocked and never worried about anything. And if anyone did come in you'd ask if they'd like some tea. The people in Goose Village cared about each other, and they helped each other. If I ever needed help in the Village there was always someone there. The closeness was really indescribable. I have never seen anything that compares with this in other communities.

"…we'd go down to the Lachine Canal

and hang around.

We'd watch the ships that came in

from all over the world.

I remember marveling at the ships:

how big they seemed, how rusty they were,

how something that size could navigate the canal.

Although we were not supposed to, we would also

sometimes sneak rides on Black's Bridge

as it swung open for the ships

at the Lachine Canal's first set of locks.

We would be just inches away from the ships!

Sometimes we'd talk to and yell back and forth

at the guys on the ships."

Ed DiZazzo

Ed DiZazzo

Ed lived in the Village between the ages of 5 and 13. He excelled academically, finishing first in his class at St. Ann's Boys' School. Ed then went on to study at Loyola High School, Loyola College and then the University of Ottawa where he earned a Masters degree in Clinical Psychology.

Ed retired from the Public Service of Canada in 2009 after serving for over 30 years. Ed was widely recognized and respected both as a clinical psychologist and senior executive.

Ed now resides on a 25-acre farm with his spouse, Christine. The farm is located in South Mountain, Ontario—40 minutes south of Ottawa. Ed is deeply involved in his community. He is a volunteer board member or member of the executive of five separate community action and service organizations.

Photo: Ed at Griffintown's St. Ann Park. 2011.

"Years later, it finally dawned on me why my memories of Goose Village are so evocative and precious to me now, despite the comparatively short time I spent there. Not only were they important formative years that exposed me to both the power and comfort of community, the Village has become special because, unlike most people who can walk the streets of their old neighborhoods, we Goose Villagers can never go home again. Little did I appreciate when I left, how in the grand scheme of things, just how much significance Goose Village would ultimately have for me."

I was born at the Montreal General Hospital in 1947. I lived on 5th Avenue in Verdun until I was five. We moved to Goose Village at that point. I attended school at St. Alphonsus in Goose Village at first, then St. Ann's Boys' School in Griffintown. When I started high school at Loyola I commuted from the Village for a short time, but soon after that we moved back to Verdun.

My father's name was Anthony DiZazzo and my mother's maiden name was Viola Starnino. My grandmother's name was Annie Geraldi. She came from Caserta Province in Italy and became a Canadian citizen by marriage when she married Edward Starnino.

At first, my grandmother lived in Providence, Rhode Island but then she moved to Canada. I don't know the precise time frame within which she lived in Rhode Island, but I do know that while in the States she worked at French's Mustard. After moving to Canada she and her husband bought a corner store in Goose Village with living quarters above the store. She also owned the duplex in Verdun where I lived until I was five. When we lived in the duplex my parents and grandmother were on the main floor. My great grandmother lived in the finished basement and my uncle and his wife lived upstairs.

Baby Edward. 1947.

My folks split up in 1952 when this was a real rarity in the Italian community. Shortly after that happened I moved to the Village with my grandmother, great-grandmother, and for a while, my father. After the divorce, I kept in regular contact with my parents but was essentially raised by my grandmother. She ran the grocery store with the help of her brother and my uncle.

My mother and father both had stable and lengthy careers in Montreal. My mother worked for Eaton's and my father worked for the Montreal Transit Commission where he started as a bus driver and later became an Inspector. My mother worked initially as an elevator operator at Eaton's and then in the complaints department, working well past the normal retirement age.

My grandfather worked on the docks in Montreal but he died in 1947 of a ruptured spleen. I don't know how he incurred that injury but I remember my grandmother recounting the story of how "everyone in Goose Village" came to give blood.

When I was growing up in the Village I was very fortunate compared to many other kids in the area. I never wanted for any of the basics. I could just go downstairs to the store and help myself to any kind of food I wanted which often included such treats as beans and fried baloney. In a sense, I was rather oblivious to the poverty around me. I remember once when I was very young I was walking to school and met a boy I knew carrying a container of popcorn. I went home that day and asked my grandmother why I never got popcorn to eat with my lunch. She looked at me and said, "Well, maybe that *was* his lunch".

Most of the fathers in the Village were involved in work at various places around Goose Village and the eastern end of the Lachine Canal; the factories, the coal yards, the meat packing plants, the railroad. These were often tiring, hard-labour jobs, and most of the men worked long hours.

We all lived very close together in the Village. It was mostly row houses and flats. In the good weather, you'd see people sitting at their open windows looking out over the street. In the summer, the doors would often be wide open too. No one ever locked their doors. When you were growing up in the Village you'd hear the chatter and the laughter, but you'd also hear the arguments.

Upon reflection, my grandmother was obviously a fairly influential person in the Village. Without a doubt her position as sponsor to many Italians from the old country, storeowner and landlord contributed to her position in the Village. She was kind of like a godmother in the community. People would regularly come to my grandmother, for example, and ask her to pray for them or their relatives. I also remember her talking on the phone for hours to people that

L-R: Ed's grandfather and grandmother Starnino, uncle Florindo (Floyd) and his mother Yolanda, seated. 1937.

L-R: Floyd, grandmother and Yolanda. 1941.

would call for help. She would look into things for them like trying to help them get jobs or navigate a system that spoke no Italian. She would be at the store from early morning until closing and sometimes later. She treated every customer the same way. She was really a person people could talk to. She was kind and helpful at a time when the corner stores like my grandmother's operated on credit and provided all the day-to-day needs of the Villagers. When she died one of the people that cried the most at the funeral was the man who worked for her when he was a delivery boy as a kid. He kept in touch with my grandmother after he moved on from the store, and Christmas would never go by without a phone call from him.

She was also a central figure for all the Starninos, sponsoring many of them to Canada from Italy. The boys came first, then the parents. The extended family was very important to us. We would all visit back and forth with each other on Sundays, and whoever came to visit us always brought homemade treats like fresh bread, pastries, prosciutto, sausages, wine, etc. I remember we were one of the first families in the Village to have a television and our place was a gathering spot for all of the Starnino boys on Saturday nights for the hockey games. They would sit around watching the game and speaking loudly back and forth in Italian. I did not understand a word. Even before the game would end they'd often just fall asleep on the couches and my grand-

Grandmother Starnino's citizenship certificate. 1953.

mother would come and waken them to send them back to their own places in the Village. Many of the Starnino clan started in the Village but most of them moved on to Ahuntsic in the north end of Montreal. They moved on to good careers like electricians, insurance agents, shoemakers and tailors. Their wives typically worked in factories engaged in work like sewing.

I remember, as well, that in the summer it seemed like every Saturday I attended a big wedding with my grandmother. Most of them were Italian, but some were Irish—and most of them were customers of the store. It was as if my grandmother was on everyone's invitee list. I remember these weddings well, including sometimes the fights that would break out after the open bar was in full swing later on in the receptions.

My grandmother sold the store in 1960 and we moved back to Verdun to the duplex. The Goose Village stores at the time all had "black books" to keep track of the credit extended to virtually all Village residents. Normally, you'd sell the black book with the store but my Grandmother did not. Even at the young age that I was, I remember speaking to her about this because there was quite a bit of money involved. She simply said to me that if the people who borrowed money could afford it, they knew where to find her and they'd pay her back, and that is where the conversation ended. She was a very kind person.

When I think of my time spent at the store, and I spent a lot there helping out as best I could, I recognize that it was a pivotal point for me as an observer of human behaviour. I didn't know that this was what I was doing at the time, but it was. My sense now is that watching my grandmother deal with people all day long on a number of fronts including helping them with various personal issues could well have influenced my choice to enter the helping professions as a career.

Growing up in the Village exposed me to different kinds of people that kids in other more affluent areas of Montreal were quite unlikely to meet. I used to do store deliveries for my grandmother and I remember one customer in particular. The property she lived in really wasn't much more than a shanty. She had several young children, and one of the fellows that worked at the coal yard was there a lot. I can still picture him walking over after work covered from head to toe in coal dust. Looking back, its clear that she lived in abject poverty

Grandmother's store, and Ed's home. c. 1963.

and that it had taken a real toll on her life. This lady always had disheveled, stark white hair that stood out. She had a toothless grin and a very pronounced hooked nose. But I was seeing her through the eyes of a child at that time, and didn't really understand the poverty she endured, nor its effects. To me, at that time, her appearance simply seemed witch-like, and it always scared me when I was sent to her house.

There was another person that as kids we used to refer to as the "crazy lady". She would have been about 60 at the time. She had white and brown disheveled hair and she'd pace the sidewalk and street in front of her home wailing loudly and waving her arms about. She was a fixture on Menai Street. I learned later on that she had lost one or more of her sons in the war.

I remember another lady too. She would have been between 30 and 40. She drank all the time and constantly walked around the streets. She was always disheveled too. She chain-smoked and always had a raspy voice and smeared lipstick. She seemed a very kind lady, though, and from a child's eye point-of-view I remember her fondly.

My time in Goose Village from grades one to seven was largely centred around school. I was not a very athletic child, and I also felt some shame at being the only child without either a mother or father at home at that time. But I worked hard and found I was very good in school. I guess you could say it sort of gave me an identity. I really enjoyed excelling in school. I was quiet and I did my work well.

Joe Berlettano was an individual who did have a very positive influence on kids in the village. He was like a social worker at the Victoriatown Boys' and Girls' Club. He took us on field trips and sponsored movies and street dances and did a lot of outreach work in the Village. He was an amazing guy.

Ed in front of one of the north-end openings to the Wellington tunnel, now closed. This tunnel under the Lachine Canal was one of routes for Goose Village children to cross over to school in Griffintown. 2011.

Overall, school, together with the microcosm of life hanging out with friends in the Village, and my time spent at the store was the totality of my life in those years. Goose Village was only three streets deep and four streets wide, but, as kids, we had absolutely everything we needed—schools, playgrounds, a community centre, and friends galore! We were always in groups of three or four. In the summer we were at the playground or at each others' houses, but we had winter sports too. One was what we called "boosting" the #2 bus. Right after fresh snow fell we'd wait for the bus to turn off Bridge Street onto Britannia. As it pulled away from the stop we would run over and grab onto the bumper, scrunch down and slide along in the slick snow in our galoshes. I stopped that habit one winter when I saw a bus drive over the legs of a man who, while exiting from the back door of the bus right outside our store, slipped under the rear wheels unnoticed as the driver pulled away. I vividly recall dozens of men appearing out of nowhere trying to lift the back of the bus off his legs.

Our other winter sport was over at the Dominion Coal yards right beside the Village. If the CN Railway Police didn't drive us away we would scale this literal mountain of snow-covered coal, and using a cardboard box or toboggan, speed down the hill. The danger was less the sharp descent than the abrupt stop that occurred when the toboggan occasionally hit the metal railway tracks at the bottom, sending everyone flying.

When I think about it, I can't believe how zoned-in I was just to the Village. When I was very young, the Lachine Canal was like a fence for us. It was the outer limits—the outlying border that went to someplace else. It was the dividing line between the houses of Goose Village and industry, the machines, the factories, the big city of Montreal. Later on, it became somewhat of an adventure zone. And even when I started going through the Wellington tunnel into Griffin-town for school I did not connect at first that I was going under the Lachine Canal.

Going to St. Ann's, whether it was the girls' school or the boys' school, extended the day for the Goose Village kids. We had to walk to Griffintown or take the bus. On the bus, we had a secret deal with the driver. If we put our hands over the fare-box and pretended to drop in a ticket, he would let us ride for free. There was no school bus and he knew how poor some of the families were in the Village. Everybody knew the bus driver. His nickname was "Flirt". His was one of the shortest bus routes in the city. It would just wind through the Village, over and over, connecting with the buses coming from Griffintown and the Point.

At lunchtime in the Griff during school days we'd often eat at Gleason's. It was a small mom-and-pop diner. Mr. Gleason would let us eat our sandwiches there as long as we bought a coke or something. Then we'd go down to the Lachine Canal and hang around. We'd watch the ships that came in from all over the world. I remember marveling at the ships: how big they seemed, how rusty they were, how something that size could navigate the canal. Although we were not supposed to, we would also sometimes sneak rides on Black's Bridge as it swung open for the ships at the Lachine Canal's first set of locks. We would be just inches away from the ships! Sometimes we'd talk to and yell back and forth at the guys on the ships. I remember that at one time one of my prize possessions was a rubber shrunken head I won by playing the gumball machine in one of the stores. One of the guys on a ship asked if he could see it, so I

Graduation days. The University of Ottawa. 1971.

Left: Loyola College. 1968

threw it to him. He missed it and it fell in the canal. I didn't get it back. Those shrunken heads were a big deal.

Sometimes, at the canal, we would try to catch small fish or "pinheads" in jars. It wasn't easy. I did catch some in a jar once and took them home. I had no pets at the time. I left them on the kitchen counter but they were gone the next morning when I got up. I asked my Grandmother where my jar was and she said, "Oh, was that a jar? I thought it was a glass of water and drank it". I never said a word!

Goose Village had its share of tragedies over the years. One that stands out was the boy who was tunneling into a snow bank on the side of the street to build a fort. As he was tunneling into the huge snowbank, a city snowblower went right through the snow bank and killed him.

I lived in the Village until I was 13, but I don't remember any systemic problems between the Griffintown and Village boys. We got along fine. After we left St. Alphonsus in the village to go to St. Ann's in the Griff, there were already lots of Village boys there ahead of us. From time to time I'd have to take a circuitous route to avoid a couple of kids that were recognized as bullies, but there was no general ongoing friction between the Griff and Village boys at that time. In fact, as we got older, our axis was more or less north and south between the Village and Griffintown. I had no comfort going to the Point, though. The odd time we'd go to Centre Street in Point St. Charles was to catch a movie, or with family to buy clothing, but even at that, most people in Victoriatown made their own clothing. We had a dry goods store in the Village run by Mrs. Grenier that sold everything needed to make clothes.

Ed's grade five class photo at St. Ann's Boys' School in Griffintown. Ed is in the first row, second from the right. 1957–1958.

During my time at St. Ann's Boys' School I was very busy after school. On Tuesdays I helped at the weekly devotions at St. Ann's Church and on Wednesday I was involved in the preparation for the next week's service. The Tuesday devotions at St. Ann's were very popular. Catholics believe profoundly in praying to St. Ann. It was so big at St. Ann's in Griffintown that special buses would bring people in from all over the city so that people could pray directly to St. Ann. I remember that one of my jobs was to ensure that the various pamphlets sold by the church were available to people as they entered the church. You could say I got my first marketing experience at St. Ann's. I used to analyze my pamphlet rack when I arrived on Tuesdays. I'd find the ones I had the most of and weren't selling and then rearrange them to the top of the rack. I'd then tell people as they arrived that these were our top sellers (and they ended up being exactly that)!

When people arrived for devotions they would typically make a donation and light a candle to St. Ann. It seemed like there were 1000 candles, and maybe there were. On Wednesdays my

The bridge in the background is on the site of the old Black's Bridge. Behind that stands the decommissioned "Silo 5" grain elevator. (The Lachine Canal is drained for winter) 2011.

friend and I would return to the church right after school and our job was to take a special little tool and dig out the hardened, melted wax from every single small candle holder, wash them out and reload them with new candles to get them ready for the next week's devotions.

I was also asked to be an altar boy and a member of the choir. It wasn't that I sought out those roles, I think it was more of a leadership development effort on the part of the church. In those days you were essentially picked. I guess with my good grades they saw something. Maybe they thought I'd make a good priest. I don't know. At that time, church was very important to Catholics both in the Village and in Griffintown. Most of the people in the Village were Italian or Irish Catholics, and there were lots of Irish in the Griff. Later on, for many years, I was not involved in church life, but now I have gone full circle. I am active in the local church here in South Mountain, near Ottawa.

As Catholics, Fridays in the Village meant you ate fish. That meant going to Passaretti's, technically known as the Bridge Restaurant because it was on Bridge Street. But we never called stores or restaurants in the Village by names like that. We always referred to them by the surname of the owner—Zaleski's, Diorio's, Kaidas'—and in this case Passaretti's. Their fish and chips were famous. Because the predominantly Catholic community was supposed to abstain from eating meat on Fridays, whole families from around the Village would line up at Passaretti's on that day. They used to have an actual bathtub full of sliced potatoes behind the counter. Mr. Passarretti would reach in, grab a handful and throw them in the fryer. Anybody you talk to from the Village will remember this. I have searched from coast to coast in my travels in Canada for a fish and chips meal that rivaled my memory of that taste, and only a few greasy spoons in New-foundland ever came close to matching it.

We did not have any taverns in the Village. I don't know why. There were places like the Arrawana, a social club, near Victoriatown, and a few taverns in Griffintown, but none in the Village. Since there was no gathering place like a tavern there, maybe that contributed to the fact that on almost every street corner in the Village you'd always find a group of older guys, adults, working men, standing around "shooting the shit" and smoking. What we did have, though, were "Blind Pigs". We had at least three in the Village. I had no clue what they were at first and was intrigued by the name, but I learned later on their real purpose. A woman named Teresa used to come to the store to buy beer for the Blind Pigs. They used to get raided from time to time, but days later would be back in business.

Every now and then Frank Hanley would show up on the street. He was our representative on city council. He was a really colorful character. He'd arrive and start handing out these gold foil coins to the kids. When you took the foil off, it was a piece of bubblegum. It was a big deal when Frank would arrive. He was a real ebullient figure in Montreal.

I graduated from St. Ann's Boys' School in first place and my friend Kenny Kaidas finished close behind me. His parents owned a store near ours. At that time I wanted to go to D'arcy McGee High School with all my other friends. My father was no longer living with us at that time, but Kenny's father encouraged us both to apply for admission to Loyola High School. I had no interest at all but he convinced us to apply. We reluctantly applied and passed the entrance exams. They lasted a full day and they were exhausting. Eventually, with a lot of persuasion, we both agreed to give Loyola a try.

Kenny's father was very supportive. He told us both it was a very good place and that if we tried it for two weeks and did not like it we could go to public school. For the two weeks he took us to Loyola every day on the bus and left us at the door. As it turned out, we soon became comfortable there and made new friends. I really liked Loyola and I stayed there for all of my high school and then continued on at Loyola College for a BA in psychology. After that I went to the University of Ottawa for a Masters in Clinical Psychology.

During the summers at Loyola College I worked at the Douglas Hospital (a psychiatric hospital with some locked wards) in Verdun. After graduation from Ottawa U., I joined the Department of Psychology at the old Ottawa General Hospital for several years, and then settled into a career in the Federal Public Service in Ottawa.

Goose Village taught me the power of community. The isolation of the Village forced an inter-reliance on everybody. Surrounded by the river, the coal yards, the meat packing plant, the railyards and the towering grain mills, they all served to create what was a virtual island save for Bridge Street, which was the only way in or out. There was an "it's just us" feeling in the Village. There were about 350 families living on those few blocks in Goose Village, and it really was quite isolated. Yet, it still had everything you needed. People did not feel enveloped or trapped.

Fish and chips on Friday night at the Bridge Restaurant. c. 1963

I was 13 when I left. I totally missed the significance a couple of years later when I first heard that the Village was slated for destruction. I was at Loyola High School at the time, and that was just about as far away from the Village as you could get and most of my close friends had already moved away from there as well. "Too bad", I thought. "Where will the remaining residents all go? Oh well…OK…, we are going to get a world's fair built on the site!"

Years later, it finally dawned on me why my memories of Goose Village are so evocative and precious to me now despite the comparatively short time I spent there. Not only were they important formative years that exposed me to both the power and comfort of community, the Village has become special because, unlike most people who can walk the streets of their old neighborhoods, we Goose Villagers can never go home again. Little did I appreciate when I left, how in the grand scheme of things, just how much significance Goose Village would ultimately have for me.

At home in South Mountain, Ontario. 2011.

"In the `thirties and `forties

I loved growing up in the Point.

It was a very close-knit community.

You knew so many people.

Extended families were all just a few minutes

walk away from each other.

I had four aunts on my mother's side

and six on my father's side all within a short walk

—Paris Street, Knox, Coleraine, Grand Trunk.

You'd be walking home from school

with some of your cousins

and could just drop in,

or they'd come to your house."

Joe Timmons

Joe Timmons

Joe Timmons grew up in Point St. Charles. Joe and his wife, Cathy, now live in Mille-Isles in Quebec's Laurentian mountains. The beautiful new chalet they built is on the shore of Lac Bec Scie, about an hour north of Montreal.

It is a quiet and peaceful lifestyle, far removed from the challenges and dangers Joe faced after the alarm sounded in one of the fire stations where he worked for over 30 years as a Montreal fire-fighter. Following in his father's footsteps Joe fought some of Montreal's biggest and sometimes tragic fires. Joe retired as a District Chief in 1987.

Photo: Joe representing the Montreal Fire Department at the St. Patrick's Day Parade. 1986.

"From as early as I can remember, all I wanted to do was be a firefighter like my father. We were very close."

I was born in Point St. Charles in 1933. I lived there for 23 years. When I was growing up we lived at various places in the Point. We lived on Knox, Grand Trunk, Mullins, Ryde, Charlevoix and Fortune Street. I have one brother and five sisters, and it seemed like every time my parents had another baby we moved.

My grandfather was born in County Armagh, Ireland. My grandmother was born in County Tyrone. When my grandfather came to Canada he worked at the Lachine Canal. He was the Lockmaster at the St. Gabriel locks. He also worked on Black's Bridge; the old swing bridge located at the bottom of McGill Street at De La Commune. That's the southeast corner of Griffintown. Black's Bridge isn't there anymore. It was replaced with a stationary overpass.

My mother was born in Surrey England. My father was born on Eleanor Street in Griffintown. My father and mother met here in Montreal and got married in 1924. My dad used to tell me about the much earlier days in Griffintown and Point St. Charles. When he was young there were some places where there weren't even any sidewalks, as we know them today. Some of the sidewalks in those days were made of wood. He also talked about how when he was young, people used to keep goats and other animals in Griffintown and the Point.

Another story that my parents told me has always stuck in my mind. Its one that I think speaks in a small way as to how the people lived and looked after each other in the Point. It involved an accident where a young boy was thought to have some glass fragments in his eye. A woman, not

Joe Timmons Sr., Montreal Fire Department. 1927.

his mother, rushed over and took a look. She couldn't see any pieces of glass but suspected there may be some very tiny fragments in the eye. She held the youngster's eye open and gently licked the eyeball. As it turned out the child was OK. This would have been almost 100 years ago now. Maybe what she did was something people learned to do at that time in situations of eye injuries. But it's an example of what people will tell you about the area. In the Point, Goose Village and the Griff we looked out for each other, whether family or not.

My mother worked at Dominion Industries Limited during the war years. It was a munitions factory in Verdun. It was only one street over from the Point. My father was a career firefighter with the City of Montreal and he worked, at one time or another, at all of the stations in Griffintown, Point St. Charles and Goose Village.

In the 'thirties and 'forties I loved growing up in the Point. It was a very close-knit community. You knew so many people. Extended families were all just a few minutes walk away from each other. I had four aunts on my mother's side and six on my father's side all within a short walk—Paris Street, Knox, Coleraine, Grand Trunk. You'd be walking home from school with some of your cousins and could just drop in, or they'd come to your house.

When you played you were out on the street with your friends. Sometimes a cousin would come over and stay at your house for two or three days. Then maybe you'd sleep over at a cousin's place. The Point was a good place to live. When you made friends, you stuck with them. A lot of people in the Point, including me, got married to Point people. You all grew up together, went to the same schools and played together. You knew all the families living close by and most of them were just hard working families that did the best they could, sometimes under difficult circumstances. For example, a lot of families had a lot of kids, and I mean a lot of kids. One family on the corner of Pacific and Knox, a French family, had 18 or 19 kids. There was another family close by on Ryde Street that had 16 or 17 kids. The father was a garbage man. Particularly on the French side of the Point there were a lot of very big families.

J. Timmons Jr. (age 12) on top of the fire truck with his father's team. 1945.

Joe's father (third from the left) outside the Mill Street station, across the canal from Griffintown and just to the north of Goose Village. The building is still there, but it is no longer in service as a fire station. 1951.

From as early as I can remember, all I wanted to do was be a firefighter like my father. We were very close. I used to spend as much spare time as I could with my dad at the various stations where he worked. It was easy for me because we always lived within walking distance of the stations. I used to drop in before school and hang around. At lunchtime, I'd hurry home, pick up my lunch, as well as my father's, then hustle over to the station and have lunch with him there. After school I would go to the station again and then walk home with my father after work. As I got a little bit older I was even allowed to sleep at the stations sometimes. I was like a mascot in the station when I was young. I just couldn't spend enough time there.

At that time I was going to Canon O'Meara School in the Point. The Brothers used to lock the doors after school started. So, if you were late, either in the morning or afternoon, you couldn't get in. Sometimes my dad would kick me out of the fire station after lunch telling me I'd be late, so I'd leave. But what I'd do is just go a couple of blocks from the station and wait until it was too late to get into school and then go back and tell him I didn't make it. He'd look at me

Joe's father and the rest of his Station Three (Griffintown) team. Joe's father is pictured standing beside the bell on the near-side running board of the truck in the centre of this photo. The building pictured on the right (now demolished) housed St. Ann's Boys' School, as well as the St. Ann's Young Men's Association. 1950.

and say "well, you better just stay here, but don't tell your mother about this". Then he would write me some kind of note for the next morning.

At Canon O'Meara you learned your stuff. I liked Brother Mell a lot. He was one of the younger Brothers. Brother Iraenus was always getting me strapped, though. I didn't like doing homework very much and he would always send me down to the office for the strap. There was an alleyway behind the school. It was about 20 feet wide. It had a chain link fence that separated us from the French school. I remember a lot of fights after school, but I never got caught.

When I was young, and before I went to work at CN, I had some great times at my dad's fire stations. In those days there were no sirens on the trucks. Instead, the trucks all had big bells on the right side of the cabs near the windows. The Officer on the passenger side of the cab, usually a lieutenant or a captain, would ring the bell all the way to the fire. Sometimes the stations would

Joe's father driving one of the first ladder trucks. 1932.

be short one or two men and the alarm would go off. Everyone would rush to the trucks and sometimes one of the lieutenants or the captain would tell me to get in one of them and ring the bell on the way to the fire.

Other times the District Chief would get in his red fire-department car to go to a fire and he'd let me get in and ride with him. After we reached the fire, the Chief would leave and I'd be in the car alone. I can still remember the faces of the kids at those fires when they would look inside the car and see someone my age sitting there. I loved my time at the stations when I was a kid. And because I spent so much time at the stations I got to know all the men. To this day, I can look at my father's old group photos or pictures of fires and name almost all of the men. Back in my father's day, and to some extent in mine, there were quite a few guys from the Point

The Griffintown fire station of Joe's youth still serves the area. 2010.

Right: Station Three, Griffintown. 2013.

and Griffintown in the fire department. In the old pictures you can see a lot of names that were common in the Point and Griffintown.

There are so many stories revolving around the fire department and not all of them are just about the actual fires. For example, they used to have street dances in Griffintown and they'd hold them right beside Station Three on Young Street. The problem was that these dances would often end up in big donnybrooks. I remember one time I was in the station during a street dance and a huge fight broke out. It didn't take long before other people from the houses around the station heard the commotion and ran over to get involved. The streets were just jammed. I was only 12 or 13 and I can remember being scared that the fight would start branching out and into the station. Some guys had run inside when the fight started and were hiding under the fire trucks. By the time it was over three guys were laid out in the lieutenant's office after being knocked unconscious. I can still remember the firefighters giving them smelling salts to try and bring them around. What a scene!

The other thing that used to happen fairly regularly was that if an alarm went off and the Griffintown kids heard the sirens going, they'd rush over to the station. If they found it empty they'd start climbing all over things, making calls on the telephone, answering calls, racing upstairs and sliding down the fire-pole. It was quite something. I was there when the alarm went off for the 1946 fire at the CPR sheds on the wharf at Berri and Commissioner in the Old Port. A big crowd of kids came over after the trucks left for that fire. One of them answered the phone and started talking and yelling a lot of gibberish into the receiver, but it was a lieutenant from another station that was calling. The lieutenant called the police. Seven cars arrived and

The old Mill Street station, 2013.

blocked the place off. There were kids running everywhere. I ran upstairs and locked myself in a room until I thought it was safe. Other kids ran straight up to the top floor and jumped from the fire station across to the nearby roofs to escape. They knew all the tricks. After a while everything had quieted down and so I opened the door. As soon as I did a policeman grabbed me. They had three of us at that point —probably the last three. The Officer told us to stand still and he went to a nearby phone to report in. One of the kids with me ran downstairs and told a waiting police officer that he was "Lieutenant Timmons' son", so the policeman says, "OK, get out of here". He bolts. That left me with one other. They threw us in the back of a police car. On the way to the station they got a call to pick someone up off the street on St. Antoine. They threw this fellow in the back with us and he was covered in blood. I had no idea who it was but apparently he had been thrown down a flight of stairs. Anyway, we arrive at the station and there is a whole mob of Griffintown adults outside. They were all yelling and chanting at the police to release the kids that had been picked up. It was near Christmas and Mickey Boyle was dressed up like Santa Claus. Like I said, they're all yelling to let us go, and that is exactly what happened. The station captain just shook his head and told us all to get out. I guess you could call it "Santa to the rescue"!

After I finished grade seven I went right to work as an office boy for the Canadian National Railway. I worked my way up to be a car tracer. Car tracers tried to keep track of all the railway cars across Canada and help make sure they were where they were supposed to be. We would try to ensure that we could tell businesses where their goods were and when they would arrive at their destination. But all the time I was at CN I knew that some day I was going to be a firefighter.

When I was older and made it into the Fire Department, I even met my future wife at one of the stations. My brother was in a church group and he was out with a crowd of the young members about our age one evening. It was a very cold autumn night. As they were walking home past Station 15 where I was working at the time he suggested to his friends that they drop in and warm up. He knew I was on duty. Anyway, they all came in and I recognized all of them except one girl who I thought was very cute. I found out her name and the rest is history. I got married to my wife Cathy. The night we met she told me she lived on Fortune Street. Well, wouldn't you know it, at about 3:00 a.m. on that very same shift we got a call to go to a fire on Fortune Street. To this day I tease her about how badly she must have wanted to see me again that she'd start a fire on her own street to get me over there!

My father had quite a career in the fire department. Like mine, his interest in the fire department started early and he'd laugh when he'd tell the story of how once he jumped out the window of the St. Ann's Boys' School during class to run over and see a fire. He joined the department in 1927. They were still using horses then. He would tell the story of how when they first motorized the department he was told he'd be the driver of the pumper in his station. He asked "why me, I don't even know how to drive?" "That's OK", the captain said, "you're the only one here that doesn't drink!"

My father earned his lieutenancy after 16 years. In those days, your first promotion (lieutenant) put you in charge of one of the ladder trucks, so that was his primary responsibility. In those days the ladder trucks weren't like the ones we have today. Back then, the ladders were portable. They hung from the side of the truck. You'd have to carry them from the truck to the fire and raise them by hand. When he got promoted it also meant he was second in command of Station 15 in the Point for a short time. Then he moved on to Station Three in Griffintown for seven years. Later on he became a Lieutenant First Grade and was posted to the Mill Street Station at the edge of Goose Village. He was there from 1951–1958.

My father's work in the Fire Department often had him stationed very near the Lachine Canal. Over the years I know he was involved in pulling a lot of bodies out of that canal. I don't know the exact number between, say, the 1930s and the time the canal finally closed, but my estimate based on anything I have heard in discussion would be in the range of about two per year. The department had a small rowboat that they'd tow over from the Mill Street Station and put in the canal. Two firefighters would get in it and one would work a grappling hook to search for the body or retrieve it from the surface.

The Point, Griffintown and Goose Village stations were always busy. So was the old Station Ten right downtown near Guy Street. He worked there too. My father attended some very historic and very tragic fires. Probably the most famous of all these fires was the bomber crash in Griffintown during world war two. My father was at that fire. What happened was a Polish flight crew was ferrying a bomber to Europe from the Cartierville airport. Very soon after they left they got engine trouble and they knew they were going down. So did the people at the tower in Cartierville. They were heading south toward the river at the time. They tried to reach the river to ditch the plane but didn't make it. They came down in Griffintown. First, they clipped the roof of the Griffintown Boys' Club, and then they went on and crashed into a three-storey tenement building. It was demolished. You could see where the plane finally came to rest. My dad took me over to the crash site the next day. Just before the plane finally stopped it hit a warehouse and you could see the circular hole in the bricks where the nose of the plane hit. The area was still hot at the time and there was really nothing left that resembled a plane. It had all just fallen in on itself during the fire, but you could still see that hole in the warehouse wall where the plane stopped. A piece of the plane was found on the roof of the Boys' Club. The experts say that if it hadn't clipped the Boys' Club they would have made it to the river. In the end the whole crew was killed and so were eight Griffintowners. My father found a small coin near the remains of one of the crewmembers. It wasn't a Canadian coin. It was burned black and it had been bent badly out of shape in the crash.

Firefighters at the Liberator airplane crash site. 1944.

Another fire that people still talk about is the 1956 St. Gabriel's Church fire on Centre Street in the Point. St. Gabriel's is the English Catholic church in the Point. That fire was just a couple of months before I got on the department. I was in the Savoy theatre with my brother Bill when the fire broke out. My sister called the theatre and actually got them to stop the show and ask for "Bill or Joe to please call home". She had been listening to my little radio at home that I had set up so that I could pick up fire calls. My brother and I raced out and I got my camera. My father was the last man out of that fire. He was up in the belfry when the decision was made to get everyone out. He told me that the fire at the time was just rolling across the inside of roof. As he came down he was making sure all the firefighters were out of the church. When he got downstairs there was only one other person left in the building. It was a nun. She was over at the altar trying to gather up and save some of the religious artifacts. He made his way over to her, took her gently by the arm and walked her down the main aisle of St. Gabriel's and out the front door. My father was known for his great sense of humor and when they reached the front door and walked outside where everyone was waiting he turned to the nun and said, "Look, it's just like we're getting married!" The nun was Sister Alice. Her job was to look after the altar. She always did that. Whenever we'd see her she would still get a chuckle when she thought of my father.

Another story that I've heard told many times about my father was when he was on a call one year on Ascension Day. That's forty days after Easter. It is an important day for practicing Catholics. In any event, he was at the top of a ladder rescuing a woman from several floors up in a burning tenement. She was at the window. My father was telling her to get on the ladder. She was very agitated and she said to my father... "Its Ascension Day. I'm not even fully dressed. I can't come out like this". My father told her that "Well, it may be Ascension Day, but one thing for sure is that you're descending with me!"

Back in those days, or for that matter, even my day, the firefighters didn't have the communications that they have now. In my father's day it was all done by phone or by sending messages back and forth from the red fireboxes at the scene. It was difficult to judge the severity of fires when the calls came in by machine via code on strips of paper. So in the early days the department tried to play it safe rather than sorry. They just sent a lot of vehicles when an alarm came in. The trucks weren't as sophisticated back then either so you'd have to send more trucks to accomplish the same thing you'd do today with fewer vehicles. In my father's time, sometimes you'd see over 15 pieces of equipment at a fire—even a minor fire.

When I applied to the department you had to be 21 to be a firefighter. So, when I turned twenty-one I applied. I went down to the headquarters and honestly, I thought there must have been 1000 guys there. The first thing you had to do was get measured, so I stepped up. Whoever was doing it looked at me and said, "5'-6 and ¾ you're out!" You had to be 5'-7. In those days recruiting intakes took place only every two years, so that was it for me for that period. I kept working at CNR, but I knew I was going to try again. So I started working out more and going to the YMCA trying to do things that I thought at the time might make me a little bit taller.

Anyway, I waited the two years and the next intake was scheduled. When my turn came to get measured I stepped up against the wall and did the best I could to stand tall—"5'-7 and a hair", he said, "move on to the written test". I passed the written test with ease and was on my way to being a firefighter and living my dream. There was a battery of other tests as well: medical, physical, aptitude etc., but I passed them all. Tests were always very easy for me in the fire department and I'll tell you one of the reasons why. When I was growing up the department used to prepare these training question kits for the firefighters. What they'd do is pull together around 200 or so questions and answers and each firefighter would have to copy them out and then have them reviewed by a senior officer. This was serious stuff. If you didn't do this and keep up the work you could be sent to a far-off station or something as a message to shape up. The men were allowed to submit their work for review by typewriter. Well, I used to type up my father's questions and answers for him. I always did this. I did it for years. So, over the years of doing this, as well as the years of hanging around the stations, I learned a lot well before I even joined. Eventually I was promoted to District Chief, and honestly, I think that the work I did with my father for all those early years helped me because I have a very good memory and a lot of that stuff really stayed with me.

There were just over 40 people in my training class in 1956. By that time most of the recruits were French. There was only me and one other English guy in the class and we sat beside each other. The instruction was all in French. I could get along in French, but he wasn't that strong. I remember the person in charge told me to make sure that my buddy got the information he needed in English so that he wouldn't have to repeat everything in two languages.

Just before I started on the job, the firefighters were working 72 hour per week. At the time I started it had just been dropped to 56 hours per week. Some years later it was dropped again to 42 hours per week. The thing was that every time the hours of work were dropped it meant the department had to increase in size to offer the same service. So every time the hours of work dropped you'd have a huge recruiting intake of around 400 or so men. My own training class was part of one of those big intakes. My father retired in 1963, so we actually served in the department for seven year at the same time.

I remember that I was at an event once and I bumped into Frank Hanley. I was well into my career by this point. He asked me what I did for a living. I told him I was a firefighter. "Oh yes", he said, "I remember, I got you your job!" I looked at him and said, "No way Frank, I got this job on my own!" Frank was quite a guy. He was a provincial member of the legislature and city alderman at the same time, and I don't think he missed one funeral in the Point. He was a very active guy and he did get a lot done for his riding. When Camillien Houde was the Mayor, he really liked Frank Hanley.

A day in the station for us was always busy. You'd often get ten or twelve calls a day. If we weren't on the road, we'd be doing things like conducting training exercises, cleaning the trucks, washing the cars, or cleaning the station. The stations were supposed to be spotless and we had regular inspections. Without exaggeration, I can remember washing the chief's car as many as seven times a day. In the winter in Montreal with the snow and slush, every time a vehicle would go out it would come in dirty. I'd wash the Chief's car down and *chamois* the whole thing. Once a week even the engines and undercarriages of the vehicles were scheduled for cleaning with fuel oil. I can remember some District Chiefs coming in and sliding under the trucks on a small flat buggy to inspect the whole undercarriage for cleanliness. I remember very well another job we used to get. The ladders we used in the early days were wooden and they were painted red. Relatively regularly we'd have to repaint them. But the thing was that first we'd have to strip the paint that was already on them. The Lieutenant would break a bottle and hand each of us a piece of broken glass. Then we'd painstakingly scrape off all the red paint and repaint the ladders. We stayed busy.

When I started we didn't have masks. In fact I was in the department for quite a while before they started to trickle in. I remember when I was transferred to the Notre-Dame-de-Grâce Station in the west end that finally they had received two masks. But when they arrived, none of the guys wanted to use them. At that time it just wasn't done. Guys used to take pride in staying inside a fire in adverse conditions and not coming outside. They wanted to save the buildings and save lives. And some of the men had an incredible capacity to handle the smoke. One guy, Gerry, never came out until the fire was over. Guys like him were known as "chimneys". Gerry could take the smoke longer then anyone. I can still remember him spitting blood three days after a fire. He died of cancer. It's not like that any more. Everyone has a mask now. When the alarm goes off the guys jump into their fire gear and head to the truck. When they sit down,

Point St. Charles Fire Station no. 15 is still in operation on rue de la Sucrerie. 2014.

Right: The old Hibernia Street Fire Station is now a library. 2014.

their backs are against an equipment rig that they harness themselves into. It includes an air pack and a mask. Everyone has a mask. No one goes in a building without one today.

From the time I was a child and all during my career, I remember a lot of fires around the Point, Goose Village and Griffintown. Industrial fires were always a big threat there, as well as in places like old Montreal. Before the 'forties or so you didn't see sprinklers like we have today. The Canada Packers fire, the Hollander fire, The Sherwin Williams explosion—these were all big fires.

Back in the day there were some real fire hazards for people living in the Point, Griffintown and Goose Village areas. As well as the industrial fires, you had real challenges in the houses. Most of the row houses or flats were heated with coal or oil. Coal was far safer than oil. In both cases though, the heat was transmitted via these big round pipes that went from the burner across the ceilings and through to the various rooms. Sometimes these things would get cherry red from the heat. They'd get so hot they'd cause fires in the walls. Sometimes we'd get called in because of a fire that had already started. Other times we'd get a call to try and do something about the red-hot pipes. You'd use asbestos mitts and wet down the pipes with cold wraps. The oil stoves were really dangerous if you weren't careful. Some people had a big 45-gallon drum out on their balcony and the oil companies would deliver the oil. Oil would drip trough a tube into the burner in the house. It would usually be a copper tube. Other burners would have a gallon-or-so-sized drum beside the stove that you'd fill with oil and the oil would drip from there to the burner. To start the drip, whether from outside or inside, you'd turn a valve, wait for a few drips then light it. Well, sometimes people would start the drip, forget about it and then remember when the burner plate was full. Then they'd light it anyway and it would just be too much heat. Honestly, I have been called to houses where these stoves were jumping. Very dangerous!

Sometimes the fires in tightly-knit communities like Griffintown or the Village could hit very close to home for people, our family included. And this was the case in one of these oil fires.

When I was around 13, I was at the station and the alarm went off. It was a fire that had started on Dalhousie Street in Griffintown. The trucks left and I ran outside. I saw the trucks turn onto Dalhousie and I saw one of the plugmen jump off to hook up the hose to the fireplug. That meant it was the real thing so I took off after them. I got there in time to see my father carrying out a woman who had been caught in the fire. She had been very badly burned. She had been pouring oil into the drum beside the stove and must have lost control somehow because the thing went up in flames. It was really bad. People were aghast at the extent of the injuries when they saw her in my father's arms. Her face was badly burned and her legs were covered in blisters. She died a few hours later in the hospital. It was only the next day that we learned that she was my father's cousin. We were told that even if she had survived the fire she would have been blind. Her two children were carried out of that fire as well, but unfortunately, neither of them survived.

In the Point there are a lot of three-storey tenements and they can pose real problems in a fire. Often, during fires in these places, it calls for weaving the hose up through hallways, as well as staircases. The hallways can sometimes extend from the front of the building to the back. Sometimes the pathway up and down can even include exterior balconies. I was fighting a fire once in one of these situations and a balcony gave way on me. It was at a derelict building and it was at one of the Victoria Day fires that were set off in the Point. I fell around 15 feet directly onto concrete. I broke my teeth, cracked some ribs and was knocked unconscious. My helmet was shattered. My men didn't even know I had fallen. They had their hands full. They told me that they looked back down the hall and I had just vanished. After they found me and I regained consciousness they sat me down and propped me up against the back of one of the trucks. My face was covered in blood and people told me I just sat there motionless. My Captain came roaring up behind the truck in his car. He told me later that when he pulled up and saw me leaning against the truck he thought, for sure, I was dead! The Saturday before that very fire, the department had buried District Chief Filiatrault. He fell off the roof of an apartment building up in NDG (Notre-Dame-de-Grâce). It can all happen very quickly. If my memory serves me correctly, over the 31 years that I was on the Fire Department, the City lost 37 firefighters. It's a dangerous job.

One job I had for a while was driver for a District Chief. Each Chief had one of the red department cars and a driver. I'd take him everywhere. At fires I'd be at his side and he'd assess the situation, direct the efforts, and give me commands to relay to Headquarters every ten minutes. He'd be sending equipment back to the station if it wasn't needed, or asking me to call for more from the firebox. The Chiefs always had to make sure that Headquarters knew what was going on at fires. With the communications we have now, there are much better processes in place. I really learned a lot when I was in that job. I saw how many different fires played out from the command standpoint. It is a whole different situation than when you are inside a burning building. All you see on the inside is what's right there.

During my career I was stationed several times in the Point. As I got into more senior positions I was in charge of the fire service for the Point/Griffintown areas, a well as other areas of Montreal. I saw a number of tragedies in the department and many close calls. Roofs, walls

Bill (left) and Joe (right), proudly flanking their father, Joe Timmons Sr. Date unknown.

and floors caving in are always a very serious threat for firefighters and it can come down to seconds in making the decision to evacuate before cave-ins. The fire at the Unitarian Church on Sherbrooke Street right downtown was just such a fire. It happened on May 25, 1987. I was there. It was 31 years after I had joined the department.

When you're at a big fire like that, one person is in charge of the inside and one person is in charge of the outside. I was in charge of the inside of the Unitarian Church fire. I had 15 firefighters with me. The fire was arson and it had been started right in the middle of the church. It was blazing from underneath the floor and elsewhere. To kill a fire underneath a floor you drill a hole in the floor and put a semicircular nozzle through so you can send the water in on an angle. It's called a bent cellar pipe. You try to wash down the fire from underneath. We were doing that and also attacking the fire in various other ways too. As time passed I reached the conclusion that the battle had been lost and that we couldn't save the church. I told the men to start packing up. You don't like doing that because you always want to save the building. I went outside to advise the Division Chief. He was the overall commander of the fire at that point. He asked me if I could just give him a couple more minutes to try an idea he had to save the building. He said that there was some more equipment on its way. I said "OK…a couple of minutes, but if I think

Joe enjoying retirement at the helm of his boat. 2012.

it is hopeless, we're coming out", and I went back in. But as soon as I got back inside I could see that things were deteriorating fairly quickly. It was just too late. No matter what, we were not going to be successful, so I immediately turned and went back to advise my boss that it was over and the men inside could soon be in danger. They needed to come out. Just as I reached him our Assistant Chief arrived and heard my opinion. Without a moment's hesitation he said, "If that's what Joe says, get them out!" By the time I got back inside I could see the fire glowing up the inside of the walls of the church and all around where the wall joined the floors. It was really bad. I could see signs of the floor beginning to sag as well. I called to the men to drop everything and evacuate immediately and no sooner had I done that than the roof began to creak and fail. Then, it was a race for life. As soon as we heard that sound we all bolted for the front door hoping we could make it before the roof completely caved in and crushed us. It was about 40-50 feet high. We all made it out the big front doors as the roof tumbled down. When the roof comes down in a building like that, the walls will sometimes fall outward; and the church was made of stone, so getting crushed on the inside isn't the only threat. Knowing this, once everyone got outside some of the men hurled themselves under the fire trucks in front of the church. I threw myself down the front stairs, tore some ligaments in the process, but managed to make it across the street. I was convinced I was going to be covered in stone trying to make it to the other side. In this case, however, the roof fell within the stone walls of the church and all of the firefighters that were working inside were safe. A few more seconds inside the church and likely all 16 of us would have been killed. If a wall, roof or floor collapses on a firefighter there is really very little hope.

But in the end it was a very sad day for the Montreal Fire Department. We lost two firefighters that were ventilating the fire from the outside. When the roof collapsed, they were high on an aerial ladder at the southeast corner of the building on Sherbrooke Street. As the roof tumbled, the overhang caught the ladder and both men were carried to their deaths. Their names were Jean-Pierre Longpré and Pierre Letourneau.

People think that steel is safer than wood in fires like this. What the average person doesn't realize is that steel begins to fail at 1000 degrees. Big wooden beams will just keep burning until they eventually collapse. When you are fighting a fire its hard to know with steel exactly when the beams will hit that 1000 degrees and then start to fail, but 90 minutes is a pretty good yardstick.

That was the situation at the Unitarian fire. Most of the church was wood at the top, but steel beams were used in an extension. When they gave out the whole roof came down.

Cave-ins are one of the worst things that can happen. I remember another one where a firefighter was trapped in the debris for hours. He was in great pain during this time. It was very sad. Rescuers managed to burrow through to him with a female doctor to deliver morphine and to try and get him out. Eventually they were successful but he subsequently died in the hospital the same night. Two other firefighters died at that fire as well.

Whoever is on the ground in command in those situations has the final say and it can be a very, very difficult call because you always want to stop the fire. You always want to save the building.

As it turned out, the Unitarian Church was my last big fire. In the seven-month period be-

Joe and Cathy at their surprise retirement party. 1987.

tween that fire and my retirement, I probably attended about 20-30 other fires. But I was 53, and I had devoted 31 years to the service. I loved it dearly and I'd do it all over again in a minute if I had the chance. But my wife, Cathy, and I talked it over and we just reached the decision that it was time. I had a great career. So did my brother, Bill. He joined the Westmount Fire Department when he was 21 and he finished his career there as Chief.

I always tried to look after the safety of the firefighters who were under my command—always. I also got along very well with my men, but it came as a complete surprise when rank-and-file firefighters hosted a surprise retirement party for me. Typically the guys on the line didn't do that for more senior managers, or what we called "Major" staff. It was a Friday night and I thought my wife and I were going for dinner. As it turned out, the firefighters had an elaborate process set up for me starting with a chauffeured drive past all my old stations where the men were all lined up and waving while the sirens sounded. Then we went on to the party. Part of it was filmed. I didn't expect it and I was profoundly moved and grateful. They gave me many thoughtful and meaningful gifts. I had no time in advance to prepare a speech or anything. When I was eventually called to the podium, off I went and things went fine. At that time it was the biggest retirement party ever in the fire department. They sold 250 tickets to firefighters from all over the city, as well as to family members and some other close friends that were not from the fire department. It was quite a night. As I said, all I ever wanted to do from the time I was a young boy was be a firefighter. I lived my dream. I was very fortunate. I followed in my father's footsteps.

"I do not know of another district or area

that the people

who come from there

identify with it

like the people who

come from the Point…

You can take the kid out of the Point,

but you cannot take the Point out of the kid!"

Mike Spears

Mike Spears

Mike Spears grew up in the Point. He was an outstanding athlete and participated in several sports. Mike boxed in the inaugural Golden Gloves Tournament in 1956. He played both Midget and Juvenile football for Point St. Charles and was awarded the most valuable lineman trophy for three years in a row. His juvenile teams won two consecutive provincial championships. Mike's reputation earned him invitations to three Montreal *Alouettes* Canadian training camps.

Mike joined the Westmount Police Department in 1964 and was promoted twice. After the amalgamation of the island of Montreal's suburban forces with the Montreal Police, Mike rose to the level of Chief Inspector and served in this capacity for the last 16 years of his career. Mike retired in 1996.

Mike has a long history of involvement with highly successful athletic programs and charitable organizations both in Point St. Charles and elsewhere in Montreal. He is always on the lookout to provide support to St. Gabriel's Parish and has served in support of the Irish community for years. Mike has served as both Vice-President and President of Montreal's United Irish Societies and as Vice-President of the Erin Sports Association. In 1983 Mike was selected Chief Reviewing Officer of the St. Patrick's Day Parade in Montreal. In 1988, Mike was honoured as Montreal's Irishman of the Year. In 2010, Mike was inducted into the Point St. Charles Hall of Recognition.

"When I canvas for volunteers, mostly friends from the Point or the Griff and West End, the answer is: *What do you want me to do and when do I start?* —not— *I would like to but...*"

Mike has deep roots in the Point and is proud of his Irish heritage. Mike makes regular trips to Ireland and remains in contact with the many friends he has made there through athletic exchanges and other activities.

Photo: Mike Spears at the "Walk to the Stone". 2012.

Mike (right) with his brother Kenny. 1948.

I was born July 1, 1942 on Albert St. (now Lionel Groulx) in the West End and baptized at St. Anthony's Parish. I am the middle of three children: older brother Kenny (1937–2010), five years my senior and my sister Doreen who is nine years younger.

I did not know my maternal grandparents but I distinctly remember my father's mother. She lived on Mullins St. and then on 4th Avenue in Verdun. We used to bike to visit her and hear her thick Irish brogue. She was born and raised in Belfast, was married three times and had ten children. She buried three husbands and eight children. The only two to outlive her was my dad and my Uncle Gerald. They were the two youngest. My dad died at 58 and my uncle about 65. My grandmother was about 85 when she died. My grandparents were retired and I never knew what they did for a living.

I have only had contact with my father's family on my grandmother's side. She was born and raised in Belfast, had been married twice over there and had some children born and died there. I only remember three uncles, two of which were born in Ireland and my Uncle Gerald and father who were born in the Point.

I go to Ireland quite often and visit distant cousins. We have kept in contact and I have a great time when I go over. They still live in Belfast in a Republican area known as Andersontown. My parents were both born and raised in the Point.

We moved to the Point when I was an infant. We first lived at 555 Magdalen Street in a six-room two-storey house. My mother, father, brother and I lived in three bedrooms upstairs. Charlie, who owned the place, lived downstairs where we had access to the kitchen and bathroom.

After a couple of years my parents separated and my brother was sent to live with my aunt and uncle, my mother's sister, on St. Hubert Street, near Jarry, and Ma went to work as a live-in maid (in-service) with me in Westmount. I believe it was on Westmount Avenue near King George Park. That lasted for about one year. My parents got back together and we all moved to 613 Magdalen Street. My sister was born there. I lived there until 1962 or 1963. During this time my parents separated a few times. My mother moved to Egan Avenue in Verdun.

Growing up in the Point, I went to Canon O'Meara School on Laprairie Street. The French School, St. Charles was on Island Street and the school yards were back-to-back. Our starting and finishing times were about 15 minutes different, to avoid any conflicts. Needless to say, it cut down on the clashes, but they did occur. Nothing serious, the odd punch in the head — or run

Mike and his mother. 1949.

Mike's grade-five class photo at Canon O'Meara. In the back row of boys standing, Mike is third from the right. 1954.

like hell. You won some and lost some but there was no hatred, just something to do. At school, it was run by religious Brothers but there were also lay teachers. The Brothers lived in a four-storey building next door. There was also an outdoor rink. At the time there was corporal punishment, usually a strap or pointer on the hands or a smack on the back of the head. I don't think anyone was scarred from the experience. It was the form of discipline at the time. You didn't go home and tell your parents the teacher or principal hit you because you would get it again from them. They would say, "He didn't hit you for no reason". I have fond memories of those days and I still see some guys I went to school with from the first grade on. The stories get better all the time.

St. Gabriel's Church is on the corner of Centre and Laprairie. On the first Friday of the month we would be brought to the church to go to confession and we were expected to go to Mass on Sundays. I made my First Communion and Confirmation at St. Gabriel's and became an altar boy. The good thing about being an altar boy was when there was a funeral during the week; you

The now-restored St. Gabriel Lock, where Mike's father once worked. This view looks east toward the Port of Montreal. 2011.

could leave school to serve the Mass and earn a dime. A lot of times you would tell the teacher you had a funeral to serve, which was not true and you got out of school for an hour or two.

After the seventh grade I went to Darcy McGee High School. There were three of us who went to McGee: Jackie Watt, Frank Hanley Junior and I. The rest went to St. Thomas Aquinas. The three of us would say McGee took only the best. To get to McGee, which was on Pine Avenue and Jeanne Mance, we would take the Wellington streetcar to the Craig terminus, and then the Park Avenue Street car to Pine Avenue. Darcy McGee High School was run by a religious order of Brothers, and the nuns ran the girls side. I had good times at McGee. The guys from the Point, a few from the Village and Griffintown hung out together. I do not remember a single person other than the guys I mentioned.

Growing up in the Point, the club for children played a major role in their lives. Personally, almost every day after school I would go to the 79th Battery which was located on Wellington between Congregation and Sebastopol. It was run by Mr. Patty Geary, Bobby Geary's father. There was a membership fee but very few people could afford it—however, everyone got a membership. There would be activities such as woodworking, painting, and all kinds of sports. You would go home for supper and return back to the club to play floor hockey, basketball,

MIKE SPEARS

1960

Point St. Charles Football Club

Above and facing page: Parts of a football game program of one of Mike's Point St. Charles teams. 1960.

boxing, ping pong or whatever. Your age determined what time you had to go home. It kept a lot of us out of trouble. You listened to Mr. Geary more than your parents.

In the summer time it was Hogan's Bath on Wellington. The man responsible was Doc Lamothe. Once again there was an entrance fee and you rented a white bathing suit that tied on the side. If you were short of money, which happened quite often, Doc would let you in. If you caused trouble you would be barred for a week or two and he remembered who and for how long. Today Hogan's Bath is condominiums.

Like I mentioned earlier, my parents were separated quite often. My father had a problem with the drink and it caused him a lot of difficulties. When he was sober, he was a great guy and a good worker. He worked for all the major companies: CNR, CPR, Northern Electric, Redpath Sugar, Dow Brewery, Sherwin Williams, Lachine Canal and others. Most of the companies —he was there two or three times. He lost the jobs due to not showing up to work, due to the drink. When he worked for the Lachine Canal, it was at the locks on des Seigneurs St. I would bring him his lunch and watch the bridge turn when a ship went through. He also worked as a checker at the Montreal Port.

If you liked to drink you could not live in a better place than the Point, we had taverns all over the place. In a three-block area near my house, there were three taverns: Palomino at Wellington and Richmond, Bucket of Blood, at Wellington and Congregation (later Magdalen and Wellington), two doors from my house, and Westlake's, at Congregation and Favard. On Friday nights there usually were fights at the Bucket and my father was involved in a lot of them. He was pretty good with his hands having boxed growing up. More than once the police were at our door, either because of his fighting or him causing trouble in the house. Because of his reputation, sometimes there were two or three police cars outside, which attracted all the kids on the street; it was embarrassing at times, but no one ever mentioned it after it was over. He died at 58 of lung cancer.

My mother had to work to make ends meet. She cleaned houses and after my sister was born, got a job on the night shift at the Royal Bank head office on St. James and St. Peter as a cleaner. I had to be home before 11:00 PM to mind my sister. More than once, after my mother left I would wrap her up and bring her to a party and get her back home before 7:00 am. My

Point St. Charles Football Club

23	Tom Geary	21	Bill Wilson	63	Chuck Canning
10	Jim Geary	22	Gerald Harold	64	Bill Kennedy
11	Brian Murray	44	Kevin Killen	70	R. Knight
12	Pete MacKenzie	45	John Kamel	71	Ken Bellemare
14	Dave Tagieff	48	Bob Smith	72	Marius Mattio
15	Ken Rowcliffe	50	Hugh Baxter	74	J. Donovin
16	Toni Christiano	53	Alex Baronstiff (Asst.)	75	Ron "Nipper" Charles
17	Robert Wall	54	Mike Spears	76	Sid Halifax
18	John Elliott	60	Bill O'Donnell	77	George Morrison
19	Lorne Murdock	61	Art Evans	78	Bill Maynes
20	John Gravel (Capt.)	62	Garry Lawson		

Head Coach - Bill Earle Asst. Coach - R.G. Moore Line Coach - Bill Rowan

mother still kept her regular customers cleaning their houses. After 10-12 years, she got a job in housekeeping on the day shift at the Royal Victoria Hospital. I lowered her age on her birth certificate in order for her to get the job. She stayed at the Royal Bank for about a month, fearing the hospital would find out about her age and fire her. After doing both jobs for about a month, she quit the bank.

She retired from the hospital at 65 years old, she still cleaned a few houses—the last one she gave up, she was in her 80's. She was not afraid of work. She used to say "Work never killed anyone". She lived a healthy life and died peacefully at 94½ years old. We did not have much money growing up. I remember selling bottles to buy 15 cents of bologna, a few slices of cheese and a loaf of bread. She kept the house spotless and we were always clean.

There was no question of an allowance so you had to make your own spending money. My friends and I would collect bottles, newspapers and scrap metal from the CNR tracks which we would sell at a scrap yard on Farm Street. Sometimes the scrap metal we found on the CNR tracks, the CNR did not think it was scrap and the police would bring us home.

I got my first job at O'Flaherty's grocery store on Bourgeoys and Favard Street weighing and bagging potatoes. I was nine or ten years old and was paid 1½ cents every ten-pound bag. I did that for a while and then got promoted to bagging the groceries at the cash. My brother also worked there. We would deliver circulars door-to-door on Mondays to make extra money. You had to be creative to make some spending money. Like I said, there was no such thing as an allowance from your parents.

Around 1955 the Point St. Charles Boys' and Girls' Club opened thanks to the generosity of Mr. J.W. McConnell. At the time it was the most modern facility of its kind in Canada. The 79th Battery had closed. Mr. Patty Geary became the Director of the new club. It had all the facilities you could want: game room, swimming pool, double gym, boxing club, weight room and various workshops. After school and after supper it was the place to go.

Boxing was a sport that I liked, probably due to my father's experience. At the time boxing was a popular sport in the poorer areas; very inexpensive to participate in. Just bring yourself, some courage, discipline and desire. The wealthier areas such as Westmount and Town of Mount Royal would find sports such as tennis and figure skating. The cost to participate was expensive. In its first year the club hosted the *Golden Gloves*. I fought in the 90-pound category, won my first two bouts and fought a fellow from the Village, Ronnie Ferguson in the final. To put it mildly, he whipped me. I still see Ronnie now and then some 55 years later and we laugh.

Even with the activities available to me, I still found time to get into trouble and more than once I found myself in the back seat of a police car. Back then the police cars were two doors and your entrance to the back seat was not comfortable when the policeman helped you. They would bring you to Station 11, Shearer and Grand Trunk, call your parents to come and get you or drive you home. I was more afraid of *that* than the police.

When I was around 15 years old some men started a football team with the Boys' Club as a meeting place. I went with some friends and met the head coach, Billy Earle. We were told when the first practice would take place and to bring any equipment we had. I went with no equipment and started to practice. Most of us did not have a clue as to what to do but there were a few guys who were natural athletes and caught on quickly. By the time the season started we fielded a team, and lost more games than we won, but were getting better all the time. Just before the playoffs the league suspended us for having an over-age player.

The following year we moved up a category. We got super uniforms, green and gold, similar to the Green Bay Packers and Edmonton Eskimos. We now had an idea how to play, and with the coaching of Billy Earle and his assistants we became the team to beat. Our practices were extremely hard and tough. The field had a little grass but most of it was just dirt. When we played "away" games on nice grass fields, it was like playing on a mattress. Like I said, we had a few really talented guys but most of all we were just regular players. Billy Earle out-coached all the other teams thus and so we went on to win the Provincial Championship.

The people of the Point really supported us. We had large crowds at our games and I think the visiting teams were slightly intimidated. The following year we repeated and won the Provincial Championship again. Billy Earle took a mixed bunch of adolescents—some a little wacky, maybe a lot wacky—and brought them to become a well-disciplined winning team.

He taught everyone responsibility, discipline and respect. If you did not come to practice and did not have a good reason you didn't play; no matter whom you were or how good you were. We were not a physically big team, we had a couple of big guys but were smaller than most teams. The guys were physically tough, loved to hit and had a strong desire to win. You take that with the coaching ability of Billy Earle and you get Provincial Champions. The following year there were financial problems and we could not field a team. It was decided that we would go to Verdun, and between the Verdun team and our team, the Verdun organization would enter a team in the Junior category. The team was called the Verdun Braves and our field was the Verdun Stadium, next to the Verdun Auditorium, where our dressing rooms were.

A lot of players from the Point went out to Verdun and the head coach was Billy Earle. Bobby Geary had sort of retired from playing for the *Alouettes* due to injuries and he was the line coach. There were two sorts of groups, the Verdun guys and the Point guys. Practices were quite lively. After about three or four weeks of practices the players were selected. I would say the majority of the team was made up from the guys from the Point. We were younger than the other teams. It was like a juvenile team playing in the junior category.

Our first regular season game was against the NDG Maple Leafs (Notre-Dame-de-Grâce) at their home field Trenholm Park on a Friday night. They were the Dominion Champions the previous year. People were saying we would finally get whipped. At half time, the score was tied 7-7. I think they won the game by a touchdown. Needless to say, to us it was a win and a few of us went up town to the Cavendish Club and celebrated. The late George O'Reilly was the waiter saying "I hope you guys never win, if this is how you act when losing". I played another year in Verdun. We had a competitive team, but did not win any titles. I had won the Outstanding Linesman Award three out of five years and as I mentioned previously, we were not a physically big team. An example, I played offensive guard and weighed 165 to 185 pounds.

At that time the Montreal *Alouettes* held a Canadian training camp where they invited 72 players to attend the two-week training camp. At the camp, there were scouts from some American colleges and at the end some players got scholarships or were invited out to the big camp with all the regular pros. I was invited to attend the Canadian camp three times, 1961, '62 and '63. In the invitational letter it gave you the coordinates and, most important, to report in top physical condition as you went directly into heavy practice—full equipment with contact. The training facilities were at Jarry Park. At the medical, you had 71 jocks and me. The players were split up by their positions. I was with the guards and the centers. Everyone was naked except for their jockey shorts. I weighed 165 pounds; the average weight of the guys was about 220 pounds. I knew it was going to be a long two weeks when one of the coaches came up to me and said it was for guards and centers. I told him I was a guard, he rolled his eyes and said good luck.

The next day the practices started. I was the only player from my team but I knew a few players from the Verdun Shamcats, the senior team. The practices were extremely tough. The biggest differences I found were the calibre of the players and the size. There were 72 of the best Canadian amateurs around Montreal and area. These guys wanted to play for the *Als* and I was there for the experience, never once did I think I would play pro football. The coaches already had a good idea of which players would go further. Guys like me were there to try our best, a slight chance to be chosen, but mostly to be competition for the good ones. In 1962 I returned to the camp, a little heavier, 185 pounds and in pretty good shape. That year Bobby Geary, who had played for Calgary and Montreal but suffered a knee injury, and missed a season, was on a comeback. Also Terry Evenshen, who lived down the street from me in the Point, was there.

On the first evening of the practice, while walking from the clubhouse to the field, Terry and I were walking together and a fellow bumped into us. He and Terry got into a fight. When we reached the field, the head coach Perry Moss gathered everyone together and said he liked what he just saw (the fight) and he wanted more of that spirit to be shown. Needless to say, that practice there were fights all over the place. At a few practices I was going against Bobby Geary and I must say he was the meanest, toughest and most determined athlete I ever met. During the Red and White game, I must have done something well because the next day I was mentioned in the Montreal Gazette along with Geary and Evenshen and a couple of others. Geary played a few more years with the *Als* and when he retired, became the General Manager. Evenshen got a scholarship to Utah University, and returned to play for the Calgary Stampeders and Montreal *Alouettes*. He had an outstanding career.

When I left high school, like many other people in the Point, I worked at the CNR. My Uncle Gerald, an engineer at the CNR sent me to see someone at the Personnel Office and I started the following day. I worked as a mail boy in the viaduct situated on Inspector Street under the tracks that lead to Central Station. After one year, I applied to a plumbing supply company, EMCO Ltd. located at 8355 Jeanne Mance St. I left the CNR and worked at EMCO for three years, first in the warehouse and then in the office doing pricing and quotations. It was convenient as it was just north of Jarry Park where the *Als* held their Canadian camp. I met my first wife at EMCO and we were married shortly after I joined the police. She was a French Canadian girl from the Villeray district. We had a son, Patrick, who is now 41 years old.

During my time at EMCO, some guys I knew in the Point were firemen for the City of Westmount and they told me that I should apply to the police department. This interested me because of the job security and pension plan. I completed the application and was called for an interview with the personnel manager. Later I received a letter inviting me to a written test to be held one evening at the police station. I completed the written test with about 20 or 30 other candidates. A few weeks later I received a letter inviting me to an interview with the Police Chief. When I went, the Chief was absent and the Deputy did the interview.

I felt good after each stage. I was relaxed, I had a job which paid more than the starting salary for a policeman, and at that time there were a lot of jobs available. Another couple of weeks went by and I received a telephone call from Mr. Grant, the personnel manager, saying I had the job and "When could I start?" I thought someone was playing a joke, so I told him I would call him right back, which I did. I gave two weeks' notice and started in Westmount in June of 1963.

I didn't start as a sworn-in regular constable, but as a special constable or a Park Ranger as they were known. You were not armed and you patrolled the parks. You were in a uniform similar to a regular constable but the only equipment you had was a night stick, flashlight and the police call box key. From June through September, I patrolled Summit Park which is where the Westmount lookout is. It is a beautiful wooded area which the city stocked with pheasants. I worked from 12:00 noon until 21:00 with Mondays and Tuesdays off. It was kind of boring, no

THE WESTMOUNT Examiner

Making not just your house but all of Westmount your home

Vol. XLIII, No. 27   Westmount 215, P.Q., Thursday, July 8, 1971   10¢

Asks notifications

Métro expropriations data sought by mayor

Sept. Fair has Centaur, Youtheatre

Another dimension has been added to this year's September Fair with the promise of drama.

Two groups have announced they will take part in the community-wide effort at the ice rink Sept. , which will raise funds for both junior and senior citizen activities.

One is Westmount's own Youtheatre, which is reported ready to put on a show for young people.

The other is Centaur Theatre, which is said to be planning a display of costumes drawn from its extensive accumulation from two years of performances, changed almost monthly, at the old stock exchange downtown.

For anyone interested in lending effort or talent to the fair, a meeting is to be held next Thursday evening, July 15, at 8 pm in Victoria Hall.

$186 lifted from purse

One hundred and sixty-eight dollars was stolen from the purse of a woman shopper in Steinberg's supermarket in Alexis Nihon Plaza on Wednesday of last week. The woman said she discovered her purse, which was in a shopping cart, open with her wallet missing.

Police report that thefts of this nature are common because women become engrossed in shopping and do not pay attention to their purses which they often leave in shopping carts.

NEW LIEUTENANT: After just a year as a sergeant, Lieut. Michael B. Spears Monday night was promoted to that rank by resolution of city council. Lieut. Spears, who joined the Westmount police-fire department only seven years ago as one of the city's first public safety officers—as distinct from constable or fireman—is at 29 one of the youngest local commissioned-rank officers in some time. His excellence in competitive examinations for the vacancy overcame his low points in seniority.

11 lifters

Eleven persons charged with shop-lifting in the Alexis Nihon Plaza Miracle Mart since June appeared in Westmount Municipal Court yesterday morning. All but one pleaded guilty and received various sentences.

Mayor Peter M. McEntyre has asked Lucien L'Allier, chairman and general manager of the Montreal Urban Community Transit Commission, to notify "as soon as possible" any citizens of Westmount who might be affected by expropriations of property for the projected westward extension of the Metro system.

The mayor's letter, written last Tuesday, was released at his suggestion by city council Monday night. It was written at council's suggestion at its last meeting June 21, after the mayor had revealed that a diagonal swath from Greene avenue and de Maisonneuve boulevard almost to Clarke avenue and St. Catherine street would have to be expropriated for an open-cut portion of right-of-way construction on the east-west Metro line's extension to Verdun.

At the present end-of-line at Greene, the roof of the tunnel is just below the street surface and the distance to Clarke and St. Catherine is believed by engineers to be needed to gain sufficient depth to commence underground tunnelling toward St. Henry and beyond.

Concerned residents

Following publication of the mayor's revelation in The Examiner two weeks ago, numerous phone calls from concerned residents were received at this office, at city hall and at the MUCTC. Little new information has been made available since by any source.

The mayor told Mr. L'Allier in his letter that Westmount recognizes the need for the extension of the system "to provide Metro service for thousands of citizens within the Urban Community. It is inevitable, however, that some persons will have to be displaced to permit construction of the new facilities.

"Being deeply interested in the well-being of our citizens, we trust that the proceedings will be undertaken with as little dislocation and inconvenience as possible," His Worship said.

Next Week's Weather
By ERIC NEAL

Westmount, Out

City seeks curbing over 'wate

Westmount, in cahoots decided to blow the whistle soaking residents of the su supplies water.

Local taxpayers pay a s by the City of Montreal, bas their properties, ostensibly f

Speak up, Father

Father Brennan at St. Leon's Church will have to speak up this Sunday.

He reported to Westmount Police Monday evening that someone had stolen the two microphones on the altar plus the amplifier to which they were attached.

The gear was valued at $500.

Nothing else appeared to have been taken.

Addict had 2 grammes of heroin

Jean Saulnier, 33 of Montreal, was arrested by Westmount Police in Westmount Park at 4:50 pm Sunday in possession of 2 grammes of heroin to which, on Monday, he pleaded guilty before Judge Claude Wagner in Court of Sessions downtown.

Saulnier, who was sentenced to two years in a special treatment centre in British Columbia, was one of several drug addicts dealt with at the same time, leading Judge Wagner, former Quebec minister of justice, to declare that capital punishment should be reinstated for drug traffickers.

Today's World

crime, but I had my picture taken hundreds of times by tourists from the tour buses. The hours were good for me because the One and Two Club had just opened on Butler Street and I could go after work, stay until closing and still have no trouble getting to work for noon the next day. October, November and December I patrolled King George and Westmount Park. The hours and weekly days off were better. In January 1964 I was sworn in as a regular constable and after six or eight weeks training, including fire training, I was put on a shift and started working in a police car and on the beat. You were teamed up with another constable on the beat. Although Westmount used one-man patrol cars, you were never put alone for about a year. Westmount is a small area, approximately one square mile and a population of about 25,000. There were 75 members in the department, possibly the highest rate per 1,000 citizens in Canada.

The department was very military-like; the officers mostly ex-military. The crime rate was low; traffic enforcement took up a large part of your shift. But it was the period of the separatist movement and the mailbox bombings. Westmount was targeted because of its mostly wealthy English-speaking population. At the time, Westmount Police were autonomous, having our own x-ray equipment and bomb disposal truck. If a bomb was discovered, the Army was called.

The most frequent crimes were residential breaking and entering, some of which were of substantial loss. The most frequent calls were burglar alarms. You could not compare the Point to Westmount. In Westmount you did not see kids playing ball hockey on the streets or getting calls for kids ringing doorbells or being mischievous in other ways. Very few calls for domestic problems or men fighting in the laneways were made.

Prior to the integration of the police department in 1972, I was promoted twice, to Sergeant and then Lieutenant. In 1978 I was promoted to Captain and transferred to Station 54, St. Leonard and Ville D'Anjou. In 1980 I was promoted to Inspector and transferred to Headquarters and then Director at Station 22 in Verdun. The district covered Verdun, Ville Emard and Côte Saint-Paul. Now I was back close to my roots. The culture was similar to the Point. In the Point, the 24th of May was a big celebration. It was officially Victoria Day but in the Point it was Bonfire Night. There were bonfires in the middle of the streets and a lot of firecrackers, etc. There were police all over the place and the fire trucks just went from fire to fire. In Verdun the same thing happened but was limited to Hickson Avenue.

Another district I worked that was similar to the Point was 52, Hochelaga/Maisonneuve Street which covered Sherbrooke South to the St. Lawrence, Parthenais East to Dickson. It was similar to the Point, blue collar workers, except 95% French Canadians. Except for the language it was the Point. The people were proud of their district, they didn't live in Montreal, they lived in Hochelaga/Maisonneuve.

After 32 years, I ended my career in District 13, Dorval. I was very fortunate in the Police Department having reached the rank of Chief Inspector at the age of 37 and retiring at 53 years old. My growing up in the Point was a critical part of my success in the Police force. You had, in your baggage, experience most people would never have. You had respect for people, the wealthy or the regular every-day guy or girl, or the down-and-out. You knew and appreciated the value of a dollar and you had the loyalty to what you believed in, plus perseverance to achieve your goals.

As I previously mentioned, I liked the sport of boxing, like a lot of guys in the Point. During my years in the Police, I would frequent various boxing gyms, starting with the Point—and when that closed I went to the Montreal West Boxing Club. The trainer was an Irish native Sean Duffin. Sean and I became good friends. Boxing is an excellent sport for getting in shape, plus Sean would have me spar with some of the novice boxers and once in a while the more experienced guys. In 1976-78 I even filled in for a guy on short notice on a card in St. Thomas Moore Church Hall in Verdun. The organizer was Ronnie Ferguson who had whipped me in the *Golden Gloves* back in 1955.

In 1981 or 82 the Quebec Amateur Boxing Association called Sean asking for his help with a team from Ireland coming to Montreal to fight against a Canadian team. The event was scheduled for the Claude Robillard arena and they wanted Sean to spread the word amongst the Irish Community, sell tickets and look after the Irish team. Sean asked me and a few guys for help. The show was a success and I spent about a week with the Irish boxers, trainers and managers. I still meet some of the guys when I go to Ireland.

The following year I was in Belfast on holidays and a Canadian team was there for two fights, one in Derry and another in Belfast. The Canadian team met me and asked if I could help them deal with the Irish organization because of the language, which I did. While dealing with the Irish organization I met Jim Noonan who worked full time for the Ireland's Youth Training Program (YTP). It is a program subsidized by the Government which trains youths who are not academically strong but have other skills to become carpenters, plumbers, hairdressers, and waitresses and so on. I will speak more on this later.

Over the years, Keith Matticks, a LaSalle businessman and personal friend, approached me about starting a boxing club in LaSalle. I thought it was a great idea and we were off. Keith negotiated a space in the LaSalle Arena and his business, LaSalle Canvas and Rope supplied all the equipment. We got Sean Duffin as the head trainer and Keith, myself and Jimmy Carroll all got our trainers' permits to help Sean.

The club was a success and we gradually backed off. The club is still operating, being run by younger guys who love boxing and helping teenagers. During those years, we organized two more boxing shows between Ireland and Canada. One held at LaSalle Arena and the other at LaSalle Catholic High School. Both shows were a success. We had more time to organize and get support from the United Irish Societies and the Erin Sports Association. Like I said prior, I developed long-standing friendships with the Irish teams and I still see some of these men when I visit Belfast.

As I mentioned previously, I met Jim Noonan when I was on holidays in Belfast. Jim was with the Irish boxing team, and over a few Guinnesses, he told me he worked in the Youth Training Program (Y.T.P.) which is subsidized by the Government. It trains teens 16 to 19 who are not academically strong but have skills in various trades such as carpentry, plumbing, hairdressing and so on. It covers teens from Ireland, Northern Ireland, boys and girls and both communities, Catholic and Protestant. They send groups of teens to various European countries for training. He asked if I could do something if he wanted to send a group to Montreal; I, thinking this was idle talk over a pint, said I was sure I could help in Montreal. I never thought any more of it.

Members of the Erin Sports Association tip their hats to the Chief Reviewing Officer at the St. Patrick's Day Parade. 2013.

Several months later Jim called me and said he was sending two Supervisors (women) to Montreal for a feasibility study on the possibility of sending a group to Montreal. They would arrive in a week and stay for ten days. They would like to visit some families who would billet the youths and employers who would take them on board for eight weeks to give them training and work experience. This caught me completely by surprise. I called my friend Denis Dougherty, formerly from Griffintown and the Point, told him about the situation and he got on board. We contacted a few families in the Point and former Point people who lived in LaSalle and West Island and they agreed to meet the Supervisors from Ireland and say they would billet a boy or a girl for eight weeks. We did the same with some employers. These people were a *façade*. The two girls from Ireland went back and wrote up their report which was fantastic. Jim submitted his report to the authorities and he got the necessary funding.

Denis and I went to Ireland, met the youths involved and their parents. We gave a description of Montreal, its customs, climate and social life. It was a start of five groups coming to Montreal between 1989 and 1999. There would be 17 to 18 youths and two Supervisors for a stay of six to eight weeks.

It was a lot of work and involved a lot of volunteers. All the volunteers were personal friends of Denis and I, most were former people from the Point. These programs developed life-long relationships between some of the youths and their families, who have since visited each other, attended weddings or christenings and correspond regularly. Now when I visit Ireland, I meet some of them who are now married and have children. They all say, their Canadian experience changed their lives, memories forever. Between the boxers and trainees approximately 120 young people came to Montreal.

In 1988 I joined the United Irish Societies of Montreal. Their mandate is to run the St. Patrick's Day Parade. They also have an entertainment group that puts on shows at hospitals and old-age homes. They annually give out Christmas food baskets to the needy. I was President in 1994 and 1995. After I retired, I was less involved as I spend winters in Florida, which is the period when all their activities take place.

I joined the Erin Sports Association in 1987. It is a group of men, almost entirely from the South West area, Griffintown, Village, Point and West End. It was founded in the Point in 1931. It is a non-profit organization. All it's fund raising goes to support charity or sporting groups in the South West area of Montreal. They were one of the original organizations to support Aces Football Team in the Point which was started by two Montreal Policemen, George Widz and Ron Durand. George still runs the Aces Organization in the Point.

When it comes to making donations to various groups, I always put up the name of St. Gabriel's Church and I get plenty of support from the guys. In 2002 we started an annual barbeque at the church. I was named Chairman and each year I get 18 to 20 of the guys who cook, set up and take down all the tables and chairs. We raised around $2,500 which is totally donated to the church. It has become an annual tradition.

In 2006 I started a Tuesday lunch held at the Erin Club on Hickson Avenue. Once again the guys volunteered their help and we serve 30 to 40 meals every Tuesday from May to November, except July and August. There is no charge for the delicious hot meal. Donations are accepted for St. Gabriel's Parish. In the last five years, $35,000 was raised and donated. Due to my health issues, there were no lunches in 2011.

Once again, most of the people who attended are former Point residents. I have been fortunate to be able to give back a little of what I received growing up. In the process I have been honoured in many ways:

Chief Reviewing Officer for the St. Patrick's Parade in 1983
Irishman of the year in 1988
Hall of Recognition in Point St. Charles in 2010
Boxing trophy in my name, LaSalle Boxing Club in 2011
Recognized in Erin Sports Club in 2011
Recognized at St. Gabriel's BBQ in 2011

Mr. Bill Earle, football coach in the Point and later in Verdun had a great influence in my life. He played a key role in me sitting in the front seat of a police car rather than in the back seat. Mr. Russ Swailes of the Westmount Police Department was an inspiration and example for me in my career in the Police department.

I have one son, Patrick, and one granddaughter Felicia. I now live in LaSalle with my long-time companion Audrey Baldo.

Growing up in the Point gave me the means to become a person who received a lot in life and gave back a little. I have friends I have known for 50 to 60 years who I see and socialize with on a regular basis. I had occasions to be in situations to organize different things. The most important ingredient in the organization is the volunteers who do 90% of the work. When I canvas for volunteers mostly friends from the Point or the Griff and West End the answer is… "What do you want me to do and when do I start?", not, "I would like to but…"

I do not know of another district or area that the people who come from there identify with it like the people who come from the Point. An example of this is an annual Slow Pitch Softball Tournament which is organized by Jackie Geary who has surrounded himself by a distinctive group of volunteers. It has been going on for several years and was held at the ball diamonds on Ash Avenue until 2006 when the City of Montreal closed the field. It was moved to Therrien Park in Verdun. It is held the beginning of August and attended by hundreds of people, some who travel a good distance, mostly former Point residents. They raise about $65,000 annually which is donated to the Children's Wish Foundation. Their slogan is **"It is who we are".** That sums it up real well, what the Point is all about.

You can take the kid out of the Point, but you cannot take the Point out of the kid!

Erin Sports Association volunteers at the annual BBQ in support of St. Gabriel's Parish. Mike is first on the right (second row). 2013.

Erin Sports Association team at the Children's Wish Tournament. Mike is the first on the right, back row. 2014.

"When we were growing up

we spent a lot of time around the kitchen table

because that was where the stove was,

and it was usually nice and warm

and we were together as a family.

We did not have any central heating in those days.

There was a coal stove in the kitchen

and this was our main source of heating.

Growing up I remember we got our first television in 1954.

The first television show I ever watched was *I Love Lucy*.

Also, we were one of the few people on the street

that had a telephone.

It was a party line

so we had to share with our neighbors."

Amelia Palazzo

Amelia (Gaglietta) Palazzo

Amelia's father came directly from Italy to Goose Village. The family lived there for 33 years until the expropriation. Amelia and her two sisters (Roberta and Antonia) lived in Goose Village until the very last days. Amelia was 16 when the family left the Village and moved to Verdun.

Amelia and her sisters, all of whom are in Montreal, remain very close.

Photo: 2008.

"I am very proud and happy to have lived in the Village with my family where I made my childhood friends. Two of them became my lifelong friends —Linda Frainetti and Theresa Shanahan."

I was born in 1947 at Ste. Justine's Hospital in Montreal. My sisters were both born in Montreal as well. Our parents both came from Italy as adults. My father's name was Gaetano Gaglietta and he came from Galluccio, Caserta, Italy in 1931. He was a highly skilled stonemason. He had a profession when he came to Canada. My father moved into the Village when he arrived and that is where he stayed until the demolition. My mother, Maria Mancini, from Guglionesi, Campobasso, and my father Gaetano, met through a mutual friend in Montreal. In those days there was not as much courtship as today. They married, and soon after, started our family.

Before my parents married, my mother worked in the garment industry in and around the Mile End and St. Lawrence area. She worked for a company that made men's suits. She often recounted how well she was treated by her employers. They really liked her, and her dedicated work.

Other than his profession, my father did not have very much when he was in Italy or when he first came to Canada. But when he started working in Montreal he saved his money and as soon as he could he bought our first home on Menai Street. Over the years he also bought some property in the Point. He'd buy a place, then fix it up and rent it. My father also always sent money back to Italy to his family. Sometimes we would go without, but he always found a way to send money back home. He worked very hard. He worked for himself all over the Village and

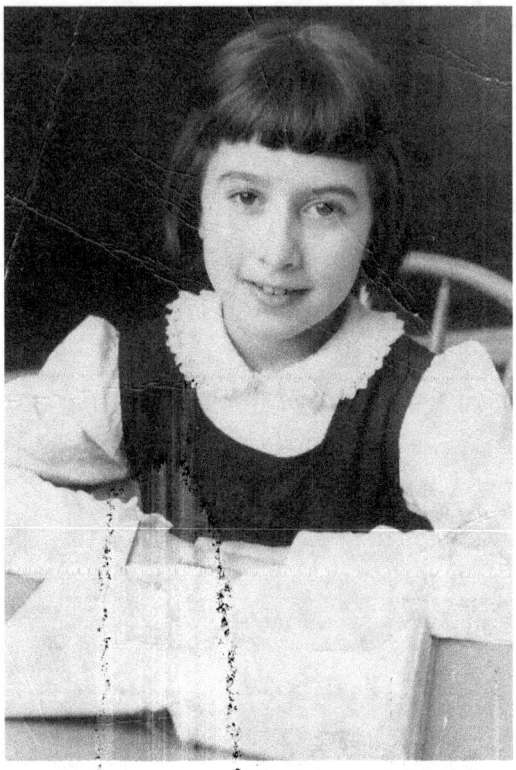

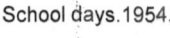

School days. 1954.

Amelia's parents, Gaetano Gaglietta and Maria Mancini. 1945.

the Point doing repairs. People from all around the Village and the Point knew him and would call him if there was any work to be done. They trusted my father as he was an honest and good worker. He also did a lot of work on some churches in Point St. Charles.

I went to St. Alphonsus School in the Village, then St. Ann's Girls' School in Griffintown. St. Ann's was run by the nuns from the Congrégation de Notre-Dame. Most of the teachers were nuns, but we did have a few lay teachers. It was very strong. After that I went to St. Patrick's High School up near St. Patrick's Cathedral. We really received an excellent education there. The teachers were strict, but the education was like that of a private school, and employers in Montreal knew it. I didn't have to look for a job. I was offered one as soon as I graduated. I remember that for my first day of work, a company employee came to our house in Verdun and took me to work.

Needless to say, my mother and father had the greatest influence on me growing up. Aside from my parents there was Sister Columba, my grade-school teacher at St. Alphonsus School. As a child I was very shy when I started school. Sister Columba saw this and she used to make me read out loud in front of the classroom. At the time, I thought she did not like me. But in the end, I realized she had my best interests at heart. She became one of the people that had the greatest

A three-storey "shed" in Goose Village. c. 1963.

influence on me. Then, later on, there was Father Kearney. He was the parish priest at St. Ann's Church in Griffintown. The kids of the area loved him. He could be seen every day on the steps of St. Ann's Church, and as children we would always go up and talk to him. He was also an influence on me.

Overall, I'd say that when I was younger I had quite a sheltered childhood. For example, there were dances held at the Victoriatown Boys' Club, but I was never allowed to go. What I remember is that we did a lot of family outings. My parents were very religious people, so a lot of the places we'd visit were religious in nature, and we went to church every Sunday. When we moved to Verdun we went to a French church. On the weekends our parents would take us to places like the St. Joseph's Oratory. My Dad would take us all around the Oratory and explain the architecture and the stone masonry to us. He would explain how something was really well done or where something could have been improved upon. They also had a really nice picnic ground that we'd go to at the Oratory. Sometimes my mother would pack a lunch and we would eat there.

Every June after school got out we would all go on a trip to St.-Anne-de-Beaupré near Quebec City. The cathedral there is very beautiful. We would leave on a Saturday morning and go to Windsor Station where we would take the train. My father would explain everything to us along the way. On the Sunday morning we would go to Mass, do some souvenir shopping and then come home on the train. It was only one night away but for us it was a big event. It certainly isn't like that any more. Today, kids expect Disneyland.

My parents would also take us every year to the Italian Festival in Little Italy—the Feast of St. Anthony. It was always in the middle of June up in Mile End. There were processions, games for the kids, bands, and lots of food such as paninis, pizza and ice cream. It was always a lot of fun. We'd go to Notre-Dame-de-la-Défense Church in Little Italy. It is an absolutely beautiful church as well. My parents were married there. Then, later on, that is where I was married.

My father would also take us to places like the Botanical Gardens in Montreal, as well as to Mount Royal. When we went to Mount Royal he would always take us to the restaurant right beside Beaver Lake. We would also walk up to the lookout. We used to always go to Belmont Park right after school got out for the summer as well. I guess you could say it was kind of like a reward. I have very fond memories of Belmont Park.

When we were growing up we spent a lot of time around the kitchen table because that was where the stove was, and it was usually nice and warm and we were together as a family. We did not have any central heating in those days. There was a coal stove in the kitchen and this was our main source of heating. Growing up I remember we got our first television in 1954. The first television show I ever watched was *I Love Lucy*. Also, we were one of the few people on the street that had a telephone. It was a party line so we had to share with our neighbors.

When we were growing up we had lots of friends in the area. We'd play hide and seek and there were a lot of places to hide. People built coverings for their stairs in the back of their houses. They used planks and we called these places "the sheds". Sometimes they would be three stories high. They always seemed very spooky to us on the inside.

I remember also that when I was young I honestly believed that some places in the Village were haunted. For example, we all thought one house on Forfar Street was haunted. An old lady

The gymnasium of the Victoriatown Boys' Club provided a venue for Goose Village residents to attend Mass within the Village. c. 1963.

lived there and she was a recluse. Sometimes we'd dare each other to go and knock on her door and run away.

My mother was a good cook and she always prepared home-made food. One of my favourites was our breakfast of Italian crusty bread with garlic and olive oil. My mother always cooked with olive oil and garlic. Today, people sing the praises of olive oil. And when the school bus took us home for lunch, my mother would always have something warm for us to eat right away like home-made pizza. My favourite was home-made French fries, which she wrapped up in wax paper like a cone. My mother baked and cooked almost everything from scratch, like her pasta, pizza and bread. When we came home after school it was the same. She always had a snack for us before we sat down and did our homework. Then, we would go out and play for a while and it would be dinnertime. Sunday dinners were our special treats. My mother would always make

Amelia (centre), with her sisters Antoinetta (left) and Bertina. 2008.

something like her home-made pasta such as *fettuccine* or *cavatelli* with her favourite sauce, which included home-made meatballs, *braciole* and Italian sausage. Today, homemade pasta is considered a luxury. I guess we were lucky because we had it most of the time.

Like so many people in the Village, my father had a small garden in the back yard. He'd grow tomatoes, eggplant, lettuce and peppers etc. In the Village, and then later on in Verdun, we always had a garden. My mother would use some of what my father grew to prepare her tomato preserves. During the year my mother would use these preserves to make her sauce for Sunday dinners. On the other hand, my father always made his own wine, and he was always proud to share it with his family and friends.

My mother was fine with leaving the Village when it was announced it would be demolished, whereas my father wasn't happy. To him, the Village was like one big family. My sister, Antonia, sometimes tells the story of how she took a new friend from Verdun to see our old house in the village. She did not know the Village had already been demolished by that time. When she got there everything had been reduced to rubble. Years and years before that, though, my father had installed a small marble step at the entry to our house. My sister figured out roughly where the house would have been, searched the rubble and she found a piece of that marble. She took it home to our father and when he saw it he became emotional. What was also sad was that when the Village was expropriated and demolished our father wasn't given what his property was worth. No one in the Village got fair value for their homes.

I am very proud and happy to have lived in the Village with my family where I made my childhood friends. Two of them became my lifelong friends—Linda Frainetti and Theresa Shanahan.

L-R: Amelia with "friends for life", Linda Frainetti and Theresa Norris. 2001.

"… people seeking to understand the Point

and the surrounding communities

should know that the Lachine Canal was the way

to enter America through to the Great Lakes.

It provided employment for people

who worked at the Montreal harbour.

It permitted the transport of manufactured goods

to and from all kinds of industries. It made Montreal

Canada's industrial and commercial center at the time…

It served as the importation and exportation facility

for large quantities of products that transited

through the Montreal harbour.

The industries along the Lachine Canal

gave work to thousands of people,

mostly living in and around the Point."

Bertrand Bégin

Bertrand Bégin

Bertrand Bégin lived on d'Argenson Street for 25 years before moving to Verdun.

Bertrand graduated from St. Charles School in the Point. Then, in consideration of a religious life and donning the robe of the Brother, Bertrand set off to Mont de LaSalle, an institution in Laval run by the Frères des écoles chrétiennes. This religious order was established in 1680 in Reims, France and is dedicated to teaching.

Bertrand's interests changed after two years at the seminary and he returned to the Point where, soon after, he set his sights on a business career.

Bertrand is now retired and lives a ten-minute drive from the Point.

Photo: Bertrand outside the "Fine Pointe". 2012.

"The Point was our Village.
We felt secure walking the streets."

I was born on February 14, 1937 on the 3rd floor at 1228 d'Argenson Street in the Point. My parents had already been living there since 1932. My mother gave birth six times but the first three babies were stillborn. I was the fourth and the first to survive. I had a younger brother born in 1939. He joined the Army but was killed when hit by a car when he was 18. My younger sister was born in 1945. She currently lives in Laval. I have one son, André, and one grandson, Emile.

When I was two or three years old the flat on the second floor of our building became available, and we moved in. We lived there until the landlord asked us to leave because he needed the flat for his son who was getting married. This was in 1962. I was 25 at that time. Shortly after that I got married and moved to Verdun.

My grandfather on my mother's side had a farm in Sainte-Philomène, now called Mercier. It is near Châteauguay over on the south shore. His wife died giving birth in 1910. My grandfather on my father's side, Georges Bégin, was a cabinet maker and carpenter; he lived in Lambton, in the Eastern Townships. Lambton is about two and a half hours east of Montreal. He died when I was around five years old. I am told that he would sometimes barter for the goods he needed for his cabinet making. For example, he would exchange molasses for the raw planks he would otherwise have to buy. His wife Mélanie died in 1955 in Lambton.

Grandparents Georges and Mélanie, Bertrand and younger brother Andre. c.1943.

My father, Lucien, grew up in Lambton as well. He told me he left home at 14 years of age to go to work as lumberjack. I don't know all the details of this but I do know he spent some time as a lumberjack in the Abitibi region of Quebec. He also drove a taxi for a while. When he was around 32 he got a job as a forklift operator at Robert Mitchell Co. This was a steel company with operations in Saint-Henri and St. Laurent. Over the years he worked in both locations. He stayed there until he stopped working. He never had an accident with the forklift. He used to get awards for this.

My mother, Lucienne, grew up in Sainte-Philomène. She was the eldest of six children. I remember her telling me a few times how very hard she worked on the family farm. She was only ten years old when her mother died. She immediately left school and from that point on, until she moved to Saint-Henri for a job, she helped raise her brothers and sisters. Her first job in Montreal was with an oil company, Joseph Elie.

She later worked at her aunt's grocery store in Saint-Henri. It was on the corner of Greene Avenue and Delisle. That is the location of the Lionel Groulx subway station now. My father used to buy his tobacco at the corner store on the way to work in Saint-Henri. That is how my mother and father first met. At that time my father was living in the Point.

I started school at St. Gabriel's Annex on Centre Street in the Point. From the second to the seventh grade I attended St. Charles School on Island Street. I was in the choir at St. Charles and we'd sing at Mass on Sunday mornings, as well as at Vespers on Sunday evenings at 7:00 p.m. As a reward the Brothers would take us on trips. One year we went to Ottawa to visit Parliament. Other times we'd go on picnics to places like Ile Bizard.

St. Charles was back-to-back with the English Catholic School in the Point and I remember that sometimes when there was a fight between one of the French kids and one of the English kids in the Point, they would become good friends afterwards. I also remember a time at St. Charles when a number of us were asked to help in removing postage stamps from envelopes where they had been soaked in water for some time. As I recall, the stamps would have been of some value. There were many boxes of these stamps.

After St. Charles, I decided to go to Mont de LaSalle in Laval, just north of Montreal. This was a private institution run by the same congregation that taught at St. Charles School. One of the Brothers had approached me when I was at St. Charles and suggested to me that I would be a good candidate. The life at Mont de LaSalle

1226 D'Argenson, where Bertrand grew up. 2012.

was about preparing for a religious life. The 100 or so boys that were there at any given time were all preparing to be Brothers and to join the congregation of the Frères des écoles chrétiennes. One of the main differences between a Brother and a priest is that Brothers do not lead Mass.

The Laval institution was opened in 1917 after the Brothers left the original Mont de La Salle on Maisonneuve. The site of the original institution is where the Montreal Botanical Gardens now stand. You can still see the marks from the old Mont de LaSalle foundations at the Botanical Gardens. The name of the founder of the Botanical Gardens in Montreal was Marie-Victorin. The Brothers at Mont de LaSalle were always quick to remind us that he was a member of the congregation.

The congregation was totally devoted to education of children, hence their name, the Frères des écoles chrétiennes. They had institutions in other countries such as Japan and Haiti, and I remember meeting Brothers who were about to go on mission. I also remember once that a Japanese Brother came to live with us to learn French.

At Mont de LaSalle we had Mass every morning delivered by a priest assigned to the institution by the Bishop from the region. We also had a daily conference led by the Director of Mont de LaSalle. It lasted about 20 minutes or so and would address various topics. Sometimes the conferences would be fairly light in nature. Other times we would be reminded of the future moment of our death when we would have to show what good we had done in life. The Director would suggest, for example that we picture ourselves on our deathbed surrounded by candles, reflecting on what we had done in life. This was fairly heavy for 12-year-olds.

313

Bertrand's mother Lucienne at her aunt's grocery store in St-Henri. 1930.

Bertrand (on the right) with his mother and father, and little brother André. 1940.

The Brothers constantly motivated us to try and do something of great value in our lives. We were told at Mont de LaSalle that in order to prepare for a life of teaching we must develop ourselves into walking encyclopedias. When we were at Mont de LaSalle we were permitted to see our parents for two hours per month. A member of the congregation also read all our incoming and outgoing letters. We also had to write our own wills when we arrived at the institution.

During the summer the Brothers from Mont de LaSalle would take us to Saint-Jérôme, up in the Laurentians where they had a summer camp. There we would be outside most of the time playing or relaxing.

We used to have regular individual meetings with the Director to discuss how we were getting along and what we thought about the future. I remember that late in my second year the Director asked me, "Where do you see yourself in ten years?". I responded that I saw myself "sitting by the fireplace with my wife". Given the goals of Mont de LaSalle he asked me, "Well, what are you doing here?". He was right.

Bertrand (first row, first on the left) with his classmates at St. Charles school. 1949.

By that point I had decided not to proceed to become a Brother in the congregation. The next step would have meant a move to Saint-Jérôme, donning a robe of the congregation and undergoing a year of retreat and meditation. After that I would have undergone two years of training to become a Brother and a teacher. I was just too young then to know what I wanted to do in life, but I did know that becoming a Brother was not for me. So I left after the second year. Of all the Brothers at Mont de LaSalle I would say that Brother Laurent was probably the one who had the greatest influence on me. He was my teacher in 1949.

When I left Mont de LaSalle I went home to the Point. My father told me that I could do whatever I wanted or study wherever I wanted, but that I had to learn English. I decided to go to O'Sullivan Business College. It was located on the corner of Church and Wellington in Verdun. I could get there on foot. It was only about a 15-minute walk from where we lived in the Point and one of my close friends was already at the college. The pace was quite relaxed and I learned bookkeeping and typing as well as other skills. I also learned to speak English.

After two years at the college I went to work. I worked in banking for five years then moved to a real estate property management firm for five years. After that I went to work for Firestone Tire. I worked for Firestone for almost 20 years spending time in sales, credit management and audit. Many of my friends in the Point also went on to various good jobs and careers such as insurance, policing, government, television and sales.

When I was growing up in the Point I wasn't involved in sports very much. I had a few good friends and one of the things we liked to do was go fishing. My friend, Jean, was the real expert and he was very well equipped with fishing gear. He got me interested. A typical fishing day would involve hitchhiking over to Châteauguay on the south shore. I remember we used stop at the Indian reserve, Caughnawauga (now Kanawake) for a soft drink on the way. When we got to Châteauguay we would rent a small boat and row out into Lake St. Louis. He was always more lucky than I was. Then we'd hitchhike back to the Point.

On Saturday, when I was young, I can remember often going over to the Atwater market with my "Express" wagon where I would wait for people to come out with their arms full of bags of groceries. I'd offer to carry the bags home for them in the wagon for a quarter or whatever they would offer me. One Saturday I remember one of the Brothers from St. Charles came out with his groceries. He asked me to bring them to the residence with him. When we got there, he said "See me on Monday at the canteen". I expected a nice treat like chocolate milk or maybe even more. He gave me a small bottle of white milk.

Until I went to work and started to bring in some money we didn't have a refrigerator. That's where my wagon came into the picture again. Before we got the fridge, I remember taking my wagon to go and pick up ice in the summer. I used to go to a place in Saint-Henri, on Doré Street, or to Thibault's on Butler Street.

Among my friends, when I was 10-13 years of age I remember young Robert Côté to be, even at that age, a determined character, as well as a very well-mannered young man. I remember his telling me how he could learn school lessons by heart easily, which was a headache for me, since I was not so good at remembering lessons word for word. So I was not surprised later when I learned through the various media of the career we know he had, both in police and as a city alderman. I sure like to mention now how I knew Robert since that time, whenever the subject of police and defusing bombs, comes into the conversation

We had no television when I was young. I don't think we got one until the mid-'fifties. We had a radio, though, and I used to listen to children's serial shows like *Madeleine et Pierre*. On Saturdays the family would tune into the New York Metropolitan Opera and that got me interested in classical music. We also had a record player and a collection of records.

When I was young I spent a lot of time in what we called the "shed". It was where my father kept his tools. It was also where we stored the coal and wood for heating. I liked to play with old radios, taking them apart, or using different parts to build crystal radios. They consisted mainly of an empty cigar box, a coil that we made of wire on an empty toilet paper roll, and what we called a crystal. In those days we were always playing with things like yoyos, tops, marbles, bolo bats, and many of the kids had a penknife in their pockets. This was something our parents and grandparents had a habit of carrying.

At the Parish church on Sunday afternoons we used to have movies for ten cents each. I enjoyed that. And when I got a little older I liked going to the movie theatres. In the Point at that time we had the Centre Theatre on Centre Street and the Vogue on Charlevoix. Apparently the same person owned them both. Across the canal on Notre Dame Street going eastward from Charlevoix we had the Corona and the Lido. The Corona has live shows now. Going west from Charlevoix on Notre Dame we had the Cartier theatre. From Atwater, going eastward on St. Catherine there was the Seville, Strand, Electra, Princess, Alouette, Orpheum, Champlain, Loews, and the Arcade. In Verdun, there was the Savoy, Fifth Avenue, Park, and the Verdun Palace. I went to all of these theatres when I was young. It was one of my favourite pastimes. The pictures were mostly in English, which I did not understand all that well at first, but the action on the screen and the sight of actors that I liked kept my interest. I remember clearly that the first time I went to a theatre it was to see *Frankenstein Meets the Wolfman*. It was at the Centre Theatre in the Point. I sat through the movie three times that day.

I also enjoyed taking long walks, and St.

Across from the Pointe-Saint-Charles side of the Lachine Canal and just a couple of blocks from Bertrand's home, the Atwater Market tower is visible to the right, as are new condos on either side. Today, the scene has small pleasure craft rather than the cargo freighters of Bertrand's youth. 2011.

Joseph's Oratory on Mount Royal was often the destination. My pals and I also used to walk a circuit where we would walk east from the Point, cross the St. Lawrence River over the Jacques Cartier Bridge to the south shore, then walk west and cross back over to the Point via the Victoria Bridge.

I remember also that in the summer some organizers used to set up a boxing ring at Grand Trunk Park in the middle of the Point. This would happen once or twice a week. They would hold boxing and wrestling matches in the evenings. This would usually attract a bunch of people.

The Lachine Canal was always present in our minds in the Point. We were not supposed to be there. It could be a dangerous place. I had a friend named Lionel and he drowned in the Lachine Canal. His dog drowned with him. I was told that the reason the dog drowned was that it would not leave Lionel's body. We'd play there anyway. We liked to play in the lumberyards right along the sides of the canal. These were big lumberyards. I'd say 100 meters or so long. In some cases

The building that once served as the Vogue Theatre on Charlevoix Street. 2012.

the piles of lumber would be around ten feet high. We would go in the yards and do different things with the planks, like building bridges between the piles. If any of the guardians caught us they would have us leave, usually in a hurry!

In the future, people seeking to understand the Point and the surrounding communities should know that the Lachine Canal was the way to enter America, through to the Great Lakes. It provided employment for people who worked at the Montreal harbour. It permitted the transport of manufactured goods to and from all kinds of industries. It made Montreal Canada's industrial and commercial center at the time. The canal was essential to many industries. It served as the importation and exportation facility for large quantities of products that transited through the Montreal harbour. The industries along the Lachine Canal gave work to thousands of people, mostly living in and around the Point. One of my aunts worked at the Northern, as did my sweetheart at the time, and her brother. I will always remember, in particular, the sound of the sirens of the Corvettes as these vessels went through the canal. The siren sound was different from the usual loud and low foghorn sounds of the merchant ships.

We lived at the west end of the streetcar line. The Number-Two streetcar went back and forth through the Point all day. This brings to mind another one of the sounds of the Point that I remember. After they reached the end of the line near our place the streetcar would reverse direction and go back the other way. They did this by backing up 90 degrees on d'Argenson, then going forward and turning back 90 degrees the other way. The tracks would spring loudly into position twice to allow this maneuver. The loud clanging noise would wake us up if the windows were open in the summer. We also lived near Sherwin Williams, the paint manufacturer. It was right behind our house. I was in Lambton when the big explosion happened in 1943, but I remember the neighbors telling us it was the result of an experiment that went bad.

I don't remember much about Griffintown other than St. Ann's Church where the park and the plaque is located at present. I remember St. Ann's because on the Thursday before Easter, Holy Thursday, we would often visit seven churches. This was a tradition that the Brothers at St. Charles School encouraged us to follow.

The first things that come to mind when I think of Goose Village are Expo 67 and also Canada Packers. You could buy your meat directly from Canada Packers. They had a storefront operation right on Mill Street so we used to go there to get our meat. It was cheaper than if you bought it at a store. And no doubt you have heard of the terrible smells from the slaughterhouse that we experienced and Goose Village residents had to cope with.

My cousin worked for the City of Montreal when the Village was being demolished. He was assigned to dismantle the city park at Goose Village. He told me that at lunchtime he visited the empty houses slated for demolition. He remembers seeing bathtubs in basements that were used to grow soya plants. I can also imagine the stress that the people living around there had to bear when having to move away from their usual surroundings.

What were the best things about growing up in the Point in the 'forties and 'fifties? Well, the young people of the Point had the Brothers. They had a big influence on the Catholic boys of the Point. They coached those who had the talent to get a better education. They were totally devoted to teaching, I would say seven days a week.

In those days the children of the Point could also always rely on a mother waiting for them at home, and we seldom heard of unemployed people around us. The Point was our village, we felt secure walking the streets at any time. We knew, and talked to our neighbors. It was the kind of place where the corner store or restaurant owner knew if the children were spending pennies they ought not to have, and would report it to the parents. For the poorest people in the Point there were milk-drops. We had hospitals nearby and there were several doctors in the Point. We had two doctors on Centre Street, one on Laprairie and one on Notre Dame that I can remember. And in those days they would come to your house if you were sick. On the other hand, there was also the almighty religion that was very controlling, forcing families to have children without considering women's health or a family's capacity to feed or educate their children.

Having looked forward to an early retirement at 55, I decided to do something different with my life. At the suggestion of a friend, I decided to give free time to *Le Havre*, an aid center. After attending the proper training, I spent most of 20 years, two or three days a week at this new occupation. Beside listening to people confiding to me about their lives, the Center's main vocation, I also did their bookkeeping and helped, at times, with the training of new members.

I have never hesitated to say that I am from the Point, but I know that's not the case with everyone. I remember I had girlfriend at one time who was originally from Cornwall, but living in Montreal. We were at a party once and someone asked me where I was from. I told them I was from the Point. I wondered if I might meet someone else at the party from the Point. Later on in the evening my girlfriend asked me, "Why would you want to tell anyone you are from the Point?"

And relatively recently something similar happened that made me feel quite uncomfortable. I was out with a few old boyhood pals from the Point and one of them said, "How about we go for a walk around the Point and see the old places?" One of my friends responded, "Why would we want to walk around that place?" Since then, I have just never really felt comfortable with him.

"Just as an example of what is happening in the Point now,

you can look at the Productive House project

on Châteauguay Street.

It has a platinum rating with the

Canada Green Energy Council's LEED Program...

[an architect] bought the original property

and built a highly energy-efficient condo/townhouse complex

that takes advantage of solar and geothermal energy.

It even has a small bakery on the property,

constituted as a club rather than a business enterprise,

and the heat generated in the bakery

heats the green house on the roof in the winter.

It can produce 300 loaves of bread a day

and it serves condo residents and locals.

Every unit has its own garden plot

to grow whatever they want."

Réal Normandeau

Réal Normandeau

Réal is a third-generation resident of Pointe-Saint-Charles. He is employed by the City of Montreal as an Economic Development Officer specializing in real estate.

Réal's family has deep roots in the Point. His grandfather started out as a blacksmith in the Point and went on to build a large and successful business in one of Pointe-Saint-Charles' busiest locations. Réal's father was a co-founder of La Caisse Populaire Saint-Charles.

Photo: 2011.

I was born in the Point in 1952 and lived there for the first 26 years of my life. I moved away for 22 years but decided to return. I currently live in the house where I grew up. My father had it built in 1956. It is a triplex, actually, and it

"The Point's future looks very, very bright! Griffintown is exploding …the Point is next."

is only a short walk from the Caisse Populaire Saint-Charles which my father co-founded, and where he spent most of his career. Both my parents grew up in the Point.

My Grandfather was from the Point as well. He died in 1949, so I never knew him. He was a blacksmith and he opened his business in the Point. It was very centrally located on the corner of Charlevoix and Châteauguay. I'm not sure of the date but it would have been some time in the 1920s. In those days the traffic in the Point was mostly horses, wagons and carts. He started out shoeing horses and doing all the things blacksmiths do, but he also fixed wagons and other heavier equipment. He became very proficient at welding. This led to increased demand for his services, as well as growing business interests in various aspects of heavy equipment maintenance and repair. The business he eventually built was what we refer to in Montreal as a heavy equipment garage. It wasn't the kind that sold gasoline.

As the garage grew so did the range of work. He did transmissions, bodywork, and a whole range of other repairs. He had many large contracts including the Quebec Provincial Police, Canada Packers from over in Goose Village, Imperial Oil and Loiselle Petroleum. If one of the Canada Packers trucks blew a transmission or something like that, they'd bring it to my grandfather. If someone broke one of the big plows on the front of their snowplow truck, they'd bring it in and my grandfather would fix it up. He also did some walk-in business on cars and

This building on Centre Street once served as the Post Office. 2014.

other vehicles. The property was eventually expropriated during the second wave of development for the Montreal subway. The buildings are no longer there.

I had other relatives that owned businesses in the Point as well. Corner stores were everywhere in the Point and Goose Village back then. At the intersection of St. Charles and Charlevoix my great uncle and grandmother owned a grocery store on one corner, and across the street my other great uncle owned a variety store. It sold all sorts of things from small toys to confectionaries. We didn't have supermarkets around back then like we do today. In those days the corner stores served most of people's needs. When you drive around the Point you can still see the tell-tale angled *façades* on the corners of buildings showing many of the locations that once housed either a corner store or a tavern. We had lots of taverns in the Point when I was young. I stayed out of the Point taverns when I was growing up. I stuck to places like university pubs when I did go for a beer.

I went to school at first at St. Charles School on Island Street. The Louis Riel Long-Term Care Centre replaced the school when it was torn down. St. Charles was a very good school. The teachers there were excellent. After St. Charles I was fortunate enough to attend Collège Mont

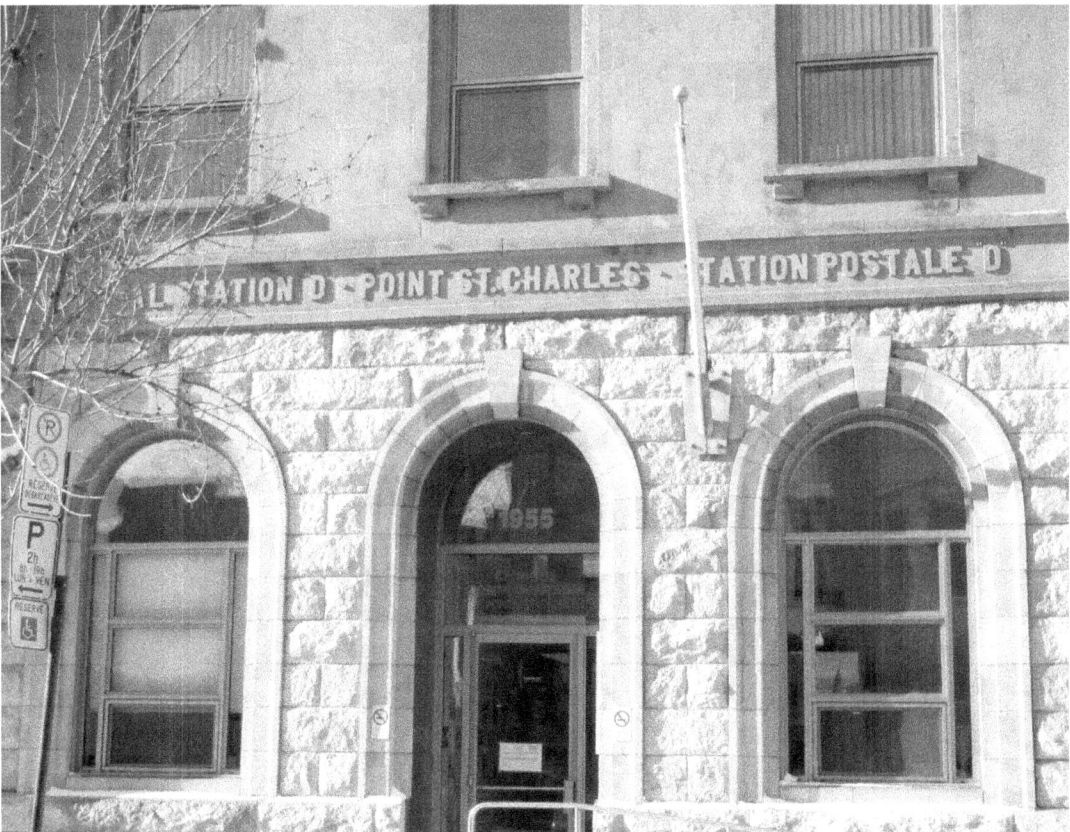

Old Centre Street Post Office. 2014.

St. Louis for high school and I really enjoyed that period. Mont St. Louis is a French Catholic private school. There are several others like it in the Montreal area including: the Collège de Montréal up on Sherbrooke Street, Brébeuf College, Collège Notre Dame, and Collège de St. Jean Eude, run by the Eudistes. Collège St. Ignace, and there are others elsewhere in Quebec. Some are still owned and run by various Catholic orders such as the Jesuits and, as I said, the Eudistes. The education at these colleges is very rigorous and typically it is classical in nature.

By the time I had finished at Mont St. Louis, the CEGEP system had just been implemented in Quebec, so before attending university I went to CEGEP St. Laurent. That's where I started to focus in on geography and began to develop a real interest in topics like urban planning. I enjoyed my time at St. Laurent very much. It was an excellent college and I took part in many activities including football. Collège St. Laurent is located right beside Vanier College. Vanier serves English-speaking students.

After I graduated I moved on to the Université du Québec and studied at the Montreal campus. This is where I concentrated my studies even more in the areas of geography, urban planning, real estate and related areas with the idea of establishing a career somewhere in the

The Productive House project on Châteauguay Street. 2014.

field. It worked out well. I have always been involved in some aspect of real estate. I started out with the real estate firm, A.E Lepage, then spent seven years with the Bank of Montreal where I worked on establishing sites for bank offices. After that I moved to the Montreal Urban Community, which covered the island of Montreal. I spent some time with Montreal International as well. This is an organization funded by the City of Montreal, the Quebec government and the Federal government. The goal of Montreal International is to attract investment to the Montreal region. Seven years ago I began working for the City of Montreal and I focus on a variety of projects related to real estate and economic development.

What was it like growing up in the Point? Well, during the period that is sometimes referred to as the golden years, the Point was a place where almost everyone had a job. The people of the Point were never going to be millionaires, but they worked hard to raise their families decently. I enjoyed growing up in the Point. It was kind of like living in a small village. Everyone knew each other. A lot of the activities for the French kids centred around the Parish. We had very good facilities there. We used the large basement at the Parish for a lot of activities including double feature films on Sundays. We had a skating rink nearby as well. We always had good skating rinks

The Productive House redevelopment towards the left of the photo respects the original streetscape: there is little external indication of the extensive nature of the changes. 2014.

in the Point. There were well-organized hockey teams we could play on as well. I remember playing hockey often against teams like Leo's Boys. That organization catered to the English boys from the Point. There were the other options for us as well like the Hogan Bath. For the most part, it was the English kids that took part in the activities at the Point's Boys' and Girls' Club over on Ash Street. It seemed like back then, the English side of the Point was a little better organized for kids' activities than us.

St. Charles Parish had a lot of influence in those days. I remember that around 1964 the City was thinking about constructing a freeway through the Point. The plan would have resulted in the highway going right through Marguerite Bourgeoys Park. There was a lot of resistance to this idea and a locally prominent nun in the Point at the time is reputed to have told City of Montreal officials that they would build the freeway "over my dead body". The City didn't pursue the idea any further.

When I started going to school in the Point, the Lachine Canal was still open. The Point was busy and heavy with industry. In those days, Northern Electric was recognized as the biggest industrial building in Canada, or what we referred to at the time as the Dominion. It was so busy that the City used to have to put on special buses that would line up around the Northern Building to take people home. There was no way the regular bus schedule could handle the outflow of workers.

It was in the 'sixties and 'seventies that things began to decay in the Point. Before the Lachine Canal closed and the factories started shutting down, there were successful small businesses all along Centre Street and Charlevoix. You used to be able to walk down Centre Street and buy a pair of shoes. We had a very good men's clothing store and many other similar establishments. In the earlier days we had several banks in the Point. There was a Montreal City and District Savings Bank. It was bought by Laurentian, then closed. What is now the Dépanneur Samy, was a Banque Nationale. Northern Electric had its own Credit Union. It closed. We also had a Bank of Montreal. It closed down. The Caisse Populaire Saint-Charles is now the only institution of its sort still operating in the Point. We used to have a big post office in the Point but that was closed down too. The building is still there and it is quite beautiful. Today, there is just a small Canada Post Kiosk in the local IGA grocery store. The small hardware store I used to go to with my father is still there, but I don't know how they do it.

After the canal started to shut down, slowly but surely businesses started to close and people started leaving. The population shrank dramatically. As it dropped from around 30,000 to 15,000, it was really some of the poorest people that stayed on. By around the early 'nineties as much as 50% of the population of the Point was on some sort of social assistance. It was a stressful and difficult period for the Point. Times were tough. People were finding themselves in jail that had never had any problems before. There would be an argument at home and some sort of altercation. The police would get called and someone who had never had any issues before would end up in jail.

Today, though, things are looking up in the Point. There are many new developments. Lots of renovations have been completed and more are starting all the time. People want to live near the centre of the city. The Point is within walking distance of a lot of Montreal's amenities and it has its own subway stop. Development will also continue along the banks of the Lachine Canal. Parks Canada has already invested significantly in support of initiatives like the bicycle path along the canal and rebuilding locks. Through years of neglect after the closing of the canal, the lock doors would not even open. Now you can see pleasure boats moving through the canal.

The work on the Lachine Canal isn't as far advanced yet as canal systems like the Rideau that goes from Ottawa to the St. Lawrence River. There aren't as many amenities along the Lachine Canal. On the Rideau there are many places that you can tie up your boat and stop at restaurants etc. The people and institutions involved in the Lachine Canal improvement efforts are exercising great care in how they go about their work, including issuing licenses.

Canal improvements will continue over the long term and there are still a few quality building lots available for development of some sort alongside the canal and relatively close to the Point and Saint-Henri. They can range in size from 30,000 to 210,000 square feet. Farther west, going out to Lachine though, a lot of this land is quite contaminated due to the various industries that operated there for decades. It would be very costly for a private investor to clean up some of these lots for development. I think that to engage in anything meaningful, in those situations you'd need some sort of government intervention.

The City of Montreal recognizes the important heritage and architecture of Pointe-Saint-Charles and is very rigorous regarding what commercial developers can and can't do. For example, we have a three-stage process for any developer seeking to demolish an existing building and then rebuild. If anyone wants to do this, they must have a clear plan of what will replace the existing building and it must conform to a number of requirements. The City doesn't just want one condo after another going up with no supporting retail, green space and other amenities. Also, many of the existing buildings are simply protected because of their heritage value. The borough is very strict. Everything submitted must have a full architectural plan. As I said, it's a three- stage process for developers and sometimes a proposal won't even get past the first stage.

Just as an example of what is happening in the Point now, you can look at the Productive House project on Châteauguay Street. It has a platinum rating with the Canada Green Energy Council's LEED Program, which stands for Leadership in Energy and Environmental Design. From the outside, the complex just looks like a well-done Pointe-

Réal outside the Fine Pointe restaurant on Centre Street. 2013.

Saint-Charles row house renovation with new doors, new windows and some brickwork etc. You'd never know what was on the other side of the old carriage entrance. What happened was that a well-known architect by the name of Rune Kongshaug bought the original property and built a highly energy-efficient condo/ townhouse complex that takes advantage of solar and geothermal energy. It even has a small bakery on the property, constituted as a club rather than a business enterprise, and the heat generated in the bakery heats the green house on the roof in the winter. It can produce 300 loaves of bread a day and it serves condo residents and locals. Every unit has its own garden plot to grow whatever they want. At the old carriageway entrance an electric car is plugged in and people can rent the car when they need it. Mr. Kongshaug retains one of these townhouses in the Point as one of his bases of operation. He is convinced that this approach to redevelopment is the key to a sustainable future. He doesn't even own a car himself. Although Mr. Kanshaug develops projects only in Montreal and New York, he travels and maintains relations with other experts and successful promoters in highly sustainable development all over the world.

My own brother recognized the potential of the Point many years ago. When he finished his degree in the mid-'seventies he decided to start buying, renovating and renting dwellings in the Point. At one time he owned 60 separate units. He bought and renovated every single one himself.

Homage is paid both to the people and industrial history of southwest Montreal in various ways, such as the naming of these two parks in Point St.
Left: Railwayman Park; Right: Boilermaker Park. (author's translations). 2012.

He learned how to do it on the fly. He completely renovated these units—inside and out. A lot of them didn't even have baths. On the outside, he'd put in new doors and windows and fix any exterior problems, but his work retained the heritage and architecture of the original buildings. He has since sold all of them and is now a homebuilder. He has built in Candiac, Ile Perrot and Saint-Zotique, a small municipality near Coteau-du-Lac and Valleyfield.

History has shown us that as immigration patterns change, so do the profiles of various communities, and the Point is an example of this. At present, I would say that the groups that are growing the most rapidly in the Point are from areas such as India and Sri Lanka. You can see this quite clearly in some of the retail establishments that are opening in places like Centre Street. About eight or nine years ago, a mosque was also built in the Point as well. At the same time, we are seeing a lot of young professionals coming in. Typically, they are looking for highly renovated units.

I think things are really looking up for Pointe-Saint-Charles. In fact, quite a number of vacant lots have been purchased lately in anticipation of increasing interest in the Point. As more people move in, we'll see more renovations, more stores and more new housing. I expect to see improvements in parks, green spaces and, of course, the improvement work on the Lachine Canal will continue. As things progress, the City will realize a strengthening tax base in the area and the cycle will continue.

The Future of Pointe-Saint-Charles looks very, very bright! Griffintown is exploding…the Point is next.

Two brick condominiums at the northern end of Griffintown frame a downtown Montreal high-rise. 2013.

The Presentation Brothers

Today, Quebec's public education system is secular. This wasn't the case when contributors to this book attended school.

Given the historically strong Roman Catholic presence in the Point, Griffintown and Goose Village, together with the fact that most contributors to this book were schooled, in part, by members of religious orders, I felt it important to profile at least one such order and hear from some members that remember the era under discussion. I chose the Presentation Brothers. As readers will already have seen, members of this specific order taught several contributors to this work.

The Presentation Brothers are Christian missionaries headquartered in County Cork, Ireland. The order is dedicated to teaching, and their help is typically called upon to support poor, disadvantaged communities. The first Presentation Brothers to arrive in Canada assumed responsibility for Chauveau School in Point St. Charles in 1910. Ultimately, the school was renamed Canon O'Meara in honour of one of the people who originally approached the Presentation Brothers in Ireland for help in Canada. According to the Presentation Brothers' Canadian Centenary publication, there was a pressing need at the time for high-quality English education for Catholic children, and they agreed to help.

From their Chauveau starting point, the Presentation Brothers went on to serve as either teachers or administrators elsewhere in Montreal and Quebec, as well as in Ontario and British Columbia. By the early 1950s more than 70 active members of the congregation were working in Quebec, but by 1985 only 20 remained in the Province. The last active Presentation Brother left Quebec in 2001—91 years after the arrival of the first contingent in Point St. Charles.

At the time I was conducting the research for this book there were three remaining members of the order in Canada: Brother Henry Spencer, Brother Ivan Verba and Brother Philip Giroux. Brother Henry Spencer remains in a school setting, and does so on a voluntary basis. He is part of the Chaplaincy team at Brébeuf College in Toronto. Brother Ivan Verba is also in Toronto and acts as the Presentation Brothers' Superior and Provincial Bursar. Brother Philip Giroux was 94 years old when I met him and was living in a Toronto retirement home managed by a religious order. I decided to approach Brothers Philip Giroux and Henry Spencer, and they kindly agreed to meet. So too, did Leo Purcell, who served with the Presentation Brothers (Brother Stephen) for over 20 years and taught at Canon O'Meara in Point St. Charles from 1949–1951, the last two years of the Presentation Brothers' involvement with the school. Leo resides in Montreal.

Oral histories follow for Henry Spencer and Leo Purcell. Brother Philip, however, was not in very good health when we met in 2012 and he passed away in 2013. In the short time we spent together Brother Philip did tell me that after graduating from St. Patrick's High School in Sherbrooke, which was run by the Presentation Brothers, he committed to the order and a lifetime of teaching. Brother Philip taught at Montreal schools such as Daniel O'Connell and Montreal Catholic High School. He also served as Principal of Verdun Catholic High School. Brendan Deegan knew Brother Philip for years. Until Brother Philip's passing, Brendan kept in touch and drove from Montreal to Toronto at regular intervals to visit him. Says Brendan:

"One of the vows taken by Presentation Brothers upon initiation is that of poverty, and Brother Philip was the most committed, honest and selfless man I have ever known. I have never heard him mention any personal need".

"The two words of *poor* and *teach*

were the two ideas

that the congregation

focused on."

Leo Purcell

Leo Purcell

Leo Purcell was born in Nova Scotia in 1932. By 1945 he was studying with the Presentation Brothers in Longeuil, Quebec. Leo became a Brother (Stephen) and by 1949 he was teaching at Canon O'Meara in Point St. Charles. He taught there until the Presentation Brothers withdrew from Canon O'Meara two years later. Leo went on to a variety of other assignments in Montreal, Montebello (Quebec) and Navrongo, Ghana.

"My focus when I arrived at Canon O'Meara was to learn how to teach, and how to respond to the children. For their part, they were just trying to get through another school day and meet the teacher's demands. I spent a great deal of time preparing for my classes, trying to devise ways of making the new material interesting and of getting it across."

Canon O'Meara School on Laprairie St. in the Point was, in a way, my basic training camp. As a young 17-year-old I developed my early teaching skills there in front of a fifth-grade class of boys for the school year 1949-50. The following year I started with another fifth grade but was moved into seventh grade before Christmas. This shift created some tension for me. Students of seventh grade had to write provincial exams at the end of the school year, which, if they were successful, would allow them to enter high school. I saw this as an added challenge because the final evaluation of the students was taken out of my hands. More care had to be taken in the teaching of the curriculum to insure that all the areas were well covered.

I took my first breath in 1932 in the small town of Mulgrave, NS. My father was also born there. His father was Irish and mother Scottish. My mother was born in Sydney, NS. Both her parents were Acadian, brought up in the beautiful Margaree Valley, Cape Breton. We were eight children—four boys and four girls. I was number five. My very early school years were relatively smooth and uneventful. But somewhere around fifth grade the fog started to roll in and schooling became a big struggle. I staggered through to the eighth grade with the constant threat of failing. I was discouraged and depressed.

The fact that I became a teacher at all is a bit ironic, since I promised myself when I was failing academically that if I ever got out of school I would never go back. The year before I finished grade eight my cousin, who was a Presentation Brother teaching in Montreal, came to Mulgrave to visit his family, and mentioned to my parents that if any of the boys would like to attend high school in Longueuil and maybe become a Brother, he would set the wheels in motion. My mother, figuring that I might be heading for disaster if nothing was done, brought up the proposition a

The former residence of the Presentation Brothers. 2012.

Canon O'Meara School once stood in the vacant lot in the foreground, beside the now-derelict Presentation Brothers' residence. 2012.

a year later of doing just that (my father had died the previous fall from a heart attack). I was 13 at the time, and Longueuil was about 1000 miles away. I felt so low that the only way to go was up. So, in blind faith I agreed. Because my older brother was employed by the CNR at the time, I was eligible for a return rail pass to Montreal. I left Mulgrave for Longueuil on September 8, 1945. My mother's parting words were: "If you don't like it, come home; you can always come home". The return pass expired at the end of October, and I didn't go home.

The Presentation Brothers' facility in Longueuil served as both a Juniorate and a Novitiate. The Juniorate section functioned as a regular high school with classes in French, English, Latin, Mathematics. The Novitiate section prepared the new candidates who were just received into the congregation to become members according to established Canon Law. As with most houses of study belonging to religious congregations, the Presentation Brothers applied to the Provincial Government for and received recognition as a Religious Scholasticate giving them the legal right to prepare their members to sit for the provincial examinations for a teaching certificate—the Complementary Diploma after one year of study following the completion of grade nine; the Superior

Diploma after two years of study. With this arrangement the Brothers and Sisters did not have to attend the regular Normal Schools. This method of certifying teachers was the general path in Quebec up until the Ministry of Education was established in the early '60s.

My years of study in Longueuil were wonderful years. One of my teachers, Brother Xavier, had a great deal to do with making these years wonderful (more later). The fog lifted, I covered a great deal of academic material in a relatively short time, and left the Novitiate as a certified teacher (Complementary Diploma) in September, 1949. I followed this with a Superior Diploma a year later.

Back to Canon O'Meara, the Presentation Brothers took charge of running the school in 1910. Several Brothers came from Ireland and some were sent to operate Chauveau School (later Canon O'Meara). The school always had lay teachers as well as Brothers. During my time the first three grades were taught by women lay teachers, as well as lay men who taught the Secondary top. This last term (secondary top) was a two-year course that allowed some pupils to finish two more years of schooling without enrolling in a regular high school. Nine years of schooling were required to get certain jobs, and to enter some of the trade apprenticeship programs.

My focus when I arrived at Canon O'Meara was to learn how to teach, and how to respond to the children. For their part, they were just trying to get through another school day and meet the teacher's demands. I spent a great deal of time preparing for my classes, trying to devise ways of making the new material interesting and of getting it across. I liked the children and was concerned about getting them through the curriculum, especially the Seventh graders. Some few continued their schooling after Seventh grade but many did not. However, it's important to point out that many of those who did not still led productive and successful lives. Three of my pupils, that I know of, became teachers.

Back to Canon O'Meara, Brother Xavier (Henry McInerney from New Jersey, USA) did his practice teaching in Canon O'Meara School as a young Presentation Brother back in the mid 1930s. For many years he taught English Literature at Catholic High. After a sojourn of three years teaching in St. John Bosco Teachers College, Navrongo, Ghana, he returned to Canada. Xavier felt that continuing to teach in Canadian schools, as he did for some 35 years, was not what he wanted to do with the rest of his life. He applied for and received a dispensation from his vows as a Brother, and enrolled in a seminary in Boston, Mass, established specifically to prepare older men for the priesthood. He was ordained, Oct. 5, 1974, and started his ministry here in Montreal. As fate would have it the Archbishop of Montreal appointed him as curate in St. Gabriel's Parish in the Point. In some strange way it seemed appropriate that the community of St. Gabriel's Parish, who welcomed the Presentation Brothers in 1910, was once more welcoming a new priest into their community who had spent most of his adult teaching as a Presentation Brother. Father Xavier wasn't with them long. He died from an angina attack in April, 1976.

Often in schools run by the Brothers, some were expected to assume other duties: taking care of the altar servers was the most common one. In larger schools coaching sports was a popular extra-curricular activity. I was asked to train the school choir, which sang mostly at the Sunday High Mass. It didn't work out very well, for the obvious reason that I didn't know what to do. In the winter I put up the rink on the parish tennis court next to the school. The school

Leo (Brother Stephen), back right, and class at Canon O'Meara School. c. 1950.

children used it after school, but public skating was popular on some evenings. The Catholic High School of Montreal, commonly referred to simply as Catholic High, administered by the Brothers, ran an annual winter carnival. Part of this one-night event was a round robin hockey tournament for the elementary schools administered by the Brothers, involving five or six teams with very short game times. Although the school population was small, and no school uniforms were available, I decided to put a team together for the carnival, and borrow the parish hockey sweaters. The Canon O'Meara boys played their best but it wasn't enough to bring home the cup presented to the winning team. Pat Duffy, well known in later years for his prowess on the football field, was by far the strongest player on our team; he sustained an injury that night. He got the end of a skate in his ribs, and it broke the skin. I took him to the Montreal General, just across the street from the Forum to be sure his lung wasn't punctured. It wasn't.

Teaching the elementary classes is, in many ways, a real blessing. One has the same 25 or so pupils for more than five hours a day. This time together helps the teacher to know the pupils and conversely helps the pupils know the teacher. In contrast, teaching at the high school level forces the teacher to teach the subject, and the individual pupils get less attention. You're assigned a class in elementary school; you're assigned a subject in high school level. If you ask an elementary teacher what he/she teaches, he/she will say: "Grade…"; the same question to a high school teacher gets the answer: "Math, Science, English Lit". etc. And at the high school level a teacher can be facing 100 to 130 pupils a day.

A few words about Catholic High: it was founded in the late 1800s with the primary purpose of preparing English Catholic students for the McGill matriculation exams. Loyola College was there but offered a general BA program. It did not offer degrees in Engineering, Law, Architecture. The School was staffed with a lay faculty. It ran into difficulties and had to close down. The pastor of St. Patrick's Parish was looking around for a religious congregation to take charge so that there would be greater stability. He was able to get an agreement with the Presentation Brothers to staff the school. This they did in 1911. The school gave the English Catholic community access to McGill, a very great asset. The school closed permanently in 1958.

With the withdrawal of the Presentation Brothers from Canon O'Meara in June of 1951 after 41 years, I was transferred to Luke Callaghan Boys' School where I taught a Seventh grade class for one year, then was transferred to Daniel O'Connell High School. For the next three years I taught First High (Religion, Math, Latin). With the completion of my Bachelor of Arts, granted by the University of Montreal in 1955, I was scheduled to teach the Math, Chemistry, Religion, Canadian History and Latin in Third Year High, and Math and Chemistry in Fourth High. This schedule stayed more or less the same for the following two years.

September 1958 saw me in Leroux High School, LaSalle, later called LaSalle Catholic Comprehensive High School (LCCHS), where I taught Math, Chemistry, Physics, and Religion in Fourth High, and Math and Chemistry in Third High. These years in LaSalle were good years. The school was just starting, interest was high in the community, and the students were keen. In September 1964 I was assigned as teaching Principal of Presentation High School in Montebello. This was a residential school, set up as a Juniorate for boys who may be thinking about becoming Brothers. This facility opened in 1947 and functioned until the late 1980s. While it registered many boys who were thinking of becoming Brothers, most of student body were boys who, for whatever reason, did not fit easily into the public system, or who needed more structure and less distraction in order to finish their schooling. The history of the school showed that while many boys graduated from the Novitiate in Longueuil to continue on the path of becoming a Brother, the majority of those young men who did go stayed for a few months or a few years, some even to the stage of getting their certification and teaching. Only four lasted more than ten years, and as of last count there is one Brother who is still a member of the Presentation Brothers; one other persevered, teaching in Africa, and dying there. If one counts success by the number of boys who went through the Juniorate and became Brothers, then it was a dismal and very expensive failure.

But there were some real successes. The numbers who received their high school leaving certificate was above average. During my two-year stay I saw several students turn their lives around and thrive in Montebello. For many of them the structure, the discipline of regular hours for study, for games, meals and sleep permitted them to concentrate on their studies, and since success breeds success, each little improvement was followed by bigger ones.

The drive for renewal in the congregations of Priests, Brothers, and Sisters across the world, once the Second Vatican Council came to a close in 1963, resulted in their members taking a good look at what their founders wanted done (when they were founded), and what these communities were doing now. The Presentation Brothers were founded to teach poor boys in Ireland the rudiments of the Catholic faith. The two words of "poor" and "teach" were the two ideas that the congregation focused on. It was very evident to anyone who bothered to look that many baptized lay Christians could do the teaching that the Brothers were doing in well-established urban and suburban communities. All religious communities were founded to be, in a sense, storm troopers, to go where others cannot or will not go. This new focus was foremost in the mind of the Brothers' Canadian Provincial Superior in1967 when Gerard Bertrand, Bishop of Navrongo, Ghana, asked for Brothers to come to his diocese and teach. Brother Xavier and I left Montreal in August, 1968, to open a new foundation in Navrongo. I returned to Canada in 1970.

"Back in the days

when we started a new mission

like that of Canon O'Meara,

there was very little money

for the Brothers to establish themselves

and run the school.

I remember Brother DePaul

telling us often that had it not been

for the kindness and support

of the people of Point St. Charles,

that the first Canon O'Meara Brothers

never would have survived."

Brother Henry Spencer

Brother Henry Spencer

Brother Henry Spencer lives in Toronto at the Presentation Brothers' residence. As noted earlier, Brother Henry remains active as a volunteer at Brébeuf College, a private, all-boys Roman Catholic school. His story is one of early and lifelong commitment to the Presentation Brothers, and his work has taken him to assignments in several countries. Brother Henry turned 80 years old in October of 2012. He is a vibrant, hard-working man. He enjoys a laugh and is a great storyteller. This is Brother Henry's story.

"Although the names of our Brothers change over time, as do the countries and schools we work in, the mission of the Presentation Brothers remains constant —education."

I was born in 1932 in County Cork, Ireland near Bantry. My father owned a farm. We had cattle, hens and chickens and mixed farming. We always had lots of milk. We were very fortunate indeed, even during the hard times.

When I was very young I attended a two-room country school. By 1948 I had completed my national school certification and I moved on to the Presentation Brothers' Boarding School. It was in Cork City and the name of the School was St. Mary's. Part of the original structure is still standing. It was truly a grand building. I remember well what we used to call the games room. It was adorned with wonderful oak carvings and it was very large with high ceilings. That is where we would gather in our spare time to play games like shuffleboard. At any given time there would have been about 80 young men at St. Mary's preparing for a life in the Presentation Brothers. I was there for two years.

After my time at St. Mary's I attended St. Theresa's College for a year. Both St. Mary's and St. Theresa's prepared us to move on to the Novitiate at Mount St. Joseph in Cork City. It was after two years at Mount St. Joseph that I made my profession of vows. Then, as it is termed, novices "live the life" for three years and take their final professional vows. I was 24 years old by the time I had completed all of my preparations to begin my duties as a teacher with the Presentation Brothers. My first assignment was at St. Joe's Elementary School in Cork City,

Ireland. I was there for two years. It was at that time that my Superior called me in and asked me, "How would you like to travel?" I said, "Yes", and in no time I was on my way to Canada.

Seven years before I came to Canada the Presentation Brothers had just finished their service with Canon O'Meara School in Point St. Charles. I will forever remember the Brothers who taught there talking about their experiences in the Point. And even today, if I hear the name of an old Canon O'Meara student I can often link the person with tales the Canon O'Meara Brothers told of boxing or something like that.

Back in the days when we started a new mission like that of Canon O'Meara, there was very little money for the Brothers to establish themselves and run the school. I remember Brother DePaul telling us often that had it not been for the kindness and support of the people of Point St. Charles, that the first Canon O'Meara Brothers never would have survived.

When I came to Canada, Brother Philip Giroux met me upon my arrival in Montreal. He assigned me to Luke Callaghan School. At the time Luke Callaghan served many new immigrants to Canada. There were a lot of Greek students and many Italian children. I was there for four years. It was challenging work and I thoroughly enjoyed the experience. For the most part I was teaching English and Religion at Luke Callaghan. After that I moved on to Verdun Catholic High School. That was at the time when St. Willibrord's in Verdun, another Presentation Brothers school, was closing and the students from there joined us at Verdun Catholic. I spent three years at Verdun and then went to teach at what would become LaSalle Catholic High School. I remember that Brother Martin Walsh was my Principal. When his schools were audited they would always come out with a sparkling review. We used to call him "Mr. Organization". He was very meticulous about the way the schools were organized.

For two years I taught at one of our schools at Montebello, Quebec, and then I was assigned as Principal to St. Peter's Parochial School in Marshall, Missouri. Marshall, at the time was a predominantly Baptist community and the Catholic population was very much in the minority. Yet everyone got along very well and the people were all very easy going. Many of the residents were farmers or ranchers, and as they used to say, "I'm from Missouri, show me". St. Peter's was an elementary school and we had about 250 students. Six Presentation Brothers worked at St. Peter's.

I was at St. Peter's for eight years when I got the call from the Superior to return to Ireland for two years to take over the Novitiate training. After that I came back to Canada in 1984 to Brébeuf College in Toronto and I have been here ever since. The Presentation Brothers took over the school from the Jesuits. I taught Latin, English, Social Studies and Religion. At age sixty-five I stopped teaching and I have been volunteering at the School ever since. In total, I have been committed to Brébeuf for 28 years now.

Although the names of our Brothers change over time, as do the countries and schools we work in, the mission of the Presentation Brothers remains constant—education. I'd say that we now have about 200 Brothers living and working in Ireland and our missions in places like Ghana and Nigeria are growing. It is difficult work. One of our female students in our Nigerian school was shot and killed just last year. It is a challenging mission but we are building schools and educating the young. We have about 40 professed Brothers novices in Africa at present and they are all Africans.

We agreed to build our most recent school in Yendi (Ghana) on the condition that it would serve both girls and boys. When we first spoke to the people of the area they explained that girls don't go to school because their job is to carry water. The girls were travelling long distances on foot to find water and then carrying it back in vessels on their heads. We told the adults of Yendi that we'd find the water but the girls must go to school. They agreed and we ensured that a well was dug—a borehole as we call it in Africa. In this case we went down 93 feet and found cold, clear water. The girls are no longer carrying water all day and most have access to computers.

About 75% of the students in our Yendi School are Muslim. We have four Brothers there now. We have a monthly collection at Brébeuf for the African schools and we are able to consistently send about $250 per month. In 2011 we took 20 of the Brébeuf students to Africa to work with the children for three weeks. It was quite an adventure for them.

The Brothers are also active at present in St. Lucia. We were in Lima, Peru for years and we currently have a mission in San Antonio, Texas where we are working with street people and the homeless. For my part, I remain very active. In addition to the work I do at Brébeuf I am involved in a variety of other initiatives. Every summer I travel to an annual six-day retreat at the Augustinian Monastery north of Toronto. I also travel to an Indian Reserve much farther north of Toronto. It is about a three-hour drive followed by a 20-min. ferry ride. I teach children, or rather prepare them for the Sacraments. There is no Catholic school, and, by and large, they do not attend church on Sundays. They get no religious training in their homes. So, I try to help the Pastor and get the kids to study the Sacraments. It is voluntary work and this will be my 25th summer up there.

Montreal

Appendix

Some Notes on Methodology

Typically, these oral histories were developed, face-to-face, over a number of sessions. My commitment to each person from the outset was that their oral history would go forward for publication only after they were completely satisfied, and approved the content.

Contributors told me their stories and I took notes. After drafting the material as relayed to me, we would meet, or in selected instances exchange e-mails to review the copy, make corrections, follow up on some topics, add new information and address additional questions. Normally, three weeks or so, between discussions permitted contributors to reflect on their stories, follow up on details, dig up old documents, look for photos or make corrections. The cycle of meeting, discussing, reviewing, reading over the narrative from start to finish, correcting etc., continued until the persons contributing were completely satisfied that their oral history was accurate and as relayed to me. After we had developed some drafts over the course of several discussions, some contributors sat down at their computers and finalized their histories themselves. The discussions in support of one oral history were conducted entirely over the phone and via e-mail. Another contributor drafted his own history based on questions that I had forwarded.

Picture credits

These picture credits are in the order that the pictures appear in the book.

Photos by Dave Flavell are indicated (JDF).

An illustration is credited where it was possible to identify the artist/photographer.

In some cases such as event or team photos, where efforts to ascertain the identity of the photographer were unsuccessful, the source of the photos is indicated as *Courtesy of (name of person who shared photo), photographer unknown* (PU).

Where there is no indication of the photographer, but the photos appear to be of the "family album" variety, they are identified as "FP" (family photo).

Photos that appear to be part of a series, but where only some can be definitively credited to a given photographer, the unidentified photos are credited as *"likely" taken by (name)."*

The street photos of Victoriatown/Goose Village credited to "Archives de la Ville de Montreal" were taken in preparation for the 1964 demolition of the neighborhood.

Cover: Fortune St. north of Wellington St., Point St. Charles. Acrylic on canvas. 2010 (JDF)

Introduction

- 1890 interpretation of Montreal (Legend added) pointing to several of the primary locations discussed in this book. Birds eye view - City of Montreal in 1889. Drawn and published by the George Bishop Eng. & Ptg. Co. (Limited). Lithographed by the George Bishop Eng Ptg. Co. (Limited). Courtesy Library and Archives Canada. MIKAN no. 413789.

- Charles E. Goad Map prepared for the 1898 Lovell's Montreal Directory (Legend added): Courtesy, McGill University (Rare Books).

- Skyline and river view from atop the Mount Royal lookout, 2013. (JDF)

- Looking across the Lachine canal from Point St. Charles to downtown Montreal, 2010. (JDF)

- Two-photograph panorama taken from the Griffintown (north) side of the Lachine Canal. Wm. Notman & Son (1896). Courtesy, McCord Museum (McGill University) Views 2941 and 2942.

- Two-photograph panorama taken from the Griffintown (north) side of the canal. Wm. Notman & Son (1896). Courtesy, McCord Museum (McGill University) Views 2943 and 2944.

- 1930 Railway yard-focused aerial (Legend added). Courtesy Library and Archives Canada. Citation: C.N.R Point St. Charles shops for George W. Reed & C0. Mikan 3402295, DAPDCAP 33184, PA-037501.

- 1920 photo of canal entrance at Lachine. McCarthy Aero Service. Courtesy, Library and Archives Canada. PA-30760.

- View of lock and Montreal harbour. Courtesy, Library and Archives Canada. Online Mikan No. 3349533.

- Ships at harbour. Courtesy, Library and Archives Canada. Archival reference no. R231-2496-X-E. Online Mikan no. 3349520. Date unknown.

- 1920 aerial view of Griffintown/easternmost point of the Lachine Canal. Courtesy, Library and Archives. Canada. Citation: Aerial view of Montreal (1) Item linked part of graphic material philatelic record R9271-5- 2-E2 no. 33228222. PA-056103.

- Aerial view of primary area of discussion (legend added). Courtesy, Natural Resources Canada, National Air Photo Library (NAPL / FTP / 108420). Circa 1970s.

- "Golden Square Mile" architecture, 2012. (JDF)

- Four Goose Village Street scenes taken shortly before the 1964 demolition. Courtesy, J. Berlettano. (PU). 1964.

- Six Griffintown photos 2010 – 2013. (JDF).
- Five Point St. Charles street photos, 2010 – 2014. (JDF)
- Six shots towards the eastern end of the Lachine Canal, 2011 - 2013. (JDF).
- Ireland Park, 2013. (JDF).
- LaSalle Tower, 2011. (JDF).
- Maison St. Gabriel in Point St. Charles (2011), and the King's ward's plaque, 2013. (JDF).
- Depiction of the Lachine Rapids. Canadian Illustrated News (1879), Vol. XIX, No. 22, Page 341. Reproduced from Library and Archives Canada's website Images in the News: Canadian Illustrated News.
- Port of Montreal looking west toward the Lachine Canal. Canadian Illustrated News (1875). Vol. XII, No. 7, (10 May, 1879). Photo: From Library and Archives Canada's website Images in the News: Canadian Illustrated News.
- Looking east during canal enlargement work at the St. Gabriel Lock. Canadian Illustrated News (1877), Vol. XVI, No. 22, Page 340. Reproduced from Library and Archives Canada's website Images in the News: Canadian Illustrated News.
- Clearing ice at the harbour and looking west toward the smokestacks of Montreal industry, a short walk away. Canadian Illustrated News (1879), Vol. XIX, No. 19, Page 293. Reproduced from Library and Archives Canada's website Images in the News: Canadian Illustrated News.

Brendan Deegan

- Katie and Brendan at a United Irish Societies event in Montreal, 2013. (JDF).
- The "Black Rock," 2010. (JDF).
- Where Brendan grew up on Laprairie Street, 2012. (JDF).
- Brendan and siblings on the front steps on Laprairie Street, 1941. Courtesy B. Deegan. (FP).
- Brendan (left) and brother Kevin at home, 1985. Courtesy, B. Deegan. (FP).
- Brendan's father (right). Dave Lampton (left). Courtesy, B. Deegan, (early 1950s). (PU).
- St. Patrick's Day. Brendan (R), brother Kevin (L) and Jack Young. Courtesy, B. Deegan, 1951. (FP).
- Brendan (right) and brother Kevin (Tennis) 1954. Courtesy B. Deegan (FP).
- Point St. Charles' St. Gabriel School, 2013 St. Patrick's Day parade, Montreal. (JDF).
- Family photograph, 1977. Courtesy, B. Deegan. (FP).
- Class photo. Courtesy, K. Deegan and the Commission Scolaire de Montreal (previously the Montreal Catholic School Commission) 1949.
- St. Gabriel's Church on Centre Street in Point St. Charles, 2010. (JDF).
- Looking west to St. Ann's Church. Photographer David Wallace Marvin, Courtesy, McCord Museum, McGill University - reference number MP-1978.186.1.4774.
- Griffintown's St. Ann's Church during 1970 demolition. Photographer David Wallace Martin, Courtesy, McCord Museum, McGill University - reference number MP-1978. 186.2482.
- Griffintown's St. Ann's Church site in winter, 2013. (JDF).
- A past parishioner at Griffintown St. Ann Park, 2011. (JDF).
- Walk to the Stone, 2012. (JDF).
- Brendan with "Paddy" and Victor Boyle on St. Patrick's Day, 2014. (JDF).
- Griffintown – St. Ann Park sign, 2010 (JDF).

Rose Villeneuve, Nee Tamburino

- Rose at home, 2011 (JDF).
- Dominion Coal Company Docks. Courtesy Library and Archives Canada. PA-56603. Photographer, Johnston, C. M. 1931.
- Coal car. Canadian National Railways Graphic Collection, 1939. Courtesy, Library and Archives Canada. PA-190750. Mikan no. 3525636. (PU).
- Women bundling cordite for naval shells at Defence Industries, Ltd. in Montreal (June 1944). Harry Rowed, National Film Board of Canada, Still Photography Division (R1196-14-7-E). Courtesy Library and Archives Canada / PA-116926.
- Working at a Montreal munitions factory. National Film Board of Canada (1943). Still Photography Division (R1196-14-7-E) Courtesy, Library and Archives Canada. Online MIKAN no. 3197048. (PU).
- Stockyard illustration. Illustrated News (1881). Vol. XXIII, Vol. 4, Page 53. Reproduced from Library and Archives Canada's website Images in the News: Canadian Illustrated News.
- St. Alphonsus School (1964). Courtesy J. Berlettano. (PU).

Roger Agnessi

- Boatswain & Ship's Diver, R. Agnessi, Royal Canadian Navy. Courtesy, R. Agnessi and the Department of National Defence, 1970.
- Roger, behind his home on Charlevoix Street, 1959. Courtesy, R. Agnessi. (FP).
- Roger (right) with his brother and cousin, 1958. Courtesy, R. Agnessi. (FP).
- Richardson's on Charlevoix Street in Point St. Charles, 2011. (JDF).
- Roger, on St. Patrick Street. Courtesy, 1959. Courtesy R. Agnessi. (FP).
- Frank Hanley. Courtesy Archives de la Ville de Montreal. VM94, Z-854. Date/(PU).
- The Wellington Tower alongside the Lachine Canal and train bridge, 2010. (JDF).
- Leo's Stable, 2010. (JDF).
- The Griffintown Horse Palace, 2011. (JDF).
- Leo Leonard, 2010. (JDF).
- Roger pointing to his old flat. 2012 (JDF).
- Roger, beside the train trestle, 2012. (JDF).
- Roger (right) at the 2012 Remembrance Day ceremony. Photographer D. McRae.

Eddy Nolan

- Eddy leading runners at Montreal's 2013 Terry Fox Run. (JDF).
- Eddy with Ian Clyde, 2013. (JDF).
- Eddy and his father getting ready. (PU).
- Chas E. Goad Co. Atlas Of Montreal (1912) Courtesy, McGill University (Rare Books).
- Aerial photo of rail yard and Nun's Island. Courtesy, Library and Archives Canada. Online MIKAN no. 3402296. Date unknown.
- Three Stockyard photographs

  1) Courtesy, Library and Archives Canada. Online MIKAN no. 3350449. Date unknown.

  2) Courtesy, Library and Archives Canada. Online MIKAN no. 3350448. Date unknown.

  3) Courtesy, Library and Archives Canada. Online MIKAN no. 3350450. Date unknown.

- Inside the railway shops in Point St. Charles (1929). Courtesy, Library and Archives Canada. Online MIKAN no. 3348631.
- Where Eddy worked part time as a youngster, 2011. (JDF).
- Eddy (left) with brother Mickey and David O'Neill, 2012. (JDF).
- Eddy and Mary outside Roslyn School, 2012. (JDF).
- Boston Marathon certificate – 1997. Courtesy E. Nolan.
- Eddy and Mary at the 2013 Terry Fox Run with the McGill University Medical School contingent. (JDF).
- Eddy completing the 2013 Terry Fox Run in Montreal. (JDF).
- Eddy's parents, Audrey and Mike "Sonny" Nolan. Courtesy, E, Nolan. (FP).

Carol (Scott) Bellware

- Carol Bellware, 2013. (JDF).
- The corner of Menai and Forfar, Goose Village. Courtesy, Archives de la Ville de Montreal VM94C270-0155. c. 1963.
- 529 Charon Street, Point St. Charles, 2014. (JDF).
- Fire Insurance Plan, Peck, Benny & Co. Chas. E Goad, Civil Engineer, Montreal (1897). Courtesy, Library and Archives Canada. Archival reference no. R6990-810-8-E. MIKAN no. 3912365.
- Carol's daughter Kelly and Carol's father Philip Scott. Courtesy Carol Bellware (FP).
- Carol's father (left), Philip Scott on Remembrance Day (2013) (JDF).
- Point St. Charles YMCA, 2014. (JDF).
- Carol at the podium, 1954. Courtesy C. Bellware & Library and Archives Canada, Montreal Star fonds (graphic material) R11284-0-4-E. Accession no. 1980-108 NPC. (PU).
- Point St. Charles "Rockettes," 1956/'57 season. Courtesy, C. Bellware. (PU).
- The Lorne School building in Point St. Charles (2012). (JDF).
- Lorne School books. Courtesy, C. Bellware. (JDF).
- Point St. Charles' Saint Columba House, 2010. (JDF).
- The old Grace Church building, 2014. (JDF).
- Family get-together, 1946. Courtesy, C. Bellware. (FP).
- Carol and team at book launch, 2013. (JDF).
- Point St. Charles architecture, 2014. (JDF).

Terry McCarthy

- Terry McCarthy, 2013. (JDF).
- Young Terry McCarthy in Griffintown. Courtesy, T. McCarthy (FP).
- The old Darling Brothers Foundry building. 2010 (JDF).
- Past Steel Company of Canada building (now a condo), 2011. (JDF).
- Cork Factory in Griffintown, 2010. (JDF).
- Canal, Charlevoix Bridge and Stelco site, 2014. (JDF).
- Past St. Henri sites of Stelco and Dominion Textile, 2014. (JDF).
- Past Simmons site, 2014. (JDF).
- Past site of Canada Malting, 2014. (JDF).

Theresa Norris, Nee Shanahan

- Theresa (Shanahan) Norris, 2013. Courtesy, T. Norris. (FP).
- The Shanahan twins with grandmother Giovanetti. Courtesy, T. Norris, 1949. (FP).
- Theresa with dad on St. Patrick's Day, 1953. Courtesy, T. Norris. (FP).
- School photo, Courtesy, T. Norris and the Commission Scolaire de Montreal (previously the Montreal Catholic School Commission). 1957.
- Theresa and husband, Doug, 2012. Courtesy T. Norris. (FP).
- Goose Village architecture. Courtesy, Archives de la Ville de Montreal VM94C270-0655. c. 1963.

Tom Shanahan

- Tom Shanahan atop Mount Royal, 2010. Courtesy, T. Norris. (FP).
- The twins. Courtesy, T. Norris, 1948 (FP).
- The Shanahan family in Goose village, 1950. Courtesy, T. Norris. (FP).
- Tom and his father on St. Patrick's Day, 1953. Courtesy, T. Norris. (FP).
- Children outside a Goose Village scrap yard. Courtesy, Archives de la Ville de Montreal, VM04C270-0332. c. 1963.
- School photo. Courtesy, T. Norris and the Commission Scolaire de Montreal (previously the Montreal Catholic School Commission). 1958.
- Tom and his mother, 2011. (JDF).
- 1964 view of the Point St. Charles rail yards adjacent to Goose Village. Courtesy J. Berlettano. (PU).

Joe Berlettano

- Joe Berlettano, 2014, Courtesy, J. Berlettano. (FP).
- Joe's mother at sewing class. Courtesy, J. Berlettano. Photo taken between September, 1955/ Spring, 1956. (PU).
- Joe Berlettano and friends on St. Patrick's Day. March 1956 or 1957 Courtesy, J. Berlettano. (PU).
- Victoriatown (Goose Village) Boys' Club. Courtesy, Archives de la Ville de Montreal, VM94C270-0170. c. 1963.
- Boys' Club with rink in foreground. Courtesy, Archives de la Ville de Montreal, VM94C270-0490. c. 1963.
- Roller-skating - 1956. Courtesy, J. Berlettano. Edward E. Sampson, photographer (with the permission of his Estate).
- Field days in the Village. 1956. Courtesy J. Berlettano. Edward E. Sampson photographer (with the permission of his Estate).
- Goose Village's "Suitmaker Blackhawks" softball team. 1956. Courtesy, J. Berlettano. (PU).
- Victoriatown softball team. 1957 – '58. Courtesy J. Berlettano. (PU).
- Soccer team.1956 or 1957. Courtesy J. Berlettano. (PU).
- A Goose Village football team. 1955. Courtesy J. Berlettano. (PU).
- National Boys' Club Week. 1959. Courtesy, J. Berlettano. Edward E. Sampson photographer (with the permission of his Estate).
- Children's party (girls). Circa 1956 – '58. Courtesy, J. Berlettano. Edward E. Sampson photographer (with the permission of his Estate).

- Children's party (boys). Circa 1956 – '58. Courtesy, J. Berlettano. (PU; likely Edward E. Sampson).
- Three Soap Box Derby racing photos in Goose Village. 1955 and/or 1956:
    1. Single cart just about to cross the finish line: Courtesy, J. Berlettano. (PU; likely Edward E. Sampson, with permission of his estate).
    2. Three carts racing down the street: Courtesy, J. Berlettano. Edward E. Sampson photographer (with the permission of his Estate).
    3. Single cart at the hay-bale: Courtesy, J. Berlettano. (PU; likely Edward E. Sampson, with permission of his estate).
- Joe and team. Circa 1956 – '59. Courtesy, J. Berlettano. Photographer Edward E. Sampson (with the permission of his Estate).
- Four Goose Village street scenes. All courtesy of J. Berlettano (1964). (PU).
- Joe and Civita at their 50 th wedding anniversary. Courtesy, J. Berlettano. (FP).

Robert Côté

- Chief Inspector Robert Côté O.C., Montreal Police, 1990.
- Robert (right) and his late brother, Claude, in front of their Centre Street home in Point St. Charles, 1949. Courtesy, R. Côté. (FP).
- Young Robert outside his old Centre Street home. Courtesy, 1948. Courtesy, R. Côté.
- Robert in front of his childhood home on Centre Street in the Point, 2011. (JDF).
- Derelict swing-bridge from Griffintown to the Point 2011. (JDF).
- St. Gabriel Church (foreground) and St. Charles Church (adjacent) on Centre Street, 2011. (JDF).
- The old Sherwin Williams Paint site, 2011. (JDF).
- The old Hogan Bath building on Wellington Street, 2011. (JDF).
- Robert (age 18) in Paris while serving in the Royal 22nd Regiment. 1954. Courtesy, R. Côté.
- Victoriatown/Goose Village World War II monument, 2011. (JDF).
- Constable Robert Côté (age 24), early in his career with the Montreal Police, 1960. Courtesy, Service de police de la Ville de Montreal.
- Now the Pub St. Charles, this was once the Pall Mall Tavern, 2011. (JDF).
- Robert beside the site of his first arrest, 2011. (JDF).

Tom Patwell

- Tom and spouse Marilyn. Courtesy, T. Patwell. (PU).
- The Griffintown Club sign. Courtesy, Bill O'Donnell, 2012. (JDF).
- Cliff Sowery. Courtesy, J. Berlettano. (PU).
- The Griffintown Grads fastball team, 1962. Courtesy, M. Harkin. (PU).
- Unloading cargo by pallet. Courtesy, Library and Archives Canada. Online MIKAN no. 3517758. Linked to Canadian National Railways graphic material (R231-1028-5-E) Date unknown.
- The Montreal harbour. circa 1927. Courtesy, Library and Archives Canada. Online MIKAN no. 3350406. Part of Canadian National Railways graphic material (R231-1028-5- E).
- Liberator bomber crash scene in Griffintown. Courtesy Library and Archives Canada. Montreal Star Fonds. PA-116062. 2.

- The Memorial Clock Tower, as well as sheds 18 and 19 (c. 1926). Courtesy, Library and Archives Canada. Online MIKAN no. 3322787Credit, Department of Interior.
- Entrance to Bickerdike Pier at the west end of the Port, 2011. (JDF).
- Containers and crane at the west end of the Port of Montreal, 2014. (JDF) Containers tacked in Point St. Charles, 2014. (JDF).
- A shed in Montreal's current-day Old Port, 2012. (JDF).
- Historic row housing across from Griffintown St Ann Park. 2011. (JDF).

Gordon McCambridge

- Gordon McCambridge, 2013. (JDF).
- CNR Express truck, Montreal (1928). Courtesy Library and Archives Canada. This item is part of the Canadian National Railways graphic material (R231-1028-5-E). Online MIKAN no. 3350498.
- Top left (2011) and right (2010): Now the property of King's Transfer Van Lines, this building once served as the residence for the Sisters of Providence and as a pre-school for Griffintown children. (JDF).
- Bottom left and right: Two photos (2011 & 2013). Eleanor Street, looking towards Ottawa Street. (JDF).
- Gordon McCambridge (left) and friends on St. Patrick's Day Parade. Courtesy, G. McCambridge.
- Graduation photos. Courtesy, G. McCambridge.
- Where Gordon first taught in Lachine. 2014. (JDF).
- St. Thomas Aquinas teachers' hockey team. Courtesy, G. McCambridge.
- Gordon and Mary McCambridge, 2013. (JDF).

Betty Dwyer, Nee Daigle

- Betty, at home, 2013. (JDF).
- Betty and family. Courtesy, B. Dwyer. Date and (PU).
- Victoria Bridge, 2013. (JDF)
- Two photographs of Bridge Street ("then and now") - looking north. 1) Historic photo (1935), courtesy, Library and Archives Canada, Canadian National Railways (Graphic material R231-1028-5-E). Online MIKAN no. 527904. 2) Contemporary photo, 2014. (JDF).

Maurice Harkin

- Maurice "Moe" Harkin, 2013. (JDF).
- Where Moe grew up, 2013. (JDF).
- Young Moe Harkin in Griffintown. Courtesy, M. Harkin. (FP) c. 1941.
- Moe and family. Courtesy M. Harkin. (FP) Circa 1941/'42.
- Hockey photo. Courtesy, M. Harkin. (PU). c. 1956/'57
- Moe's class photo (1945). Courtesy, M. Harkin and the Commission Scolaire de Montreal (previously the Montreal Catholic School Commission
- Altar boy Moe Harkin, circa 1947. Courtesy, M. Harkin. (FP)
- Moe en route carrying the crucifix. Courtesy, M. Harkin, c. 1951 (FP)
- Moe, holding the cross. Courtesy M. Harkin, c. 1951 (FP)
- William Dow and Co. Fire Insurance Plans (1903). Courtesy, Library and Archives Canada. Archival reference no. R6990-825-X-E.

Margaret Healy

- 2005 Grand Marshal Margaret Healy with grandchildren Jonathan and Matthew Showers. Photographer Peter McCabe.
- Margaret and family. Courtesy M. Healy. (FP).
- Thomas Healy alone. Courtesy, M. Healy. (PU); date unknown.
- Memorabilia, 1943. Courtesy, M. Healy. (JDF).
- Healy Bros. Ltd. Courtesy, M. Healy. (PU).
- Thomas Healy and friends beside St. Ann's Church. Courtesy M. Healy. (PU); date unknown.
- Grand Marshal Margaret Healy and the rest of the Marshals at the 2005 St. Patrick's Day Parade. Photographer Peter McCabe.
- Margaret with husband Ken O'Donnell (left) and Ireland's Ambassador to Canada, Mr. Raymond Bassett, 2013. (JDF).

Patrick Duffy

- Paddy, beside the Black Rock, 2013. (JDF).
- Redpath on St. Patrick Street in Point St. Charles, 2013. (JDF).
- Shearer Street entrance to Northern Electric building, 2011. (JDF).
- 801 Charon, 2014. (JDF).
- Paddy's Rozel Street building, 2014. (JDF).
- Canon O'Meara hockey team, 1950 - 1951. Courtesy, L. Purcell.
- Old Northern Electric Building and the Fine Pointe Restaurant, 2011. (JDF).
- Bob Geary. Courtesy, Point St. Charles YMCA. Date and (PU).
- Herb Trawick Park Sign, 2012. (JDF).
- Canadian National Railways, Point St. Charles. Courtesy, Library and Archives Canada. Online MIKAN no. 3348632 (1929).
- 1964 Juvenile football championship team reunion, 2013. (JDF).
- Making cable. Courtesy, Department of Manpower and Immigration/Library and Archives Canada (Photographer, Malak). Online MIKAN no. 4369804. Between 1930 and 1960.
- 1952 juvenile champion football team. Courtesy, P. Duffy. (PU).
- Aerial from Le Nordelec looking over St. Patrick Street and Montreal, 2013. (JDF).
- Aerial view from the old Northern building looking west over the point.

Mary Duffy, Nee Burton

- Mary Duffy, 2012 (JDF).
- Two photographs of updated Sebastopol Street housing, 2013 and 2011 respectively. (JDF)
- Photo of products showing the names, Belding and/or Corticelli, 2012. (JDF).
- Looking northwest across the canal from the old Northern Electric building., 2013. (JDF).
- Two photos of the site of Mary's past employer taken from north side of Lachine Canal, 2012. (JDF).
- Photo from Sebastopol Street across old rail yards and looking toward the Montreal skyline, 2011 (JDF).
- Looking down Sebastopol Street toward the yards, 2013. (JDF).
- Mary and Paddy Duffy at St. Gabriel's Church Hall, 2013. (JDF)

Linda Frainetti

- Linda Frainetti at home, 2011. (JDF).
- Baby Linda, 1948. Courtesy, L. Frainetti. (FP).
- Linda's grandfather, (1929), and her grandmother, (1948) holding Linda's sister, Sandra. Courtesy, L. Frainetti (FP).
- School photo, 1954. Courtesy, L. Frainetti and the Commission Scolaire de Montreal (previously the Montreal Catholic School Commission).
- Norman Snack Bar. Courtesy, J. Berlettano, 1964. (PU).
- John's Licensed Groceteria. Courtesy, Archives de la Ville de Montreal VM94C270-0204. c. 1963.
- Dominico Pace Restaurant. Courtesy, Archives de la Ville de Montreal VM94C270-0170. c. 1963.
- Pizza Rotella. Courtesy, Archives de la Ville de Montreal VM94C270-0201. c. 1963.
- Piche's grocer and butcher. Courtesy, Archives de la Ville de Montreal VM94C270-0324. c. 1963.
- Salvatore Snack Bar. Courtesy, Archives de la Ville de Montreal VM94C270-0560. c. 1963.
- Two photos (right - 2011 and left - 2012) of Benedict Labre House in Griffintown. (JDF).
- Inside a Goose Village corner store. Courtesy, Archives de la Ville de Montreal VM94C270-1095.

Ed DiZazzo

- Ed at Griffintown - St Ann Park, 2011. (JDF).
- Baby Edward. Courtesy, 1947. E. DiZazzo.
- Ed's grandfather and grandmother with Yolanda (Ed's mother) and his uncle Florindo (Floyd), 1937. Courtesy, E. DiZazzo. (FP).
- Ed's grandmother with Floyd and Yolanda, 1941. Courtesy, E. DiZazzo. (FP).
- Ed's grandmother's citizenship certificate, 1953. Courtesy, E. DiZazzo. (JDF).
- Ed's grandmother's store, and Ed's home in Goose Village. Courtesy, Archives de la Ville de Montreal, VM94C270-0584. c. 1963.
- Ed in front of the now closed Wellington Tunnel, 2011. (JDF).
- Graduation days (Loyola College, 1968 & University of Ottawa, 1971). Courtesy, E. DiZazzo. (FP).
- Ed's class photo. Courtesy, the Commission Scolaire de Montreal (previously the Montreal Catholic School Commission).
- Ed in front of "Silo 5" (grain elevator), 2011. (JDF).
- The Bridge Restaurant, Goose Village. Courtesy, Archives de la Ville de Montreal, VM94C270-0216. c. 1963.
- Ed, at home in south Mountain, Ontario, 2011. (JDF).

Joe Timmons

- Joe Timmons, 1968 St. Patrick's Day Parade in Montreal. Photographer Laureen Sweeney.
- Joe Timmons Sr., Montreal Fire Department (1927). Courtesy, J. Timmons. (PU).
- Young Joe atop the ladder truck. Circa 1945. Courtesy, J. Timmons. (PU).
- Joe's father and team outside Mill Street Station. Courtesy, J. Timmons. (PU).
- Joe's father's team outside the Griffintown Station, 1950. Courtesy, J. Timmons. (PU).

- Joe's father driving one of the first Montreal ladder trucks. Courtesy, J. Timmons. (PU).
- Two photos of the Griffintown Fire Station of Joe's youth. It still serves the area today, 2010. (JDF).
- The old Mill Street station, 2013. (JDF).
- Liberator crash, 1944. Courtesy Library and Archives Canada, Montreal Star Fonds. PA-116061.
- Today's Point St. Charles Fire Station no. 15, 2014. (JDF).
- The old Hibernia Street Fire Station is now a library, 2014. (JDF).
- Bill Timmons (left) and Joe (right), flanking their father, Joe Timmons Sr. Courtesy, J. Timmons. (FP).
- Joe, enjoying retirement at the helm of his boat, 2012. (JDF).
- Joe and Cathy at Joe's retirement party. Courtesy, J. Timmons. (PU).

Mike Spears

- Mike at the 2012 walk to the stone in Point St. Charles. (JDF).
- Mike (right) with his brother, Kenny. Courtesy M. Spears. (PU). c. 1947.
- Mike and his mother, 1949. Courtesy, M. Spears. (FP).
- Class photo, 1954. Courtesy, M. Spears and the Commission Scolaire de Montreal (previously the Montreal Catholic School Commission).
- The now restored St. Gabriel Lock, where Mike's father once worked, 2011. (JDF).
- Two photos of one of Mike's 1960 Point St. Charles football programs. Courtesy, M. Spears.
- Westmount Examiner story (1971). Courtesy Westmount Examiner.
- Members of the Erin Sports Association at the 2013 St. Patrick's Day Parade. (JDF).
- Erin Sports Association volunteers at the annual BBQ in support of St. Gabriel's Parish, 2013. (JDF).
- Erin Sports Association team at the 2014 "Wish" tournament. (JDF).

Amelia (Gaglietta) Palazzo

- Amelia (Emily) Palazzo. Courtesy, A. Palazzo, Circa 2008. (FP).
- School photo, 1954. Courtesy A. Palazzo and the Commission Scolaire de Montreal (previously the Montreal Catholic School Commission).
- Wedding of Gaetano Gaglietta and Maria Mancini, 1946. Courtesy, A. Palazzo. (PU).
- Goose Village three-storey "shed".Courtesy, Archives de la Ville de Montreal, VM94C270-0243. c. 1963.
- Victoriatown Boys' Club gymnasium arranged for Mass. Courtesy, Archives de la Ville de Montréal, VM94C270-1358. C. 1963
- Amelia (centre), with sisters Antoinetta (left) and Bertina, 2008. Courtesy, A. Palazzo. (FP).
- Friends for life. Amelia (left), Linda Frainetti (centre) and Theresa Norris, circa 2001. Courtesy. A. Palazzo. (FP).

Bertrand Bégin

- Outside the Fine Pointe Restaurant, 2012. (JDF).
- Bertrand (second from right) with grandparents Georges and Mélanie as well as brother André. Circa 1943. Courtesy, B. Begin. (FP).
- 1226 D'Argenson, Pointe-Saint-Charles, 2012. (JDF).

- Bertrand's mother, Lucienne, at the grocery store. Courtesy, B. Begin, 1930. (PU).
- Bertrand (right) with his father, mother and brother. Courtesy B. Begin, 1940. (FP).
- School photo, 1949. Courtesy B. Begin and the Commission Scolaire de Montreal (previously the Montreal Catholic School Commission).
- Lachine Canal and Atwater Market, 2011. (JDF).
- The old Vogue Theatre, 2012, (JDF).

Réal Normandeau

- Réal Normandeau, 2011. (JDF).
- Two photos of the old Point St. Charles Post Office on Centre Street, 2014. (JDF).
- Two photos of Productive House, 2014. (JDF).
- Réal outside the Fine Pointe, 2013. (JDF).
- Two photos of Point St Charles parks honoring past residents of the area, 2014. (JDF).
- Downtown high-rise framed by two Griffintown condos. 2013 (JDF).

Leo Purcell

- Leo Purcell. Courtesy, L. Purcell.
- Two photos of the old Presentation Brothers' residence on Laprairie Street, 2012. (JDF).
- Leo (Brother Stephen) and class at Canon O'Meara School, circa 1950. Courtesy L. Purcell and the Commission Scolaire de Montreal (previously the Montreal Catholic School Commission).

Henry Spencer

- Brother Henry Spencer. Courtesy, H. Spencer and Edge Imaging.

Bibliography

Ames, Sir Herbert Brown. The City Below the Hill. A Sociological Study of a Portion of the City of Montreal, Canada. The Bishop Engraving Company, Montreal 1897.

Barlow, John Matthew. The House of the Irish: Irishness, History, and Memory in Griffintown, Montreal, 1868 – 2009. A Thesis in the Department of History. Concordia University, Montreal, Quebec, Canada, March 2009

Burman, Richard. 20th Century Griffintown in Pictures. 2010.

Burns, Patricia. The Shamrock and the Shield: an oral history of Montreal. Montreal: Véhicule Press, 2005.

Coogan, Tim Pat. The Famine Plot: England's Role in Ireland's Great Tragedy. New York: Palgrave MacMillan, 2012.

Côté, Robert, O. C. Ma guerre contre le FLQ. Éditions Trait D'union, 2003.

Desloges, Yvon and Gelly, Alain. The Lachine Canal, Riding the Waves of Industrialization and Urban Development 1860 – 1950. Les éditions du septentrion, 2002. Published in collaboration with Parks Canada.

Doyle Driedger, Sharon. An Irish Heart—How a Small Immigrant Community Shaped Canada. Toronto: Harper Collins, 2010.

Dobson, Kathy. With a Closed Fist: growing up in Canada's toughest neighbourhood. Montreal: Véhicule Press, 2011.

Feltoe, Richard. Redpath: The History of a Sugarhouse. Toronto. Natural Heritage/Natural History Inc., 1991.

Fitzgerald, Patrick and Brian Lambkin. Migration in Irish History. Hampshire England: Palgrave MacMillan, 2008.

Kelly, John. The Graves are Walking. The Great Famine and the Saga of the Irish People. New York: Henry Holt and Company, 2012.

Leduc, Michel. Point St. Charles Shops. Michel D. Leduc Enr. Press. 2007.

Marrell, Nancy and Simon Dardick (editors). The Scots of Montreal: a pictorial album. Montreal: Véhicule Press, 2005.

O'Connor D'Arcy. Montreal's Irish Mafia: the true story of the infamous West End Gang. Mississauga: John Wiley & Sons, 2011.

Parks Canada. Lachine Canal, National Historic Site of Canada, Management Plan, May 2004.

Parks Canada web site. Lachine Canal—Historic Site of Canada: The Canal in Depth—a Supplier of Hydraulic Power (A New Source of Energy)—The First Ink in the Canal Network (A Commercial Necessity); The Cradle of Industrialization—A Change in Direction.

Presentation Brothers 100th Anniversary Booklet, 2010.

75e Anniversaire de la fondation de la Paroisse Saint-Charles. Montreal: 1958

Sicotte, Anne-Marie. Quartiers ouvriers d'autrefois. Sainte-Foy (Québec): Les Publication du Québec, 2004.

Montreal

The quotes on the next page are by:

BB   Bertrand Bégin
TM   Terry McCarthy
EN   Eddy Nolan
BD   Betty Dwyer
AP   Amelia Palazzo
TN   Theresa Norris

Quotes from this engaging collection of oral histories

"…the Lachine Canal was the way to enter America through to the Great Lakes. It provided employment for people who worked at the Montreal harbour and permitted the transport of manufactured goods to and from all kinds of industries. It made Montreal Canada's industrial and commercial center at the time." — BB

"A lot of our parents and grandparents came to Griffintown from Ireland and other places with very little. But with two or three generations of hard work many of us moved a long way. We worked hard. We educated our kids." — TM

"…the sounds of the trains, the kids all over the street, the baseball games down at the park…There was always the sound of people on the balconies talking to each other and calling out to others in the streets." — EN

"I can still hear the sound of the guys under the street lamps in the evening, singing in harmony. Usually it would be four of them—no musical instruments—just singing. It was just marvelous." — BD

"…we spent a lot of time around the kitchen table because that was where the stove was, and it was usually nice and warm and we were together as a family." — AP

"People worked hard, lived hard, and played hard. They were decent people who truly enjoyed their homes, their neighbourhood, and their way of life. It was a 'Village', in all senses of the word." — TN

www.ingramcontent.com/pod-product-compliance
Lightning Source LLC
Chambersburg PA
CBHW081527120626
46550CB00009B/2646